VIRALITY

VIRALITY

CONTAGION THEORY IN
THE AGE OF NETWORKS

TONY D. SAMPSON

UNIVERSITY OF MINNESOTA PRESS
Minneapolis
London

Portions of chapters 1 and 3 were previously published as "Error-Contagion: Network Hypnosis and Collective Culpability," in *Error: Glitch, Noise, and Jam in New Media Cultures*, ed. Mark Nunes (New York: Continuum, 2011).

Portions of chapters 4 and 5 were previously published as "Contagion Theory beyond the Microbe," in *C Theory: Journal of Theory, Technology, and Culture* (January 2011), http://www.ctheory.net/articles.aspx?id=675.

Published by the University of Minnesota Press
111 Third Avenue South, Suite 290
Minneapolis, MN 55401-2520
http://www.upress.umn.edu

Library of Congress Cataloging-in-Publication Data
Sampson, Tony D.
 Virality : contagion theory in the age of networks / Tony D. Sampson.
 Includes bibliographical references and index.
 ISBN 978-0-8166-7004-8 (hc : alk. paper)
 ISBN 978-0-8166-7005-5 (pb : alk. paper)
 1. Imitation. 2. Social interaction. 3. Crowds. 4. Tarde, Gabriel, 1843–1904. I. Title.
 BF357.S26 2012
 302'.41—dc23   2012008201

Printed in the United States of America on acid-free paper

The University of Minnesota is an equal-opportunity educator and employer.

20 19 18 17 16 15 14 13 12   10 9 8 7 6 5 4 3 2 1

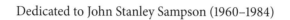
Dedicated to John Stanley Sampson (1960–1984)

Contents

Introduction

Too Much Connectivity?

Before laying down the initial groundwork for the theoretical foundations of *Virality*, it must be clearly stated that this is not the first study to have intuitively considered the ubiquity of epidemiological encounters in the so-called *age of networks*. A growing number of present-day authors, writing from social science, humanities, network science, economic, and business perspectives, have evoked a past interest in contagion theory by pondering its relevance to the current age. Some of these accounts point to the intensification in connectivity brought about by network technologies as a possible trigger for increased chances of infection from wide-ranging social, cultural, political, and economic contagions. For example, eschewing popular utopian discourses that tend to exaggerate the democratizing powers of the Internet, the social scientist Jan van Dijk warns of new vulnerabilities that arise when "network society" encounters "too much connectivity."[1] The proliferation of global transport networks makes this model of society susceptible to the spreading of biological diseases. Digital networks become volatile under the destructive potential of computer viruses and worms. Enhanced by the rapidity and extensity of technological networks, the spread of social conformity, political rumor, fads, fashions, gossip, and hype threatens to destabilize established political order. Likewise, financial contagions cascade through the capitalist economy, inspiring speculative bubbles, crashes, and aperiodic recessions.

There is, it would appear, a certain measure of consensus across the political spectrum regarding how the networked infrastructures of late

1

capitalism are interwoven with the universal logic of the epidemic. On the Left, Michael Hardt and Antonio Negri have argued that the age of globalization is synonymous with the age of contagion.[2] This is an age in which increased contact with the Other has rekindled anxieties concerning the spreading of disease and corruption since permeable boundaries of the nation-state can no longer function as a colonial hygiene shield. The spontaneity of contagious overspills thus has the potential to initiate a revolutionary renewal of global democracy. On the Right, the International Monetary Fund, the World Bank, and various leaders of the capitalist world order have pointed to the threat posed to the stability of the current neoliberal political–economic system by the capricious spreading of financial crises from nation to nation. Correlations have been made, for example, between the interlocking of global stock markets, the chaos of financial contagion, and the so-called Islamic threat to justify the ongoing War on Terror.[3]

Nonetheless, virality is not merely perceived as a threat to capitalism. It also presents certain opportunities for the refreshing of its consumerist models of wealth creation founded on a clearer understanding of how money can follow social influence as it spreads across a network. Indeed, the link between an ever-expanding form of network capitalism and the self-propagation of network virality is explicitly made through a heady concoction of business enterprise, network science, and neo-Darwinian-related literature. Like this, the *meme* and the *viral* (the marketing buzzwords of the network age) have been conjured up from an assortment of crude renderings of evolutionary theory, powerful computer-assisted contagion modeling, and business trends. It is via these various contagion models that financial crisis, social influence, innovations, fashions and fads, and even human emotion are understood to spread universally like viruses across networks.[4]

Yet arguably, as intuitive as this new epidemiological paradigm seems to be, the medical metaphors and biological analogies that underpin it present many analytical limitations. To be sure, understood as a metaphor, the *too much connectivity* thesis offers very little in terms of an ontological grasping of contagion theory. Similarly, the overgeneralization that network capitalism, or indeed resistance to it, *spreads like a disease* inadequately describes the politics of the network age.

This book sets about developing, as such, an ontological investigation of contagious relationality intended to probe *outside* the generality of metaphors and analogies. It focuses instead on three specific questions committed to more fully interrogating the claim that the age of networks is indeed the age of contagion. First, *Virality* asks, what is it that actually spreads on a network? Unlike the neo-Darwinist approach, which shores up memetics, as well as much of the viral marketing hyperbole, the discussion purposefully avoids a specified mechanism of contagion derived from analogical thinking. It draws instead on the much older social epidemiology developed by the French sociologist Gabriel Tarde in the late nineteenth century, which answers this question with a novel monadological understanding of social relationality. This is an approach intended not only to unravel the many discursive and rhetorical references to viral disease but also to highlight how discourse is intimately interwoven with a prediscursive flow of contagious affect, feelings, and emotions. Second, by addressing the question of how sociotechnical networks become viral, the book aspires to establish, following Gilles Deleuze, a topological diagrammatics of what composes the age of contagion. It is, after all, Deleuze who notes the importance of finding the appropriate abstract diagram to grasp the concrete assemblages of social power.[5] To be sure, it is my intension here to grasp such a diagram through a Tardean lens so that contagion can be seen as an exercising of a force (or many forces of relation) on the social field and displayed as relations between forces and encounters that determine features and functions apparent in that field.[6]

Third, and perhaps more crucially, *Virality* questions the language of fear and threat generally associated with the *too much connectivity* thesis. Here the discussion takes a resolutely nonrepresentational approach to its subject matter. It investigates, as such, wide-ranging implications of a kind of network virality that surpasses linguistic categories of disease and instead reaches out to explore new exploitable social assemblages of affective contagious encounter. It is, in effect, important, before moving on to conceptualize *Virality,* to linger on this third question for a while and consider the theoretical frame it suggests. To begin with, I am not suggesting that there is not a representational dimension to contagion theory. Nevertheless, and again following Deleuze, and specifically his critique of the ontological basis of representation, *Virality* endeavors to eschew the organizational capacity of linguistic categories.[7] This is because categories based on analogy and resemblance, for example, drawn from models of disease and immunology, tend to block the conceptual freedom to which this book aspires. Likewise, categories of opposition and identity, derived again in this case from biological infection and immunity, impart a concentrated rhetorical ordering of contagion theory and real practices. Nowhere is this more evident than in the problematic viral discourses surrounding network security, in which the recourse to immunological analogies and metaphors of disease shape the network space by way of igniting public anxieties concerning an epidemic "enemy" that is "undetected, and therefore potentially everywhere."[8]

In contrast, a nonrepresentational approach helps *Virality* purposefully circumvent an analytical method that stresses the significance of cultural inscriptions and meanings attributed to objects ahead of the actual relations objects have to one another.[9] Of course, objects *represent*, but as Nigel Thrift argues, "[they] do far more than represent."[10] *Virality* thus employs conceptual tools intended to focus the reader's attention on a world

> made up of all kinds of things brought in to relation with one another by [a] universe of spaces through a continuous and largely involuntary process of encounter and the often violent training that the encounter forces.[11]

To be sure, *Virality* is no metaphor. It is all about the forces of relational encounter in the social field.

Significantly, the space of encounter *Virality* explores eludes a prejudiced worldview separating human subjectivity from natural objects and organic from inorganic matter. This is a continuous space that Deleuze, like Tarde, recognizes as full of multiple monadic singularities: a spatiality within which the social, psychological, and biological are folded.[12] *Virality* is, as follows, located in an epidemiological space in which a world of things mixes with emotions, sensations, affects, and moods. In this space is a continuous "generation of neurophysiological ecosystems" boosted by the "cultural amplifiers" of objects and commodities, such as "caffeine, sentimental novels, and pornographic works," that can adapt the social in novel and unpredictable ways.[13] This is a world awash with hormones and consumer goods, making people happy or sad, sympathetic or apathetic, and a space in which affects are significantly passed on, via suggestions made by others, more and more through networks.

No Metaphor, Just Two Kinds of Virality

There are in effect two kinds of *Virality* presented in this book. On one hand, there is a distinct molarization of the contagious forces of relational encounter. These molar forces can be located in the organizational tendencies of analogical thinking that forcibly bring singularities into unified relation with each other. This relates to, for example, the universal application of epidemic models of disease across a range of contagious phenomena. *Molar virality* is, I contend, endemic to new biopolitical strategies of social power, that is, a discursive (and prediscursive) means of organizing and exerting control via, for instance, the widespread imposition of generalized immunological defenses, anomaly detection techniques, and the obligation of personal hygiene in network security. Control is therefore justified through these social inventions by way of drumming up presocial uncertainties concerning contamination. Like this, the inventions of biopower play to the vulnerabilities people feel when they encounter disease.

However, in addition to the discursive mobilization of negative emotions, biopower is further exercised through the exploitation of the entire valence of human emotion—not just through fear, panic, terror, and fright but via the positive affects that spread through a population when it encounters, for instance, the intoxication of hope, belief, joy, and even love. Methods of control, including the affective priming of social atmospheres and the preemption of a tendency for increasingly connected populations to pass on and imitate the suggestions of others, point to the potential exploitation of a susceptible and porous networked subjectivity. Importantly, these social inventions do not tap into networked subjects in the sense of self-contained or necessarily rational cognitive individuals but rather make use of embedded network subjectivity: opening it up to flows of contaminating influence and persuasive mood settings, all of which are transmitted through mostly unconscious topologies of social relation.

On the other hand, though, we need to consider a second kind of *molecular virality* located in the accidents and spontaneity of desire. This precedes the endeavor to organize the social via representational categorizations of epidemic disease or joyful encounters of hope and belief. The accidentality of collective contagion relating to mood, for example, can again be defined in Deleuzian terms as a happenstance molecular flow of desire that spreads through and disrupts social assemblages brought together, for instance, by shared beliefs and assurances. Unlike a social body composed of collective representations, this is a subrepresentational flow of events that radiates outward as a contaminating desire–event. It is this flow that assembles social wholes around an accumulation of microimitations and readies them for appropriation by social invention. Indeed, this second kind of virality introduces a significant question for contagion theory concerning just how much of the accidentality of the molecular can come under the organizational control of the molar order. In other words, how much of the happenstance of desire–events can be captured? How can beliefs be stabilized, ordered, fixed, or kept in one place? The answer, to some extent, is found in a Tardean line of flight apparent in a late capitalism geared, as it is, toward studying how small, unpredictable events can be nudged into becoming big, monstrous contagions without a guiding hand.[14] In fact, the knowledge gained from studying these capricious spillovers of contagious desire is, as Thrift suggests, helping the business enterprise, and the political strategist, consider new triggers for virality.

Resuscitating Tarde: Monads, Inseparability, and Intervention

It is necessary at this point to introduce what this book borrows from Tarde's notion of social composition. Importantly, though, such an introduction needs to be preceded by stating that *Virality* is not a restoration or revival of Tarde. I have resisted, where possible, demands simply to appraise his work or rigorously apply it to the subject matter. There are indeed better points of reference for getting to know Tarde in detail.[15] What I offer instead is a *resuscitation* of his approach. This involves a carrying forward of an interpretation of Tardean ideas so that they can be linked, transversally, to contemporary notions, breathing new life into social theory, and contagion theory, in particular. It will already be clear that Deleuze plays a central role in this resuscitation, but others not beholden to a strictly Deleuzian interpretation figure writ large. However, before placing this old figure in the full recovery position, to begin with, I want to sketch a few key aspects of Tarde's monadological account of the social and his unconventional approach to the nature–culture divide, before outlining the main thrusts and influences of his theoretical intervention.

Tarde's use of the word *social* is not to be confused with a dominant sociological viewpoint that (1) divides its subject matter into macrolevel social aggregates and microlevel individuals or (2) distinguishes itself from natural or psychological phenomena. With regard to the first point, Tarde's microsociology has been mistaken for a reduction of the social body to the atomic level of the individual, but as Tarde enthusiasts (including Deleuze and Bruno Latour) have noted, there is more to Tarde's individuation than a mere person. Indeed, Tarde's radical social monadology begins with the premise that "*every thing is* a society."[16] The social relationalities established in Tardean assemblages therefore make no distinctions between individual persons, animals, insects, bacteria, atoms, cells, or larger societies of events like markets, nations, and cities. The main point is that the social can be further boiled down to a monadological level of relation. As Latour puts it, with Tarde, "everything is individual and yet there is no individual in the etymological sense of that which cannot be further divided."[17]

Not surprisingly, compatible with Latour's actor networks as well as Deleuzian assemblage theory, Tarde's social is not concerned with the individual person or its collective representation but rather with the networks or relational flows that spread out and connect everything to everything else. To be sure, Tarde's contagion theory is all about flows or vibratory events. This is what spreads—what he calls *microimitations*—a point Deleuze and Guattari stress in their homage to his project:

> Tarde countered that collective representations presuppose exactly what needs explaining, namely "the similarity of millions of people."

That is why Tarde was interested in the world of detail, or of the infinitesimal: the little imitations, oppositions, and inventions constituting an entire realm of subrepresentative matter. Tarde's best work was his analysis of a minuscule bureaucratic innovation, or a linguistic innovation, etc. The Durkheimians answered that what Tarde did was psychology or interpsychology, not sociology. But that is true only in appearance, as a first approximation: microimitation does seem to occur between two individuals. But at the same time, and at a deeper level, it has to do not with an individual but with a flow or a wave.[18]

It is indeed this allusion to a "deeper level" of "subrepresentative" material flows to explain "the similarity of millions of people" that makes the analytical line running from Tarde to Deleuze such a compelling alternative to the macro- and microreductions of a dominant sociology erected by Émile Durkheim. This can be seen in the way that the molar–molecular distinction of assemblage theory does not produce an oppositional relationship established between two types of organization.[19] Assemblages are not constrained to big and small scales, parts and whole, organs and organism, or, significantly, individual and society.[20] Unlike Durkheim, then, who understood individuals to be the product of the societies into which they are born, molecular social assemblages are part of a continuous flow of decoded (deterritorialized) boundless monads, or singularities, as Deleuze refers to them, until that which is a singularity is recoded (territorialized) so that it relates to other singularities and therefore becomes an organized (organic) body.[21] This is the molarity of a social territory moving through the organizational levels of atoms, cells, genes, individual persons, and social wholes. Nevertheless, it is important to note that the seemingly fixed molar way of being is not a natural homogenous end state toward which all social phenomena tend.[22] Although singularities clearly "come together" in a topological diagram as an extension into space, they remain in a state of intensive molecular flux (becoming). Unlike the social functionalism of the Durkheimians, in which the homogeneity of the collective consciousness determines the individual parts, Deleuze's assemblage theory, like Tardean sociology, argues that it is the composition of singularities that determines the whole. Society is only really whole when it "has been grasped by an outside force"—as in the case when a "contained population" becomes "a subjected group" or when an individual becomes a molar person when "assigned a category."[23] From this point, Brian Massumi goes on to propose that the molar recoding of a body, as in the case of the organic social body, is in effect "the organizational model *applied* to the body."[24] Molar recoding is, as such, a mode of domination over multiplicity, order over complexity, generality over difference, and stability over instability.

With regard to the second point, *Virality* returns to aspects of Tarde's crowd theory to expose the artificiality of a nature–culture divide, that is, a disciplinary artifice frequently erected between, on one hand, the naturalness of the biological world and, on the other, the social and cultural domains the human inhabits.[25] In many ways, it is the Durkheimian paradigm that reinforces a contractual separation between the natural and social worlds, but there is also a far more distinctive cross-disciplinary cognitive turn, dating back to the Enlightenment, that misleadingly shuts off the social being from the world of relationality and therein the affects of others. In her analysis of the decline of crowd theory, Teresa Brennan notes, as such, the ominous implications of this turn toward cognition. It not only concentrated enquiry on the rational minds of a self-contained individual but also bisected biological and sociological explanations of collective social interaction.[26] The theory of the self-contained individual stresses that it is conscious cognition that determines human agency rather than natural phenomena such as emotions, feelings, and affect, which spread, often unconsciously, through social atmospheres. As Thrift similarly warns,

> For a long time, the categories of the social and the biological have bedevilled rational analysis of human cultures, producing no-go zones which are only just beginning to crumble. On the one side have stood the guardians of causes understood as "social" . . . on the other side have stood the guardians of biological causes, and ne'er the twain shall meet. Indeed, the two sides are often actively opposed to each other. Worse than the obstinacy of the distinction has been the ways in which it has disallowed research into areas of human experience which can only be explained by appealing across the divide: affects like violence, for example, or fear.[27]

What is lost in the cognitive turn corresponds with what Tarde referred to as the inseparability of volition and mechanical habit, or what Thrift now describes as "the mutual constitution" of the "social" and the "biological."[28] Yet, despite the concepts of crowd theory undergoing a sharp decline in popularity in the twentieth century, renewed interest in the foundational work of Tarde, coinciding with the onset of a new network ontology and affective turn, is nonetheless prompting their twenty-first-century return.

Along these lines, the theoretical interventions offered in this resuscitation of Tarde require the identification of a series of countersociological, evolutionary, and psychological ideas, forwarded by Durkheim, neo-Darwinians, and Freud, that tend to molarize the organizational forces of contagion. These are perhaps overambitiously positioned straw men, but in addition to escaping the cognitive turn, they represent my intention here to circumvent a multipart propensity to diminish difference under the generalizations of, for example, Durkheim's collective consciousness, neo-Darwinist evolutionary algorithms, and certain aspects of the repressive paranoia of psychoanalysis applied to group communication.

First, Tarde feverishly disputed the claims of his ever-more influential contemporary Durkheim, who favored the determination of the collective representation (expressed through emergent group consciousness and consensus) over the social anomalies and accidents from which Tarde's mostly unconscious contagious associations are derived. Throughout the discussions in *Virality*, there is, as such, a counter-Durkheimian endeavor to account for the capricious monadic accidents from which these associations emerge. Indeed, to clearly distinguish between Tarde and Durkheim, it is necessary to return to a much older spat between these two forefathers of collective sociology. This resuscitation of Tarde is, as follows, partly informed by a "momentous debate" between Tarde and Durkheim at the École des Hautes Études Sociales in 1903.[29] They disagreed on a wide range of issues and have become, in recent years, regarded as the polar opposites of sociology. As one conference blurb put it, "Durkheim has been thinned over the years to the point of becoming a straw man," whereas Tarde, "once dismissed as a naive precursor to Durkheimian sociology . . . is now increasingly brought forward as the misrecognised forerunner of a post-Durkheimian era."[30]

Second, although sometimes associated with a Darwinian theory of contagion,[31] Tardean analysis sets out a clear challenge to how Darwinism is applied to the social and, in particular, how the neo-Darwinian accounts of cultural contagion become fixed to a gene pool analogy. In sharp contrast to the delimiting logic of the mechanistic evolutionary algorithm applied in memetic contagion theory, *Virality* will side throughout with Tarde's sense of cross-hybridization that is also apparent in Deleuze's fascination with the Proust-inspired relational encounters of the wasp–orchid assemblage. Third, and finally, there is a Tardean–Deleuzian conceptual understanding of the unconscious crowd that manifestly goes up against the psychoanalytical notion of unconscious group communication. Here I argue that Tarde's references to somnambulism and hypnotic mutualism counter both the Freudian notion of group unconscious under the paranoiac influence of the family unit and the deteriorated mental unity of Gustave Le Bon's *The Crowd,* from which Freud derived many of his ideas regarding group communication. Indeed, although accused of naive psychologism, unlike his contemporary Le Bon, Tarde offers a distinct ontological shift away from an evolutionarily hardwired, self-contained, and repressed individual at the center of psychoanalysis. As Deleuze and Guattari similarly argue, Freud mistook the unconscious for Daddy's voice. He was indeed shortsighted insofar as he didn't see the relation it had to the "buzz and shove of the crowd."[32]

Desire and Invention

The next chapter will approach the complexities of Tarde's theory of social contagion in full and map its connections to contemporary epidemiological articulations. But by way of further introduction, I want to briefly bring in Tarde's notion of how desire spreads through mostly unconscious social association as a process of invention. Principally, for Tarde, the fabric of the monadological social is intimately interwoven with the spreading of two kinds of desire. In addition to more obviously indispensable needs of organic life, for example, "to drink or eat, of clothing oneself against the cold," there are "special desires, of a social origin."[33] These are desires for satisfaction, new sensations, ambitious or amorous fevers, intoxications, and ecstatic joy, among many others. Significantly, both kinds of desires propagate and contaminate according to a base law of open-ended repetition. Like this, they are "periodically reborn and newly satisfied to be reborn again, and so on and so forth indefinitely."³⁴ The point of distinction, though, is that the first kind of desire is part of the repetitive mechanical habit of the everyday, whereas the second desires "always begin as fantasies before consolidating themselves into habits." Indeed, where *Virality* takes its furthermost inspiration from Tarde is in his very early recognition that the reproduction of desire becomes a central concern of the capitalist machinic assemblages. As he writes in *Economic Psychology*,

> We should therefore distinguish, in every individual life, between periodic (and periodically linked) desires, which are both the most numerous and the most important from the standpoint of industrial production, and capricious, non-periodic, desires, which follow one another without regular repetition. It is above all on the habits of individuals that industry must count; but their passions and their whims, whose proportion is growing in our age of social crisis, are like nurseries for the new habits of tomorrow.³⁵

In Tarde's reckoning, there is no separation between biological desires and social desires; rather there is a process whereby the first becomes translated into the second, which can, when encountered and copied, take on a vital and contaminating force of its own. Arguably, this process is not a one-way street. As I will go on to argue, today's "nurseries of industry" are becoming adept at more than capturing the flow of biological and social desires. They realize, like Tarde, that the object of desire is belief. Neuromarketers, for example, endeavor to steer desire toward belief, producing counterfeit affective encounters with desire–events so that the flow of desire folds into and contaminates the repetitive and mostly unconscious mechanical habits of the everyday.

Somnambulism and Subjectivation

Central to Tarde's sociological viewpoint is a radical questioning of what constitutes social subjectivity. Instead of focusing on individuals (microlevel) or collectives (macrolevel), the Tardean approach concentrates on what it is that contagiously passes through social assemblages. Significantly, what spreads through the social (imitation–suggestibility) is, Tarde contended, mostly experienced unconsciously. *Social man is a somnambulist.* Like this, Tarde, controversially perhaps, understood social subjects to be involuntarily associated with each other via their hypnotic absorption of the contagions of others. Indeed, Tarde's social subjects appear to sleepwalk through everyday life mesmerized and contaminated by the fascinations of their social environment. Importantly, then, the somnambulist's vulnerability to hypnosis is located in the same inseparable relation between human volition (intention) and the involuntary mechanical habits of everyday life.

Of course, the concept of an agentless, half-awake subjectivity, nudged along by the force of relational encounter with contaminating events, is unsettling. As Thrift argues, in Western culture especially, Tarde's imitation–suggestion thesis is a "painful realization" because it reveals just how little of our thinking, reasoning, and emotions might actually be "ours."[36] Nonetheless, Tarde's appeal to somnambulism maps interestingly to current ideas expressed in cognitive neuroscience concerning the relation between thinking and the automatic processing of affect said to occur via mirror neurons or empathic transmissions. As the cognitive scientist George Lakoff argues, neuroscience can tell us a lot about the workings of the unconscious political mind.[37] Drawing to some extent on this contemporary support for Tarde's thesis, *Virality* makes the case for a revised notion of social subjectivity grasped according to a hypnotic sleepwalk somewhere between unconsciousness and attentive awareness. This is particularly relevant, I propose, in an age when subjectivity is increasingly embedded in technological network relations. Like this, then, Tarde's somnambulistic subjectivity prefigures an increasingly inseparable and exploitable intersection between what is experienced biologically and what is encountered socially and culturally in a network.

As a result, this Tardean resuscitation regards the social environment of the network not simply in terms of too much connectivity but as an affective atmosphere composed of subrepresentative currents flowing between a porous self and other relations. This opens up the potential for corporate and political powers to tap into a tendency toward imitation–suggestibility by measuring, priming, and manipulating the collective mood. *Virality* is therefore evident in corporate and political efforts to organize populations by way of the contagions of fear as represented through, for example, the War on Terror. However, the potential for the spreading of social power epidemics is also evident in a tendency to be automatically drawn toward and contaminated by mesmeric fascinations, passionate interests, and joyful encounters. As Tarde argued, we tend to follow (and imitate) those we love, those in whom we put faith and hope, and those whom we idolize and take glory in their fame as much as those whom we fear.[38]

To conclude this introduction, I want to better define two of the main concepts *Virality* derives from Tardean sociology.

1. The Encounter with the Event

Virality is a theory couched in an ontology of relational encounter. What I take from Tarde to support this theory is a process in which two kinds of desire-events intermingle. This can be thought of as a point of intersection at which biological desires, or basic survival needs, converge with much-imitated social inventions and performances interwoven in the everyday mechanical habits of social encounter. This is a process of imitative subjectivation that differs considerably from the neo-Darwinian genetic reproduction of subjects according to a finite survival-of-the-fittest mechanism. As I will go to argue, *Virality* is not a contagious encounter that maps onto a genetic copying mechanism. Unlike memetics, which analogically imports genetics into social processes, the contagions of *Virality* are very much social events, albeit in the unconventional way in which Tarde described the social. Crucially, the force of imitative encounter is a process of subjectivity in the making.

2. The Force of Encounter

The much-imitated social inventions that Tarde conjures up are forces (flows, vibrations, or radiations) of imitation–suggestibility that seem to take on a life of their own as they spread through a network. Herein lies the virality of a contagion theory influenced by a vitalist philosopher. But again, this is no metaphor. The force of imitation–suggestibility, related as it is to contemporary theories of presocial affective and emotional contagions, exceeds the symbolism of a self-propagating disease. The encounter with these contagious affective forces, up close or mediated at a distance, plays a significant role in the distribution of biopolitical power relations in the network age.

Although clearly overshadowed by the Durkheimian paradigm, Tarde has continued to bubble up over the years. He first reappeared in early translations in American microsociology during the early 1900s before resurfacing in France in the late 1990s. He was an obvious influence on Deleuze's difference and repetition thesis and was carried forward, with Guattari, to *A Thousand Plateaus*.[39] Maurizio Lazzarato has also brilliantly revived Tarde's notion of social invention in his work.[40] More recently, Latour has claimed Tarde as a thinker of networks and, as such, makes him a forefather of actor network theory, and many others have recently rediscovered the efficacy of Tarde's political economy, notably here, Thrift, Latour, and Lépinay; Lisa Blackman; and Christian Borch.[41] As follows, *Virality* might be seen as an expansion of Tarde's influence into the field of network culture.

The Five Chapters of *Virality*

In short, the first chapter, "Resuscitating Tarde's Diagram in the Age of Networks," expands on the ideas this book borrows from Tarde and explains how Tardean contagion theory can be profitably connected to the work of others. Here the influence on Deleuze, Latour, Thrift, and others is sifted through, reflected on, and put to work. The second chapter, "What Spreads? From Memes and Crowds to the Phantom Events of Desire and Belief," develops this Tardean sociological perspective to intervene into the medical and biological analogies that underpin the dominant form of contemporary contagion theory: memetics. Through Tarde, an alternative understanding of what it is that spreads through a network is realized outside the dogmas of neo-Darwinian evolutionary theory. The third chapter, "What Diagram? Toward a Political Economy of Desire and Contagion," continues to address the question concerning what spreads by asking what is the most appropriate diagram through which to grasp Tarde's social epidemiology. It argues that despite its prevalence in epidemic studies, the network graph problematically freezes the temporarily of the events of contagion. Using examples of financial contagion and viral marketing, the chapter sketches a topological diagram that can express the shock accidents and events of the epidemic that seem to exceed the nodes and edges of the network.

The fourth chapter, "From Terror Contagion to the Virality of Love," follows Tarde's aforementioned argument that populations are not controlled by appeals to fear alone. For Tarde, love is far more catching. The discussion therefore notes a shift from fears related to epidemic spreading, terror networks, and computer viruses to power relations formed around a biopolitical concept of viral love. Finally, chapter 5, "Tardean Hypnosis: Capture and Escape in the Age of Contagion," begins to trace the Tardean trajectory to current exercises of biopower in capitalism and related business and political enterprises. It includes a discussion of the use of new technologies in so-called neuromarketing practices intended to influence consumer decisions by tapping into and capturing the unconscious processing of feelings, emotion, and affect. The book concludes with some embryonic reflections on how to discern, resist, and perhaps escape the flows of what are mostly indiscernible currents of imitation–suggestibility.

1
Resuscitating Tarde's Diagram in the Age of Networks

As a continuation of the themes cursorily approached in the introduction, this first chapter sets out to explain the specificity of Tarde's resuscitation and how his ontological diagram lays the groundwork for *Virality*. It begins with an interpretation of the foundational sociological ideas Tarde forwarded in three key texts: *Social Laws, The Laws of Imitation,* and *Psychological Economy.* These books introduced a complex series of interwoven microrelations, the diagram of which provides a novel alternative to dominant micro- and macroreductionisms so often attributed to social, cultural, and economic relationality. The aim here is to disentangle Tarde from Durkheim's collective consciousness and unravel contested claims that try to make him a forefather of both memetics and actor network theory. *Virality* instead aligns Tarde to Deleuzian assemblage theory and connects him to a disparate series of past and present contagion theories. These include approaches to imitation and conformity, crowd manias, and contemporary perspectives drawn from cognitive neuroscience and the theory of affect. By breathing new life into these microrelations, *Virality* intends to further connect Tarde to present-day network ontology and the fresh concerns it raises about social interaction and agency.

The Imitative Ray

To fully grasp the full relevance of Tarde's epidemiological microrelations to contemporary contagion theory, it is important to understand that he

17

does not regard the social, as Durkheim did, in terms of a deterministic encounter between collectives and individuals. Indeed, comparable to the way in which Deleuze's assemblage theory approaches social complexity,[1] Tarde needs to be seen from the outset as neither a macro- nor a microreductionist. Although overall categories, like crowds, clearly exist, his diagram is all about the *relationalities* that bring things together irrelevant of a given category, scale, or unity. As Deleuze puts it, it is "within overall categories, basic lineages, or modern institutions" that Tarde's microrelations can be found. Indeed, "far from destroying these larger unities," it is the microrelation that composes the unity.[2]

With regard to macroreductionism, then, Tarde rejects Durkheim's claim that it is the generality of social facts associated with social institutions that produces powerful downward pressures able to completely define the individual as a product of the society into which she is born. In sharp contrast to Durkheim's allusion to the controlling influence of an emergent collective consciousness, guided by the formation of consensus and norms and capable of somehow self-regulating the anomalous deviances of individuality, Tarde's theory of social encounter stresses that social wholes are derived from a principally accidental repetitive succession of desire. So importantly, although Tarde does not deny that social wholes exist, he accounts for them differently by pointing to their origins in the seemingly capricious minutia of microrelations. Like this, the repetition of desire spreads out through the mostly unconscious associations and oppositional forces of imitative social encounter. He explains social relationality accordingly as composed, decomposed, and recomposed by imitative radiations of desire, appropriated by social inventions, and coming together in the shape of shared beliefs, sentiments, and performances. It is this imitative radiation that stirs the social into action and brings about constant adaptations of stability and instability. It is not, therefore, the finality of wholes, collective unities, or institutions that are causal but the molecularity of colliding microrelations of desire and belief that, as Deleuze stresses, constitute the overall category.

Now with regard to microreductionism, Tarde's microrelations should not be mistaken for a sociology operating solely at the level of the individual. Although there are ostensible similarities with the microsociology of interactionism, Tarde's focus does not begin with individual social participation or (inter)action, as conventionally embedded in the person. On the contrary, and as Deleuze again contends, the harmonics of social assembly—*what holds it all together*—are not at all predetermined by an all-embracing category of persons or interacting subjectivities but "by having recourse to minutely small relations" that spread from point to point.[3]

The relevance of Tarde to the network age needs to be understood, in this light, not in terms of individual interaction or collective participation but in terms of the microrelational forces of imitative encounters. In other words, the encounter is not bound up in individual or collective representations but relates instead to a nonbonded yet much folded monadological *world of things*. In place of the logics of a molar representation of individuality and collectivity, Tardean social space is composed in the happenstance force of differentiated and repetitious events of desire and is appropriated by social inventiveness and the logic of an innate proclivity to imitate the inventions suggested by others.[4] Unlike the organic social system preferred by Durkheim, then, it is the mostly accidental flow of difference and repetition in Tarde's diagram that brings together monads in relation to each other. We might say, following Deleuze again, that Tarde's social space is a body without organs or, rather, a body "beneath organic determination" in the sense that is in "the process of differentiation."[5]

Tarde referred to the microrelational process of differentiation in a number of ways, including currents, waves, vibrations, and flows, but here I want to begin by concentrating for a moment on his extraordinary reference to the seemingly immeasurable *imitative rays* or what "radiate[s] out imitatively."[6] This is because the imitative ray, albeit a strange conception, completely captures the complexity of the social relation Tarde sets out to describe. As will become clear, what radiates out imitatively (what spreads) should not be confused with a purely cognitive, ideological, or interpsychological transfer between individuals and organic social formations (groups, masses, etc.). The imitative ray comprises of affecting (and affected) noncognitive associations, interferences and collisions that spread outward, contaminating feelings and moods before influencing thoughts, beliefs, and actions. Moreover, the imitative ray does not travel *between* (inter) individual persons; rather, it moves *below* (infra) the cognitive awareness of social association. In fact, what becomes associated, or related, in propagation of an imitative ray does so, in the main, by way of a "dream of action"[7] or paradoxical continuum between what is associated and dissociated.

Tarde's imitative ray has, not surprisingly, been likened to actor network theory (ANT).[8] It can certainly be traced beyond the organizational properties of conscious organic life to the contaminations of nonorganic matter, too. In Tarde's epidemiological diagram, there is indeed a distinct inseparability and insensible relation established between organic life and nonorganic matter. As is the case in the contagions of assemblage theory, informed to some extent by Samuel Butler's decentered notions of an involutionary human and technological process of innovation, Tarde's epidemiology is composed from a much wider and cross-hybridized understanding of what constitutes social invention than theories that limit themselves to human relations alone.

Imitative Repetition, Opposition, and Adaptation

To explicate how imitative rays function in ongoing social invention, Tarde sets out three underpinning social laws: *imitative repetition, adaptation,* and *opposition* (see Figure 1.1). Tarde's aim is to explore the role each of these laws plays in the propagation of imitative radiations in, for example, education, language, legal codes, crime, fashion, governance, and economic regimes. All these contagions might appear to begin with "personal initiative" but are "brought into mutual relation" with one another via an encounter with a ray that is "imitated by first one and then another . . . [and] continually borrowing from one another."[9] It is helpful to quote Tarde at length to set out how these three social laws fit into the social process of radiation he envisaged:

> It is through imitative *repetition* that invention, the fundamental social *adaptation,* spreads and is strengthened, and tends, through the encounter of one of its own imitative rays with an imitative ray emanating from some other invention, old or new, either to arouse new struggles, or (perhaps directly, perhaps as a result of these struggles) to yield new and more complex inventions, which soon radiate out

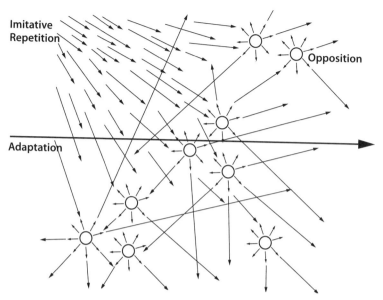

FIGURE 1.1. Repetition, adaptation, and opposition.

imitatively in turn, and so on indefinitely. Observe that the logical duel, the fundamental term in the social struggle of *opposition* . . . the fundamental term in social adaptation, requires repetition in order to become social, to become generalized and grow.[10]

As Figure 1.1 illustrates, Tarde's social is unlike the positivism of Durkheim's organic sociology. It is not a pregiven entity, but as the first, and most determining, law suggests, in among the continuum of variation experienced in social environments, there are repetitions of events that imitatively reproduce the cause point to point. *The social is not given, it is made.* The intermediary of small causes takes on what Tarde calls a "transmission of movement from one body to another," suggesting a continuous, localized, and indirect epidemiological space where social inventions are always in passage, spreading out, contaminating, and varying in size.[11] In contrast to the anomic self-regulation of Durkheim's collective social body, bodies are not fixed in Tarde's diagram. They are instead "receivers and transmitters" of flows that move through human bodies and other beings, interpreting the "feelings, affects, and attentive energy ... [and] ceaselessly moving messages of various kinds on."[12]

The middle law, opposition, is the most difficult to describe since the word itself inspires many interpretations. In fact, before approaching what Tarde meant by opposition, it is important to briefly set it apart from (1) a dialectical movement of opposition and (2) a competitive struggle for fitness between two opposing organisms. To begin with, the dialectic, famously rejected in Deleuze's Bergson-inspired ontological move away from Hegel, suggests a most improbable movement between binary opposites completely at odds with Tarde's open-ended repetition of imitative radiations and vibrating movements.[13] The ray is indeed an event that can vibrate in short bursts or infinite harmony. The ray's oppositional encounters are not negations, or negations of negations, but affective interferences, leading to an adaptive and accumulative flow of invention, imitations of invention, imitations of imitations, and so on. To put it another way, Tarde's oppositional forces have nothing to do with the competing dialectical negation of two halves leading to finality or totality, but as Deleuze and Guattari contend, it involves "the making binary of [imitative] flows."[14] This kind of opposition is entirely linked to the repetitive movement of invention—a derivation made from different flows that encounter each other and continue to productively spread out or radiate.

Locating Tarde's law of opposition in a competitive struggle for survival is equally problematic since it erroneously leads to the claim that Tarde's society of imitation maps onto social Darwinist and neo-Darwinian accounts of social evolution (the subject of my critique in the next chapter). But as Bruno Latour and Vincent *Lépinay* have recently argued, Tarde may well have "registered" Darwinism, but he is certainly not a social Darwinist and definitely not a neo-Darwinist.[15] That is to say, Tarde understood the biopower these two expressions of Darwinian competition exercise on a population. They both artificially transcend natural forces of encounter and become organizing principles, not part of the *nature of,* but *added to,* the repetitions of monads.[16] To be sure, Tarde does refer to opposition as part of a Darwinian-like struggle or "logical duel," but the competitive struggle does not take on a constitutive role in itself. It merely "provokes a tension of antagonistic forces fitted to arouse [biological and social] inventive[ness]."[17] Tardean oppositions are not therefore constrained to either dialectical or evolutionary schemas based on competition. Imitative encounters are rhythmic interruptions akin to a Bergsonist *creative involution*, if you like, occurring in the open-ended repetition of converging and diverging trends.

The third and final social law—adaptation—most definitely sets Tarde's epidemiological diagram apart from the molar overcodings of neo-Darwinian biopower. In the first instance, and in sharp contrast to Richard Dawkins's geneocentric account of encoded cultural imitation, the *meme,* Tarde offers an indirect imitative encounter between two oppositional forces: (1) those that collide and potentially stimulate adaptation and (2) those irregular rhythms that come and go according to the order of repetitive succession.[18] This latter kind of imitative force is "only in direct service to repetition."[19] It is not beholden to the course of any particular "natural" evolutionary schema guiding social reproduction. It is, unlike the meme, distinctly mechanism independent in this sense. By the same token, and in contrast to the overcoded categorizations of social functionalism, too, Tarde's law of adaptation explains how the social comes together vis-à-vis a continuum of mostly unconscious *infra* associations and encounters.[20] No downward determinacy is afforded to individuals or the unity of a collective consciousness; only the "growth in extension by imitative diffusion" and the "unifying" quality of this growth are held up as co-causal agents.[21] In addition, and part of the following discussion, Tarde clearly locates social adaptation in the productiveness of a repetitious and contagiously capricious encounter with desire-events.

To conclude this initial focus on Tarde's three laws, it is again worthwhile to observe how Deleuze and Guattari rearticulate Tarde's repetitious microrelations in the contagions and contaminations of assemblage theory:

> For in the end, the difference is not at all between the social and the individual (or interindividual), but between the molar realm of representation, individual or collective, and the molecular realm of beliefs and desires in which the distinction between the social and the individual loses all meaning since neither is attributable to individuals nor overcodable by collective signifiers.[22]

Along these lines, *Virality* draws on both Tarde's epidemiological diagram and Deleuze and Guattari's assemblage theory as a way to resist a tendency to begin social analysis at the level of molar overcodings. My intention is to provide an alternative account of social relation in which it is not the finitude of overall category but an infinitive encounter between two kinds of contagious multiplicities (molar and molecular) that becomes the focal point of the analytical gaze. Before moving on to more fully explore Tarde in relation to differences with Durkheim and influences on Deleuze, respectively, the discussion now turns to the detail of what he contended actually spread through epidemiological space.

Desire: Invention and Imitation

Unlike the medical metaphors and biological analogies adopted in the many contagion theories of the network age, which tend to grasp contagion as an anomalous disease, what spreads in Tarde's diagram becomes the distinguishing characteristic of all social relations, defined by a universal repetition of imitation. Effectively, the repetition of imitation becomes the infinitesimal rhythm of social relationality, triggered by the desire-event. In fact, we need to further explore Tarde's contention that invention and imitation appropriate desire but also reproduce a second kind of desire (see Figure 1.2).

To grasp the significance of how the three variables of desire, invention, and imitation intersect each other in the epidemiological diagram, we have to contend initially with a complex process involving, right from the outset, the repetition of everyday biological desires. These are the first kind of desire: the periodic, mechanical habits of everyday life (to eat, to drink, to dress, to make friends, to shit, to fuck, and so on). The first kind of desire is transformed, via capricious encounters with social invention (an encounter with a desiring machine or machinic assemblage), into a second kind of desire. It is very important to reaffirm that Tarde regarded these relations moving between mechanical biological habits and social action as part of an inseparable and indissoluble continuum. It is the desiring machine nevertheless that transforms the first kind into the second kind of desire and radiates these inventions outward into the social field. It is this second kind of desire to which we now refer as cultural contagion such as fashions, fads, market trends, and

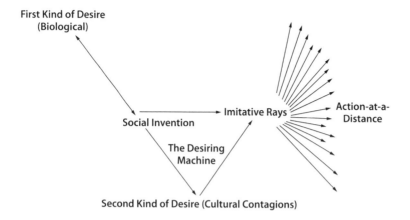

FIGURE 1.2. Two kinds of desire.

the like. The object of desire is in fact the belief in these contagions to the point where an ascending fashion, for example, becomes the custom that is followed. The important point to make about this second kind of desire is that its inventiveness is often aperiodic. Like this, fashion has a rare tendency to cascade or overspill, usurping customs.

It is the social process of imitative encounter that actualizes desire and transforms it into social invention. In other words, it is the imitative encounter that appropriates desire into the "desire to invent."[23] Inventions stemming from desire are then contagiously passed on, point to point, via radiating ideas, fascinations, passionate interests, beliefs, and any other suitable social media for imitation, feeding into a continuum of invention and further adaptations of the entire social field. This is how, for example, biological desires for nutrition, food, sex, entertainment, and amusement are appropriated, expressed, and transmitted in assemblages of social inventions, including consumer food products, religious rituals, games, novels, and the theater.[24] All this occurs, Tarde argues, against a chaotic backdrop of continuous accumulation of further "repetitions [which are] multiplications or self-spreading contagions."[25] This is how the small innovation becomes big and how contagious imitation adapts social invention according to an accumulation of invention. As Tarde argues, there is a tendency for a given invention or social adaptation to become larger and more complex by adapting itself to some other invention or adaptation, and thus create a new adaptation, which, through other encounters and logical combinations of the same sort, leads to a higher synthesis, and so on.[26]

Again, to understand the process by which the small becomes big, it is valuable to quote Tarde at length:

> We see specific desires that have been excited or sharpened by certain inventions or practical initiatives, each of which appears at a certain point from which, like a luminous body, it shoots out incessant radiations which harmoniously intersect with thousands of analogous vibrations in whose multiplicity there is an entire lack of confusion. We also see specific beliefs that have been produced by certain discoveries or hypotheses that also radiate at a variable rate and within variable limits. The order in which these inventions or discoveries appear and are developed is, in a large measure, merely capricious and accidental; but, at length, through an evitable elimination of those which are contrary to one another (i. e., of those which more or less contradict one another through some of their implicit propositions), the simultaneous group which they form becomes harmonious and coherent. Viewed thus as an expansion of waves issuing from distinct centers and as a logical arrangement of these centers and of their circles of vibration, a nation, a city, the most humble episode in the so-called poem of history, becomes a living and individual whole, a fine spectacle for the contemplation of the philosopher.[27]

Once more, it is important to note how the preceding passage illuminates Tarde's resolve that the social invention of desire has its origins in mostly capricious and accidental imitative encounters. Invention may, from time to time, take on the appearance of organic harmony and coherence, but the molarity of the living whole comes about only by way of the molecular stirring and sharpening of desires encountered in the repetition of desire-events, oppositions, and adaptations. What gets passed on in this machinic relation (the imitative ray) becomes a self-spreading social relation. These emitting rays exceed, as such, both the body of the self-contained cognitive agent (a person) and the collective consciousness. It is the movement of the ray that matters more than the tendency to cluster around it. It is, as Latour argues, the trajectory of the imitative ray that makes a difference, "not any of its provisional steps."[28] That is, what spreads passes through states of individuality and collectivity, eluding a deeply engrained tradition in Western thought in which rational agents are supposed to enter freely into relations with each other, principally unaffected by the contaminations of their neighborhood. In contrast, what spreads in Tarde's diagram does so by passing autonomously through unconscious associations.

It is necessary to further note how the extraordinary mesmeric (and rhythmical) self-spreading of the imitative ray reproduces social influence without a discernable medium of contact. This is arguably where the power dynamic resides in the Tardean diagram of epidemiological relationality. This process will be referred to hereupon as an *action-at-a-distance*. In contrast to the emergent dynamic densities that lead to Durkheim's determining collective consciousness, Tarde's diagram points to a perplexing hypnotic magnetism that exerts control over a mostly unconscious monadic social space, without a guiding hand. It is accordingly not the consensual regulation of social anomie but the overexcited magnetic forces of the imitative ray that bring things into relation with each other and constitute the overall category.

A Political Economy of Subjectivation

The problem of freewill is demonstrably apparent in Tarde's approach to political economy in *Psychological Economy*. Published in 1902, this book is a startlingly prophetic work that challenges the kind of subjectivity suggested in the self-contained and self-interested model of John Stuart Mill's *Homo Economicus*. It claims that cold-calculated decisions made regarding economic value are not the only yardstick by which to measure the economy and the human relation to it. On the contrary, economic man's desire for riches is interwoven with the passions and sentiments that relate him to the marketplace. This is a political economy of desire that brings together the fluctuations in market value, the rise and fall in testosterone and cortisol levels (market mood), and the spreading of financial crisis into a univocal imitative momentum or propensity, which, given the "reach and complexity" of contemporary communication technologies, allows for "undreamt of generative powers" in the age of networks.[29] Indeed, in their insightful appraisal of *Psychological Economy,* Latour and Lépinay make the very important point that by linking the economy to passionate interests in this way, Tarde in fact puts the political back into political economy.[30] He observes, as such, that economic relations are not merely attributable to a rationale, agentic logic guided by a prevailing *natural* law of capital. In the stead of *Homo Economicus,* we see how socioeconomic relations are differently composed of a politics of sentimental attachment, emotional association, market mood, and contagious affect.

Tarde's approach to unconscious associations and political economy has come to the attention of other writers. Borch, for instance, notes how "identities and individuality cannot be presupposed" in Tardean analysis since Tarde forwards the idea that "subjects are themselves constructed and reconstructed through economic operations." Economic exchange cannot therefore "presume the a priori existence of stable economic subjects (e.g., economic man)."[31] Blackman has, in much the same way, pointed to the notion that Tarde's political economy is also "not a matter of studying individual psychology, characterized by the abstracted, self-contained individual." In Tarde, Blackman argues, "subjects [are] open to affecting and being affected."[32] This rethinking of subjectivity (or subjectivation) as open to the affects of others is similarly approached by David Toews's account of Tarde, which further notes how the imitation of invention is "perhaps contrary to common sense" since imitation is not founded "upon [the] will or volition" of individuals but on individualities that themselves become the "media of inventions." It is indeed this imitative social media that constitute what Tarde means by participating in social practices.[33] As Toews further contends, "an actor does not 'participate' in this as we normally think of participation by means of an ego and a bodily extension." In place of free social interaction, the self becomes "a medium of creativity" in relation to the spread of social invention.[34]

Evidently, in contrast to the Enlightenment logic that continued to pervade much of the cognitive turn in sociology and psychology beginning in the twentieth century, Tarde's nineteenth-century crowd theory alternatively presents a subjectivating social medium free from human agency. Subjectivity is open to the magnetizing, mesmerizing, and contaminating affects of others. To be sure, Tarde's imitative social subjectivity is a somnambulist hypnotized by an epidemiological space Eric Alliez vividly depicts as a "cascade of successive mesmerizations."[35] The delicate inseparability in this space of imitative succession between biological flows of desire and colliding social invention renders the somnambulist vulnerable to imitation–suggestion.

It is nonetheless important to be cautious about how the unconscious individual is approached when discussing processes of imitative repetition. At one extreme, it would be possible perhaps to use Tarde to create a social space devoid of subjects, but as Borch remarks, Tarde is very concerned with analyzing the individual's inventions. However, once the invention becomes embedded in a social network of imitative relations, it takes on a "social character" that exceeds the mere interaction between one person and the next.[36]

Virality will in fact respond to the question of what spreads in the present-day network ontology by referring to a differently orientated notion of unconscious associations understood in the concept of the *networkability* of the desire-event (see chapter 3). The spreading of fashion, for example, passes through individuals, making them intervallic points of exchange, or transitive relays, passing on the desire-event, mostly unawares. These encounters with imitative repetition can therefore include a "hesitation," an "internal opposition," a decision point to adopt or reject the fashion.[37] Yet, unlike the cognitive turn toward a deciding agentic state, Tardean agency belongs here to the imitative ray in itself. It is not the deciding agent who freely enters into the network relation but the imitative ray that instead *makes* the agent part of an assemblage of relationality. Indeed, the extension of infinitely minute imitative currents, not just of contagious ideas but also of physical performances, suggestions, emotions, and affects, is "renewed a million times every moment," spreading from embedded customs to the adoption or rejection of a fashion or counterfashion.[38] It is the networkability of the desire-event that rhythmically maps the points at which desires accumulate (becoming appropriated by invention, invention becomes a multiple imitation of invention, and the imitation becomes an imitation of an imitation, etc.) so that, for example, a counterfashion (countercontagion) becomes part of an assemblage in which "opposing imitative rays interfere within the individual consciousness."[39] The ray therefore acts rhythmically on the unconscious, relating the individual to the invention by way of the force of the action-at-a-distance and opening him up to a potentially overwhelming succession of further radiations. There is no discernable medium of contact or subject–hypnotist in the network's rhythm of invention, yet individuals will unconsciously become "touched," as Tarde puts it, "by the rays of invading fashion."[40]

To understand how Tarde's imitative rays function according to an action-at-a-distance, we need to grasp how the magnetizing force of imitative encounter has a sense of rhythm. As Borch contends, "there is no doubt... that [Tarde] considered imitation processes rhythmlogically."[41] But this sense of rhythm can be decidedly offbeat. The rise and fall of certain fashions in the market, for instance, are part of an "irregular" kind of "rhythmic repetition" that is either opposed or adapted.[42] Hesitations and conflicting desires can occur in the general periodic flow of repetitive mechanical habits, but nonperiodic flows in the economy, such as undulating stocks, unpredictable rises in inflation or deflation, recession and boom time, and the very much related affective oscillations of market mood, provoke arhythmical social adaptation. Borch refers here to "rhythmic adaptations; that is, situations where the opposition generates new inventions that establish harmony rather than opposition."[43] This is not a regulating organic harmony of the collective consciousness, as Durkheim would have it, but a coming together of social relationality founded on the magnetic attraction of encounter. An example of how social relation is composed in this way is perfectly captured in Elias Canetti's description of the contagious rhythm of a dancing crowd as it acts to pull others into the "communal excitement" of a "rhythmic or throbbing crowd":[44]

> As long as they go on dancing, they exert an attraction on all in their neighborhood. Everyone within hearing joins them and remains with them. The natural thing would be for new people to go on joining them for ever, but soon there are none left and the dancers have to

conjure up increase out of their own limited numbers. They move as though there were more and more of them. Their excitement grows and reaches frenzy.[45]

Canetti argues that the social comes together not merely through a biological "urge for self-propagation" but because the dancers become part of a desire-event: they sense, they feel a desire to increase their size.[46] It is from within these excitable social assemblages that the dancing crowd becomes a social invention exerting its mesmeric and magnetic attraction on the other.

Before pursuing a similar Tardean trajectory into the network age, we need to briefly locate the desire-event in the context of the industrial age Tarde inhabited. He makes much of how the appropriation of desire is effectively sped up by the intensive concentration of urban life. The widespread spirit of innovation in the burgeoning metropolises of the late nineteenth century, for example, seems to provide new epidemiological densities, which, unlike the slow conservatism of rural populations, ensure that imitations can be "instantaneously transmitted to all minds throughout the city."[47] As follows, the invention of the locomotive cannot be taken in isolation as the result of a narrow progression of human ideas. It involves a highly complex accumulation of inventions that "once seemed foreign to one another"[48] (iron extraction and steam power) but then, from out of the quickening and thickening of social density, herald the emergence of a new technological innovation.

The usefulness of Tarde's epidemiological diagram in the study of network culture becomes apparent. As Latour declares, Tarde is the ideal "thinker of networks."[49] The proliferation of his diagram, via the Internet and the web, reaches out, as such, beyond the boundaries of the industrialized urban space, extending the inventive appropriation of desire, and what subsequently radiates out imitatively, to new social territories. To be sure, *Virality* is concerned with the reappropriation of desire in these new social territories and cultural contexts, that is, today's *nurseries of industry,* which capture fragments of the desire-event in social invention. This reappropriation is realized increasingly through the innovations of a new business enterprise that looks to place the end user (and her desires and experiences) at the center of research and development. The imitative rays these industries endeavor to emit are intended to dip below consciousness, building mostly unconscious emotional engagements between consumers, products, and brands, with the intention of triggering self-spreading imitations comparable to the magnetisms of Canetti's dancers.

The exponential growth in recent years of so-called social media networks, for example, demonstrates how inventiveness taps into the biological desire to be surrounded by friends—to increase the size of the crowd—and seize on the generative processes of the subsequent excitable social imitation to anticipate and produce novel extensions of unconscious consumption. The manifestation of the commodification of the desire for friendship is not only overlooked by the consumer (as Tarde argued, the unconscious innovator does not pay the "slightest attention in the world to the degree of difficulty or merit of the innovation in question")[50] but attention is, it seems, redirected toward a seductive series of innovations that do indeed self-spread. Along these lines, consumers of social media build their friendship networks frequently through their own innovative labors and emotional loyalties to each other and a particular social media brand. They are mostly unaware that they are part and parcel of a process of consumption at all, despite being prompted by a continuous stream of automated assists purporting to be from friends that further exploit the desire to attract more friends. Of course, the ways in which these enterprises realize hundreds of millions of dollars of revenue from the desire for friendship differ considerably from how they promote friendship in itself. They encourage friendship as a "tendency to desire what is best for the other" through expressions of feelings like sympathy, empathy, honesty, trust, mutual understanding, and compassion, which all become covertly coupled to the economic value of friendship established through data mining, customized advertising, and booming sales.[51]

The currency of the viral marketing enterprise is no longer the meme! The money now follows a trajectory comparable to Tarde's diagram. It marks out new endeavors to uncover the invisible presocial currents that relate users to each other, and the products, brands, and services they consume, in the hope of triggering profitable mesmeric cascades. Infectable emotions, feelings, and affects have in effect become the favored focal point for experience designers and neuromarketers. In the study of human–computer interaction (HCI), for example, there is a distinct trend toward measuring the social context of user experience in relation to affect and emotion.[52] The traditional theoretical framework of HCI was very much a product of a shift from behavioral to cognitive psychology in the 1970s. It involved an ongoing interdisciplinary convergence between Tayloristic engineering (time and motion and ergonomic studies) and cognitive psychology approaches to attention and memory. However, the so-called third paradigm of HCI research extends the study of human–machine coupling by linking it to a growth in know-how in cognitive psychology informed by neuroscience. Indeed, arguably allied to this third paradigm is the neuromarketer, working with attention, memory, and emotion technologies to more effectively hook up the user experience of e-commerce to biological desires and better prepare the consumer for future purchase intent (see chapter 5).

Although such manifestations of Tarde's trajectory are becoming increasingly evident in the psychology of design, there is a need to move cautiously through the psychological dimensions suggested in his diagram. Despite the protestations of Durkheimians, who argued long ago that Tarde's laws of imitation were a mere psychologism verging on spiritualism, Deleuze argues that it is "completely wrong to reduce Tarde's sociology to psychologism or even inter-psychology."[53] To begin with, the imitative ray does not equate to a distribution of mental representations between individuals. Tarde is far more concerned with how the spreading of open-ended imitative repetitions blur the self–other divide than he is with the conscious (or unconscious) sharing of images. This is certainly the flip side to Durkheim's notion that it is the collective consciousness that, through downward processes of "dynamic density," entirely determines the consciousness of the individual.[54] In contrast, Tarde's social concept points to how what spreads (the imitative ray) becomes the consciousness of the epidemiological diagram. This is a process that might be better termed an *infrapsychology*. But perhaps Latour has it right. No sociology, he contends, "was ever further from psychology than Tarde's."[55] Indeed, Tarde's diagram is not a psychology at all. It is a *relational ontology!*

From Collective Intelligence to Media Hypnosis

The ontology of relationality apparent in Tarde's diagram questions two tenets of the Durkheimian paradigm, that is, (1) what is it that brings together and regulates overall social categories and (2) how is it that social categorization can be regarded as discontinuous with psychological and biological phenomena? On one hand, Durkheim presents his theories of collective consciousness and anomie, which produce bonded relations distinct from all other categories. On the other hand, Tarde's notion of mass hypnosis identifies a distinctly nonbonded relation, lacking in human agency (collective or individual) and growing out of the happenstance of events and accidents. This is a distinction between Durkheim and Tarde already made but one that now requires further elaboration.[56]

To begin with, we must register how Durkheim understood anomie as a necessary evil a corrupted society needs to suffer to regulate itself and become whole again. Paradoxically perhaps, without anomie, there is no social need to express moral or legal rules, which are always worked out via the averaging of the opinion of the collective consciousness.[57] In other words, the emergence of deviations from the norm results in social actors formally coming together to reject what is contrary to the common good.

It is, however, Durkheim's notion of *dynamic density* that arguably makes him the forefather of an altogether different theory of social complexity and collective emergence from that suggested in Tarde's diagram. By way of his influence on Talcott Parsons's functionalism, Durkheim has subsequently been claimed by a number of authors as an early pioneer of systems theory and cybernetic approaches to the social, including notions of swarm, collective, and distributed intelligence.[58] As Durkheim contends, together we are indeed smart:

> Society is not at all the illogical or a-logical, incoherent and fantastic being which it has too often been considered. Quite on the contrary, the collective consciousness is the highest form of the psychic life, since it is the consciousness of the consciousnesses. Being placed outside of and above individual and local contingencies, it sees things

only in their permanent and essential aspects, which it crystallizes into communicable ideas. At the same time that it sees from above, it sees farther; at every moment of time, it embraces all known reality; that is why it alone can furnish the mind with the moulds which are applicable to the totality of things and which make it possible to think of them. It does not create these moulds artificially; it finds them within itself; it does nothing but become conscious of them.[59]

As follows, Durkheim was concerned with how an "increase in the volume and dynamic density of societies ... making social life more intense and widening the horizons of thought and action of each individual, profoundly modifies the basic conditions of collective life."[60] The organic glue that brings the social together is, in this light, a homeostatic process regulated by anomie, social facts, and the downward influence of collective intelligence.

In contrast, Tarde's epidemiological diagram positions the imitative ray as the pervasive factor—the elephant in the room, if you like. Unlike Durkheim's top-down determinism, Tarde appeals to the contagiousness of point-to-point social encounters, continuously adapted by local contingencies. Significantly, Tarde does not completely dismiss the idea of social wholes but argues that the whole is a manifestation of habitual repetitions of social invention and imitation prone to the occasional monstrous contagion. Imitation radiates, as such, through the porous self–other relations established in the desiring machine, building occasional bubbles fit to burst.

Yet what concretely distinguishes Tarde from Durkheim is the latter's attempt to render all things psychological, biological, and neurological categorically distinct from the social, while the former marks their inseparability. In lieu of Durkheim's concentration on social consciousness and category, Tarde's diagram comprises mostly unconscious flows of desire, passion, and imitative radiations of muscular as well as cerebral activities. In their debate together at the École des Hautes Études Sociales (the year after the publication of *Economic Psychology*), Durkheim reportedly made a particular issue of how the social sciences needed to make their subject matter separate from these other phenomena. As he puts it elsewhere,

There is between psychology and sociology the same break in con-
tinuity as there is between biology and the physical and chemical
sciences. Consequently, every time a social phenomenon is directly
explained by a psychological phenomenon, we may rest assured that
the explanation is false.[61]

Nonetheless, it is important, I contend, not to mistake Tarde's appeal
to psychological and biological phenomena as endemic to a subliminal space of the unconscious, secreted away from both collective and
individual consciousness. Infrapsychology differs considerably in this
sense from a parent–child interpsychology. It is instead a description
of a *nonconscious* that finds a better home in Deleuze's schizoid than
it does in Freud's paranoid (see chapter 2). It also seems to prefigure
current neurological explanations of the relation established between
unconscious transmissions of affect and cognitive processes such as
what is attended to, what is decided on, and (of particular interest to
neuromarketers, of course) purchase intent.[62]

   Tardean epidemiological relations can therefore be understood as
an *almost* liminal social process, likened by Tarde to the in-between
states characterized by hypnotism and somnambulism. In this diagram, categorical distinctions between psychological and biological
phenomena become inseparable from the social. To be sure, Tarde
understands unconscious associations by making "no distinction . . . between Nature and Society."[63] There is no "absolute separation," he
counters, "of this abrupt break, between the voluntary and the involuntary . . . between the conscious and the unconscious. . . . Do we not
pass," he argues, "by insensible degrees from deliberate volition to almost
mechanical habit?"[64]

   Tarde's epidemiological diagram involves the distribution of a noncognitive rather than cognitive intelligence, that is, an imitative-suggestibility
passed on in the collective nonconscious so that the affects of the other
become etched onto the body and mind of the porous self.[65] As follows,
unlike Durkheim's self-regulatory collective, Tarde draws attention to
how nonconscious intersections between social, psychological, and
biological phenomena are implicated in the propagation and diffusion
of desire in the neighborhood.

A Contested Tarde

Despite being overshadowed throughout the twentieth century by the Durkheimian social paradigm, Tarde's epidemiological diagram has surfaced in various articulations of contagion theory. In these next two sections, I want to critically engage with his line of influence in such cases, beginning with contested claims that Tarde is in fact the forefather of both memetics and actor network theory before returning to focus, in the next section, on the validity of connecting Tarde to Deleuze's assemblage theory.

Before going on to claim Tarde as a forefather of memetics, Paul Marsden begins by providing a useful sense of how he came to make imitation central to his understanding the social.[66] As a former lawyer, Tarde's interest in imitation was apparently sparked into life by his observation that crime has an epidemiological component, spreading like a fashion. He went on to study imitation as a general feature of the social, including imitation of customs, fashion, sympathy, obedience, precepts, and education. However, Marsden argues that Tarde's subsequent publication of *Les Lois de l'Imitation* can be traced back to specific Darwinian credentials some six years earlier when he published a paper titled "Darwinisme naturel et Darwinisme social" in 1884. Marsden is for that reason intent on connecting Tarde's central thesis to neo-Darwinian selectionism and the survival of the fittest mechanism in particular. Like this, he draws attention to Tarde's references to "counter-imitations," in which the career of "inherited inventions" spreads through a population according to a differential survival mechanism—processes to which Tarde refers using ostensibly Darwinian evolutionary jargon, such as "culling processes," "logical duels," and "struggles," that either accepts or rejects the imitation.[67]

Marsden is also quick to align Tarde to the efforts made by contemporary memeticians to explain the potential to engineer generative imitation. In effect, what Marsden argues connects very well to the memetic strategies so often touted by the first wave of viral marketers:

> Tarde . . . raised the possibility of engineering a successful imitation
> independently of any truth or utility that imitation may have. To

engineer a successful imitation, or meme in today's parlance, Tarde
suggested that it might suffice to present the invention (mutant
imitation) as a descendent of an endemic part of culture into which
it is to be introduced.[68]

In fact, what Marsden picks up on in this description of engineered imitation draws on Tarde's idea that to succeed, a competing fashion must
imitate ("assume the mask of") an older custom "fallen into discredit
and rejuvenate [it] for the needs of her cause."[69] On the face of it, this is
a neo-Darwinian Trojan horse, by any other name. Nonetheless, Marsden's efforts to make struggle central to Tardean epidemiology arguably
glosses over a crucial point made in "Darwinisme naturel et Darwinisme
social," in which Tarde rejects a strictly Darwinian explanation of the
social by stating that competition needed to be considered alongside
cooperation. Although neo-Darwinists, including Dawkins, have come
to agree that altruism is part of the evolution of selfish competition
("nice guys finish first"),[70] it is arguably a misreading of Tarde to fix
imitation–suggestibility to the exclusive terms of competitive struggle.
In fact, contrary to memetic selectionism, Tarde's diagram of imitation–
counterimitation does not present a simple causal accept–reject mechanism. It shows instead how counterimitations are assimilated into the
processes of social adaptation without a need for winners and losers.
As Tarde puts it,

> In counter-imitating one another, that is to say, in doing or saying
> the exact opposite of what they observe being done or said, they are
> becoming more and more assimilated.[71]

Along these lines, Tarde's diagram differs considerably from selectionist
evolution since it does not exclude a paradoxical coalescence of opposition from social adaptation.

There are indeed many deep-seated points of divergence between the
memetic unit of imitation and Tarde's diagram. I will go on to unpack
these in the next chapter, but one other is significant to this discussion:
briefly, how Tarde and memetics differently contend with the notion
of the unconscious. On one hand, the meme reduces social agency

to an unconscious induced by an evolutionary algorithm. It is in fact Marsden who tries to distance a Tardean-influenced memetics from the extremes of this psychosocial rendering of the self as constructed entirely by the meme typified in the work of both Susan Blackmore and Daniel Dennett. It is therefore important to register here the clear difference between (1) the way in which the hypnotic action-at-a-distance of Tarde's epidemiological diagrams works in-between the circuitry that connects conscious and unconscious states and (2) the way in which social relation is absolutely lost to "natural" evolutionary causes in memetics.

It is perhaps a relief, then, to discover that Tarde has more grand-children! To be sure, in his article "Gabriel Tarde and the End of the Social," Latour makes the case for being a long-lost relative in typically flamboyant style: "I have decided to share with the readers the good news that ANT actually has a forefather."[72] He provides two main interrelated reasons why this is the case, both of which will already be familiar to the reader. First, ANT and Tarde share the goal of making what Latour refers to as "the nature and society divide ... irrelevant for understanding the world of human interactions."[73] Second, Tarde's diagrammatic focus on the microrelations of imitation–suggestibility helps Latour counter "the micro/macro distinction," which "stifle[s] any attempt at understanding how society is being generated."

It is important to go over the reasoning of Latour's twofold claim to Tarde as a forefather before returning to how both relate to the development of *Virality*. At first, Latour extols Tarde for not beginning his analysis with the "social" as we have come to understand it (on either side of the nature–society divide or within a micro–macro reductionist concept). Instead, he notes how Tarde begins in a similar space of flows suggested by Deleuze's incorporeal materialism of monadology, in which desire actualizes matter, imbuing it with agency. As Latour argues,

It is with this bizarre arrangement of apparently contradictory metaphysics that we have to familiarize ourselves if we want to understand why Tarde had so completely ended the social—or refused to begin with it.[74]

Like this, Tarde's notion of agency deals alternatively with the stuff the universe is made of. His use of the word *social* does not refer at all to determining the category of collective or individual representation. On the contrary, Latour points out how Tarde, like Deleuze, considers that all societies are "assemblages of many interlocking monads."[75]

It is this refusal to reduce the social to either side of a nature–society or macro–micro divide that leads both Tarde and ANT to alternatively focus on monadological association. More precisely, in ANT, the monad is translated to the actor (scallops, microbes, door closers, and humans), and the notion of association pertains to the networkability of the monad's agency. Certainly, in this sense, and contrary to Durkheim's assertion that the big influences the small, Tarde insists that the small always holds the big. The small is, as such, always the more complex. This is seemingly counterintuitive to much of what is described in the social sciences. As Latour argues,

> We are so used in the social sciences to speak of levels of complexities, of higher order, of emergent properties, of macrostructure, of culture, societies, classes, nation states, that no matter how many times we hear the argument, we immediately forget it and start ranking local interactions from the smallest to the biggest as if we could not think without stuffing Russian dolls one neatly into the next. . . . But [for] Tarde . . . the big, the whole, the great, is not superior to the monads, it is only a simpler, more standardized, version of *one of the monad's goal[s] which has succeeded in making part of its view shared by the others.* . . . The macro is nothing but a slight extension of the micro.[76]

Social structures and levels are entirely artificial layers formed on top of a "discordant chaos" composed in the minutia of imitative social encounters. Via Tarde, Latour gainfully draws our attention, as such, to the artificialness of disciplinary distinctions commonly made between (1) the actions of agents and (2) the laws that act on agents—a distinction that may very well be further broken down into the problematics of what constitutes, on one hand, the freewill of social agency and, on the other, the causal forces of nature that act on individuals. There is no need after Tarde, Latour argues, for these "two vocabularies."[77] ANT speaks in one vocabulary composed of a world of things in association and agency.

From this I hope the ontological link between Tarde and ANT is now made clear. But by way of a further illustration, we can refer to the apposite example Tarde provides to describe the authoring of a book so as to conjure up a Tardean actor network. Tarde contends that associative innovations, like books, are not reducible to a pure division of labor, but "it is through the conscious or unconscious, assembled or dispersed, association of workers that the solidarity of labors manifests itself."[78] He continues, "One would . . . need to distinguish between all sorts of associations that converge in producing [a book]."[79] Indeed, social inventions only become "coherent" through the spreading of influence, imitations, contaminations, and routinizations. The spreading of associations therefore makes sense of the world, but moreover, it explains the social without reducing it to a controlling culture since the spreading of language and scientific innovation illustrates how it is the spread of influence itself that generates a cultural consciousness. As follows, the action-at-a-distance functioning of Tardean imitative suggestibility does not equate to a controlling culture either, but as Latour notes, it ties, or relates, one person or thing to the imitative rays of another.

Nonetheless, *Virality* differs from ANT in at least two respects: first, in how it grasps Tarde's action-at-a-distance, and second, in the prominence it awards to the force of encounter with events. To begin with, whereas actors are locked into the inscribed associations of the network, the focus moves to the disassociations suggested by the Tardean somnambulist. I do not mean here physically broken links or mental disengagements from the network, but on the contrary, the spotlight falls more brightly on the way in which nonconscious imitative rays relate one person to a world of things, largely unawares. This is an important component of the society of imitation thesis to which Latour begins to allude when he draws on Tarde's notion of the blurring of the self in relation to the other. As Tarde similarly puts it,

In any one, if we look carefully, we will find nothing but a certain number of he and she that have blurred and confounded themselves through their multiplications.[80]

Although Latour gainfully uses this quotation to dissect Tarde from individualism (and, in doing so, traces the network by looking for the actors, and in turn, understanding actors through the networks in which they are traced), the biological and psychological blurring of the self and other in social encounters seems to be purposefully avoided, perhaps in case it resides too closely to a psychoanalytical perspective or a modern-day interpsychology. As I will argue, a drift back to both a psychoanalytical unconscious or interpsychology is indeed incompatible with Tarde's diagram, but its appeal to somnambulism nonetheless infers an unconsciousness of sorts not accounted for in the associative network model. By integrating the role of the somnambulist in social association, Tarde suggests a parliament of things significantly (and paradoxically perhaps) not only associated to each other in proliferating networks but also related to each other through disassociations in which identities become blurred in their own multiplication. It is a seemingly distracted and inattentive somnambulist that is embedded in the network and whose attention is potentially steered via the exploitation of the unconscious association with the other. This is not so much a theory of association as it is a theory of persuasion and suggestibility.

In this light, Jonathon Crary's thesis on attention (and its subsequent reading of Tarde) introduces media hypnosis as a way to think through the biopolitical control of a population as an action-at-a-distance. As Crary consummately notes, there is a paradoxical relation established in both media consumption and hypnosis between, on one hand, induced inattention, distraction, and reverie and, on the other, the focusing of attention.[81] The inference of what Crary says here is certainly important to the ideas expressed in this book; that is, in a network age, when there is a concerted effort to guide the precious attention of the consumer to the increasingly fragmented sprawl of commercially networked media messages and political propaganda, appeals to a relatively small percentage of cognitive thought is fast becoming a waste of resources. As the neuromarketers and experience designers perfectly understand, to grab attention, it is better to focus resources on the neurological unconscious. It is not therefore cognitive processing power but the spontaneity of emotional responses to affective priming that drives purchase intent.

Indeed, despite Tarde's tendency to stress the accidentalness of the flows of desire in his diagram, the spontaneity of the imitative ray may, as Thrift argues, be increasingly steered by way of a mass mesmerism gone bad.[82] This is a reinvention of the somnambulist in the network age: subjectivity only half asleep and dreaming that he is in command while reciprocally engaged with the hypnotist. Whereas the Freudian subliminal interpretation of dreams locates the somnambulist as an automaton under remote control, we might be better advised to follow Alex Galloway and Eugene Thacker's alternative narcoleptic somnambulist, who performs in a liminal media space, like a surrealist engaged in automatic writing. "*I* am media," he states, "but only when [accidentally] asleep."[83] *Virality* will similarly continue to persist in thinking through the notion of a neurologically defined unconscious somnambulist, revisiting Deleuze and Guattari's equally counter-Freudian claim that the unconscious should not be mistaken for a single person. The unconscious is not, as Freud's analysis of group psychology contends, controlled by Daddy's voice. The unconscious is rather the "shove and buzz" of the crowd.[84] The unconscious is the desiring machine that opens up subjectivity to the world of affective capacities and events.

ANT is, of course, exemplary in this respect. It eludes essentializing the individual node. The opening up of the cognitive subject, the "mind-in-a-vat," to the outside world of relation is a Tardean reinvention of the social through and through.[85] Nevertheless, the second point of departure herein is well explicated by Thrift, who, while acknowledging ANT's usefulness in awarding agency to objects, emphasizing invention over cognitive reflection, and the sense it gives of a distributed personhood, criticizes its tendency to accumulate and sustain "effectivity."[86] The problem with ANT is that it tends to neutralize the intensity of events, giving precedence to "steely accumulation" over "lightning strikes" and to "sustained strategies" over "sharp movements."[87] ANT, it seems, treats accumulation as an effect or product generated by heterogeneous means. Knowledge and agency are products composed or translated within the relationality between bits and pieces from the social, technical, architectural, conceptual, and textual ad infinitum. Yet, however much the heterogeneous engineering of an actor network is regarded as a verb (to translate) rather than a noun (the Translated)—in other words, a generative process recursively reproducing itself—the character of organization it produces is always a product, an effect, or a consequence, not an event.

The Desiring Machine: Wasps and Orchids

I want now to make a significant connection between the desiring machine apparent in both Tarde's diagram and Deleuze's theory of machinic assemblage. The point of drawing attention to the machinic processes at the core of both Tarde's and Deleuze's diagrammatics of desire is to stress their significant place in a counter-neo-Darwinian concept of *cross-hybridization,* or what I will go on in this book to describe in the concept of *viral love* (see chapter 4). The main focus for now, though, is placed on Deleuze and Guattari's prominent account of the cross-kingdom lovemaking of the wasp–orchid assemblage and how it in turn relates to a decentralized power functioning in Tarde's diagram.

To fully grasp the role of the desiring machine in Tarde's diagram, it is necessary from the outset to recognize it as a dispersed process of social reproduction enabled by the capture of fragments of desire. By doing so, a clear distinction is made between the genetic model of reproduction, typified in neo-Darwinism, and the contagions, contaminations, and imitative encounters also evident in assemblage theory. "We oppose epidemic to filiation, contagion to heredity, peopling by contagion to sexual reproduction, sexual production," Deleuze and Guattari contend. Crowds (humans, animals, or insects) "proliferate by contagion, epidemics, battlefields, and catastrophes."[88] To be sure, nowhere is this distinction made more apparent than in the reproductive relation established between the orchid and the male wasp. This is an accidental involution that occurs between two species that have "nothing to do with each other," but when they meet, they change both of their destinies.[89] Before analyzing this specific assemblage, however, it is important not to limit thought to metaphorical relations it might imply since the sexual relation established between the wasp–orchid assemblage demonstrates a reproductive act of capture that occurs between different assemblages, regardless of what is categorized as "natural" or "cultural." To be sure, in the stead of constraining metaphors, it is necessary to grasp the notion of capture via the processes of territorialization (coding), deterritorialization (decoding), and reterritorialization (recoding or overcoding).

Deleuze and Guattari begin by noting how it is the orchid that attracts the male wasp by carrying on its flower the image and odor of the female wasp. The "heterogeneous elements" of the assemblage form a rhizomatic relation in which the orchid and wasp territorialize and deterritorialize each other's codes to become part of a collective "reproductive apparatus." There is, in this apparatus, a molecular contagion, or "an increase in valence, a veritable becoming-wasp of the orchid and a becoming-orchid of the wasp."[90] Contagion is defined in this apparatus by way of a convergent imitative encounter in which one assemblage captures the fragments of another's desire. In "rhizomatic fashion," the contagion "quits" one assemblage, drawing the other forward and opening it up.[91] The reproductive apparatus involves a machinic capture in which a swapping of code fragments from one machine to another leads to the emergence of "strange, unheralded new assemblages."[92]

The wasp–orchid assemblage draws attention to reproductive acts that are not centered on mating couples passing on genes but rather are part of a networked collective of mutual imitative reproducers. As one entomologist recently put it, "we need to think of mutualisms as being embedded in—and sometimes reliant upon—a wider network of species interactions."[93] This is, of course, nothing new. Deleuze and Guattari's inspiration comes not only from Proust's fascination with fat bumblebees and orchids but also from Samuel Butler's nineteenth-century *Book of Machines,* which develops such mutualisms to argue that to assume that humans and machines cannot reproduce is utterly "unscientific."[94] We might "see a machine as a whole," Butler argues. We may look on our own body and its limbs as a machine "which springs from a single center of reproductive action." We "name and individualize it." Nevertheless, we mistakenly assume that there can be "no reproductive action which does not arise from a single center."[95] As Deleuze and Guattari go on to argue, machinic assemblages not only reproduce via contagion and contamination rather than heredity reproductive sex, they also have no conceivable center or, indeed, beginning or end.[96]

The molecularity of the wasp–orchid assemblage further challenges the molar geneocentric definition of imitation as a mere act of preprogrammed copying. On one hand, molarity is modeled on the linear imitation of resemblances (becoming-the-same). Molar imitation, as Massumi argues, "respects the boundaries between molar wholes, setting up comparisons between bodies considered separately, as entities unto themselves." As follows, genes preserve the structural whole of the body in which causal functions act in "stable interaction" with other determining functions.[97] The body is defined by what remains the same, as such. On the other hand, though, molecular imitations are reproduced through the microrelations of contagion and contamination (becoming-other). Assemblages are not therefore *resembled* from past linguistic blueprints (culture) or genetic templates (nature) but *assembled* through repetitious and differentiated imitative encounters that cut through the culture–nature artifice. As indeed Tarde seems to similarly argue, imitative propagation occurs "through the inner rhythms of . . . indefinitely repeated movements, rather than through the transmission of characteristics . . . of reproduction."[98]

So reproductive stability is not a fatalistic end. Spreading out from its origins in the accidents of Tarde's diagram, the reproduction of sameness in another assemblage is never guaranteed. Oppositional collisions—the accidents and unforeseen events of social density—introduce nonlinear instabilities, interference, error, and aperiodic noise into the processes of imitative encounter. *It is these microrelations that take control of the whole* — the most deterritorialized aspects of the assemblage that takes control of the most territorialized strata.[99] The functional identity of an assemblage is only guaranteed insofar as it can ward off the wear and tear caused by further accidental encounters with events. Continuous breakdown of the concreteness of assemblages will "demand a renewal of its material components."[100] It is significantly the vulnerability and sensitivity of assemblages to contamination that makes them distinct from the assumed robust immunity of social wholes.

We can perhaps return at this point to the "psychology" apparent in Tarde's diagram and say that what spreads does not simply enter the individual via interpsychological pathways running between instinctual drives. It is rather passed on, or more exactly captured, in affective transmissions. Consider, for example, the contagiousness of yawns, smiles, or blushes, processes in which "human beings subconsciously mirror each other's actions in a constant iterative ballet of not-quite duplication."[101] As Thrift argues, affective contagions are transferred from others (and a wide variety of other objects) not via a simple mechanical process of copying but through a circuitry of feeling–response. There is a distinctive indirectness in Tarde's diagram that differs considerably from mimetic processes of representation. "There is no exact copy so our desires can never properly be ours. Rather our desires are secondhand and socially oriented." Desire is not therefore a copy of the instructions guaranteeing survival but a "passage from one state to another, as an intensity characterized by an increase or decrease in power."[102]

There is, like this, a distinct power relation in the wasp–orchid assemblage. The orchid imitates the female wasp to trick the male wasp and make it an unwitting pollinator. Significantly, unlike the genetic coding apparent in neo-Darwinist reproduction (the copying of hereditary resemblances through the genetic line of a species), the orchid's imitation of the female, as well as being an indirect and counterfeit reproductive act, is often contrary to the survival of the male wasp, who squanders both sperm and energy.[103] The female wasp certainly has very little need for the male. Like hundreds of other male insects duped by plants, their female equivalents can often reproduce without the male. In some cases, female wasps have developed more lasting relations with other plants, like the fig tree, which similarly plays host to female eggs. The *mutualism* developed between insects and plants can, on one hand, become a stabilizing vitalism that heralds new assemblages, but on the other, it is not always a harmonious relation and can endanger the delicate ecologies that bring together these new assemblages. In this context, sexual reproduction is not restricted to the passing on of a genetic code from one being to another but becomes, like the wasp and the orchid, a deterritorialized relation or symbiotic association through which desire and sensation are transmitted and captured.

Along these lines, Luciana Parisi uses the wasp–orchid assemblage to demonstrate the extension of the strata of sex beyond humanism and, in doing so, challenges the biological determinism of the neo-Darwinian paradigm: a dominant paradigm which she contends has become embedded in social, political, economic, and cultural arenas of capitalism. The problem for Parisi, as for Deleuze and Guattari previously, is that the sexuality of the selfish gene becomes the prevailing "motor of preservation and production of variation."[104] However, the relation between capitalism and sex is moving away from the centered-ness of human sexual mating, sexual organs, and sexed genes toward Butler's machinic desire. As capitalism becomes increasingly mediated through biotechnologies—cloning, for example—sexual reproduction becomes ever more disentangled from the confines of a strictly human domain. The outcome of this decoupling is an "intensification of desire in molecular relations," like those established between "a virus and a human, an animal cell and a micro-chip."[105]

Significantly, unlike an older paradigm of industrially powered capitalism, supported by a scientific method that reinforced the cul-ture–nature divide, the transversal, cross-kingdom methodologies of biopower perhaps reveal the extent to which a molecular, viral capitalism is starting to penetrate biological, cultural, and economic intersections.[106] This is a concept of biopower comparable to a benevolent orchid able to magnetize the mutual but largely involuntary desires of the wasp and simultaneously hijack and transform them into social invention. Refer-ring back to Tarde, the wasp can perhaps be rather crudely interpreted as the somnambulist who "unconsciously and involuntarily... allows an action of others to be suggested to him."[107] The orchid, conversely, provides the hypnotic point of fascination (the joyful encounter) that guides the attention and involuntary actions of the wasp by way of a distraction. What captures the attention of the somnambulist wasp is the orchid's hypnotic transmission of passions triggered by imitative tendencies. Capitalism is the wasp–orchid assemblage insofar as it conjures up a marketplace of imitative encounters in which ever more fragments of desire can be captured. A post-neo-Darwinist biopower therefore arises from out of the imitative desires of a mostly unconscious but reciprocal pollination process. The mass mesmerism of Tarde's imi-tative rays does indeed occur in moments of joyful encounter, wherein "non-conscious perception, dissociation, suggestion and suggestibility, and social influence" are not necessarily perceived as "a threat to the boundaries of an individual."[108]

It is important to grasp in Tarde's early industrial urban spaces how a magnetic pull of distraction worked on a "stupefied... state of catalepsy," in which the attention, or rather the lack of attention, of the somnambulist is

so bent upon everything they see and hear, especially upon the actions
of the human beings around them, that it is absolutely withdrawn
from everything they have previously seen and heard, or even thought
of or done. . . . Memory becomes absolutely paralyzed; all its own
spontaneity is lost. In this singular condition of intensely concentrated attention, of passive and vivid imagination, these stupefied and
fevered beings inevitably yield themselves to the magical charm of
their new environment.[109]

Here Tarde's influence on Crary's thesis is made concrete. Modern
distraction is not a disruption of natural attention but a constitutive
element of the many attempts to produce attentiveness in human subjects.[110] His diagram expresses, as such, paradoxical moments in which
points of fascinated attention are in composition with overspills of dis-
orientation, distraction, and inattention—a somnambulistic attention
deficit disorder.

If Tarde is indeed a forefather of any theoretical tradition, then that
is, as Thrift similarly argues, surely a theory of mass media persuasion
that manages to avoid reducing the spread of social influence to a function of institutional power alone.[111] Comparable to some extent to the
mass ideological apparatus of mind control, the imitative ray instills
the *feelings* that we are the originators of our own thoughts, beliefs, and
actions.[112] This is not, however, a theory of persuasion that begins with
a state of false consciousness so much as it brings together unconscious
desires into a dream of command. It is, as such, a theory of persuasion
that is no less political. However, it seems to have gained momentum in
recent "corporate impulses" of the network age before "spilling over into
political life," with politicians only just taking advantage of "a whole array
of corporate internet-related techniques" to make voters "susceptible
to the same subconscious processes of imitation."[113]

Persuasion does not have a solely semiotic charge either. Certainly,
unlike his contemporary Gustave Le Bon, whose concept of mass persuasion accorded "great power to the image as [hypnotic] organizer of
the crowd,"[114] Tarde's hypnotist is arguably nonrepresentational. Political
feeling and social action are primed and ignited instead by appeals to
hunger, sex, aggression, fear and self-preservation, hormonal fluxes,

body languages, shared rhythms, attentive energies, and entrainments, all produced during imitative encounters between the body and the event.[115]

A Connected Tarde

Before concluding this opening chapter, I want to draw particular attention to various other authors who explicitly or implicitly connect to both Tarde and the themes addressed in *Virality*. These connections include a range of past and present ideas from Milgram's social psychology approach to imitation in the 1960s to a very early study of contagious crowd behavior and financial contagion (both of which have greatly influenced the so-called new science of networks), as well as more recent references to work in cognitive neuroscience and a social theory of affect. In addition to Tarde and Deleuze, these sources offer opportune excursions by which to compare and contrast Tarde's insights and, more crucially, give prominence to the role contagion plays in reproducing power relations and social obedience in the age of networks.

Milgram's Manhattan Experiment

Nearly eighty years after Tarde's ruminations about the society of imitation, a research team headed by the social psychologist Stanley Milgram set up an experiment intended to better understand how social influence spreads through the urban crowd.[116] Mirroring to some extent Tarde's late-nineteenth-century interest in how imitative contagions propagate through social collectives mostly unawares, Milgram's experiment in 1968 was designed to stimulate the imitative behaviors of individuals as they encountered a crowd. To begin with, an actor was planted on a busy Manhattan street corner and told to look up at a tall building while the researchers observed the actions of unwitting passers-by. A few of the passers-by noticed and looked up too. However, Milgram then increased the number of skyward looking actors to five. The idea was to gauge how this increase in stimulus would influence the decision-making processes of the urbanite passers-by and to record how many more of them would subsequently imitate the skyward looking crowd. In the first test, 20 percent of the passers-by looked up, but when five actors appeared on the street corner, the number apparently jumped to 80 percent. From these results, Milgram deduced his theory of *social*

FIGURE 1.3. Students from the University of East London attempt to re-create Stanley Milgram's skyward looking people experiment. Photograph by Jeff Ellis.

proof; that is, as Figure 1.3 shows, on encountering the crowd, the individual makes a *contagious assumption* based on the quantity of evidence that there is something worth looking up at. To put it another way, the individual's imitation of others is largely dependent on his cognitive assessment of the magnitude of social influence.

As will become apparent in chapter 3, Milgram's impact on the new network sciences approach to contagion has been considerable. Not only has his work greatly influenced the models used but his ideas figure writ large in the stress given to an individual's instinctual tendency to herd or cascade, particularly in times of bubble building and subsequent financial crisis but also during the spreading of fashion and fads. In many of these accounts, imitative decisions (rationale or irrational) conforming to the social actions of others are assumed to be biologically hardwired into the brain, enabling a person to make snap judgments to avoid, for example, threats to her physical, emotional, or financial well-being. Notably, even when using online systems like e-mail, it is argued that "the human brain is *hardwired* with the proclivity to follow the lead of others."[117]

Milgram's focus on the individual's internal motivations guiding decision-making processes (*agentic states,* as he called it) clearly differs in many ways from Tarde. It is the evolutionary propensity of individuals to obey rather than to imitate that matters. He is not, as such, untypical of the aforementioned cognitive turn in the twentieth century, in this case in social psychology, in which crowd behavior was generally traced to the disposition of individuals caught up in a natural chain of command or hierarchy rather than association or disassociation. As Milgram argues, imitation leads to conformity, but obedience ultimately requires the distinct social action of the individual.[118] Whereas crowd theory ascribed contagious affect to mania and hypnosis, the cognitive turn would contrastingly dismiss such ideas as fanciful psychologism.

Nevertheless, Milgram was famously the great manipulator of the social encounter. Resembling his other famous experiments linking social conformity to authority and obedience, his triggering of crowd contagion in Manhattan was unquestionably socially engineered. He might even be considered a hypnotist of sorts, or an authentic viral marketer, insofar as he planted suggestibility, via the points of fascination provided by his skyward looking actors, into the neurological, biological, and sociological composition of the crowd. From this privileged position, Milgram not only observed but also controlled the involuntary, semiconscious, and imitative responses his experiment induced.

MacKay's Tulipomania

In 1848, at least 120 years before Milgram's Manhattan experiment, the Scottish poet and journalist Charles MacKay published *Memoirs of Extraordinary Popular Delusions and the Madness of Crowds,* in which he described a series of seventeenth-century crowd manias including the spreading of mental disease, passions, murder, religion, witchcraft, and significantly, financial contagion. In this latter case, MacKay drew particular attention to the so-called case of tulipomania in Holland in the 1630s. It all began, MacKay argues, with the passionate interests of a few rich aristocrats who desired virally infected and subsequently highly variegated tulips. Indeed, like Tarde, tulipomania is a study of how desire seems to provide the impetus for the interwoven spreading of social, cultural, and economic influence. "Many learned men," MacKay argues, "were passionately fond of tulips." This was a "rage" for possession that soon spread to the middle classes, merchants and shopkeepers, and even those of "moderate means." All levels of Dutch society began to "vie with each other in the rarity of these flowers," willing to pay preposterous prices. One Haarlem trader, MacKay notes, "was known to pay one-half of his fortune for a single root." He had no intention of selling it on again for profit but kept it for the "admiration of his acquaintances."[119]

The intensity of desire for tulips resulted in the collapse of the Dutch economic system, which spread, as financial crisis tends to do, from country to country, plunging 1630s Europe into deep recession. As Sadie Plant notes, tulipomania "was as infectious as the virus" that infected the tulip in the first place. It was "a runaway sequence of events triggered by the smallest of anomalies," which exposed an entire economic system to a malfunctioning epidemic logic.[120] It is not surprising, then, that the case is often referred to in network science as a model precursor to the virality of more recent incidents of financial contagions involving herding, cascades, and the eventual bursting of economic bubbles.

Lakoff's Political Unconscious

A resuscitated Tarde may have a considerable neuropolitical component insofar as the agency awarded to the imitative ray can be interestingly approached through a neurological relation established between emotion and cognition. This includes the location of so-called mirror neurons, which supposedly process the sharing of feelings and mood, or *empathy,* as it is known. Mirror neurons are said to be the equivalent of human-to-human "wireless communication" and have been linked to innate imitative human relations occurring between infants and adults.[121] They are located in an area of the brain called f5, which fires in response to the affects of others. Mirror neurons function best in face-to-face encounters, when there is a need to comprehend or "mind read" the "intentions of others," but they amount to more than simply recognizing a face. On one hand, they lead to the automated copying of emotions like joy, sadness, or distress. On the other hand, they fire following the avoidance of face-to-face contact, as people tend to do when lying, or following the interruption of stable emotional signals through surprise, shock, or a failure to predict.[122]

So what does this neuropolitical component consist of? Well, in the last forty years or so, political performance has seemingly drifted toward slick celebrity presentation and a media-friendly style intended to appeal more and more to voter emotions and market mood. The affective priming of political campaigns and adverts by think tanks and communication PR machines is not necessarily a new phenomenon. Politicians have been kissing babies for a long time now, but as the cognitive scientist George Lakoff argues, much of what is politically communicated today is increasingly designed to enter the political mind by dipping below consciousness and appealing directly to hardwired emotions. For example, Lakoff argues that the political machinery of the Republican Party in the United States during the G. W. Bush administration successfully monopolized much of the unconscious political mind of public opinion. It did this mainly by appealing to innate conservative desires but also through the spreading of fear and panic related to issues of national security triggered post-9/11. The War on Terror is indeed a neurological war. It is an idea "introduced under conditions of trauma and then repeated so often that it is forever in your synapses."[123]

However, the alternative politics of empathy Lakoff forwards to combat the neurological persuasion of the neo-Conservative is a Tardean diagram through and through. This is a politics of persuasion that does not function through fear alone but potentially works its influence through the empathic desire of a population to share in the feelings of others. Like this, in his 2008 election campaign, Barak Obama famously captured political territory by tapping into the empathy of the voter ready for *change* and *hope*. But more than this, Lakoff argues, voters feel Obama's joy, empathize with his bodily stance and the way he smiles and holds up his head as a result of neuronal triggering.[124]

Looking at this trend toward emphatic politics from a more fine-tuned Tardean perspective, we can see how the management of new political distractions–attractions (i.e., borrowing from Crary) requires more than just a passive neurological reception of affect. The imitative state of voter empathy, however automated in terms of biological hardwiring, is seemingly dependent on the pretesting of reciprocal social encounters. Power relations are therefore not simply constituted as old persuasion theories would have it—between institutional power and mass society—but instead necessitate the cocreation of mutual emotional engagements via premediated microrelations. As follows, empathy is a mode of Tardean assimilation that can capture the desires of voters to gain political ground.

A neurological somnambulism can, as such, be seen as part and parcel of a shift away from a distinctive Enlightenment account of the duality of rational awareness and emotional irrationality toward an inseparable unconscious–consciousness relation stimulated by both what one believes one sees, with one's own eyes, and what one dreams about.[125] Although cognitive science has tried to establish that we "know our own minds," most thought is not autonomously reflective but emanates from neurons firing in response to the spontaneous binding together of concepts. Decisions are similarly not entirely conscious. They arise from gut responses, visceral and knee-jerk reactions to affective sensory inputs. Although it seems counterintuitive to a mind that considers itself mostly rational, neuroscience claims that we are mostly unaware of the decisions we make.[126]

Thrift's Affective Contagion

The connection between Tarde and the age of networks is made abundantly clear in Thrift's recent work, where despite noting a historical fluctuation in the appeal of crowd theory, contagion theory seems to be making something of a comeback. To be sure, the nineteenth-century obsession with the crowd ends abruptly with a distinct cognitive turn in the twentieth century. In psychology, for example, the focus on the commotions of the crowd shifts toward the self-contained cognitive subject. By the 1930s, the old ideas about mass manias, hypnosis, and hallucinatory delusions made popular in Le Bon's *The Crowd* are briefly hijacked by the far Right and then become largely ignored in the social sciences when the positivism of Durkheim finally begins to take hold. As Thrift argues, Tarde's contagion theory "fell out of fashion, not least because of its emphasis on process at the expense of the substantive results of social interaction."[127] That is, until fairly recently, when inspired by the new network ontology, cultural theory started to engage again in somewhat opaque and speculative viral models of contagion.[128] Yet, as this book argues, through a resuscitation of Tarde, and an effort to reconnect him to contemporary debates, much of this obscurity might be cleared away. Here Thrift convincingly argues that "the spread of the internet has produced both a new medium and a means of getting much closer to what Tarde was trying to study."[129] Of course, the media ecologies encountered by Tarde at the end of the nineteenth century have since been massively augmented. The Internet now provides what Thrift calls a novel "prosthetic impulse," or vector, for social imitative encounters. It acts as a new kind of "neural pathway, transmitting faces and stances as well as discourse . . . [and] forging new reflexes."[130] Indeed—and in a fitting way by which to conclude this opening chapter—Thrift forwards a number of interrelated reasons (I look at just four subsequently) that support a Tardean resuscitation as essential to understanding how the network is fast becoming the new prime conductor of the biopolitical epidemic.

First, Thrift highlights the universal feature of Tarde's epidemiological encounter; that is, desire and invention are both underscored by imitation–repetition. Like Deleuze, an open-ended repetition becomes, as such, the "base of all action."[131] Again, importantly, the imitative ray is not reduced here to micro- or macrorepresentations but is part of a process of social adaptation linked to an unfastened and differentiating repetition of events. "The entities that Tarde is dealing with are not people, but innovations, understood as quanta of change with a life of their own."[132] To be sure, agency here is awarded, through Tarde's idea of the inseparability of the repetition of the mechanical habits of desire and the mostly illusory sense of individual volition, to a vital force of encounter, certainly not centered on human subjects alone. This we can see clearly in Tarde's approach to political economy, in which the individual's rational drive to produce riches is supplanted by an economy of desire in which the "circulation and distribution of riches are nothing but the effect of an imitative repetition of needs."[133] Tarde's economy is a *reciprocal radiation of exchanging desires,* related to passionate interests as well as the needs of labor.

Second, then, special attention is drawn to the way in which repetitive mechanical habit and the sense of volition (social action) become inseparable. Tarde questioned the world he experienced in the nineteenth century. Unlike the categories of sociology established by his contemporary Durkheim, Tarde introduces a complex set of associations (mostly unconscious) traveling between (and below) the artifice of a nature–society divide and therefore positioning biological entities as equidistant to "social" ones.[134] In fact, the use of the word *social* needs to be carefully approached here because for Tarde, "all phenomena is [*sic*] social phenomena, all things a society"—atoms, cells, and people are on an "equal footing."[135] Tarde therefore anticipates a time when an indivisible contract, in which social and biological causes will no longer confront each other, reappears.[136]

Third, Thrift's concept of *affective contagion* provides a contemporary take on Tarde's imitative ray, latching on to his ideas concerning how passionate interests radiate through social assemblages, mostly unawares, but adding an affective and neurological dimension. Thrift notes, as such, how Tarde's focus on the spreading of fear, sentimentality, and social disturbance infers affective crowd behavior, with a tendency of its own making.[137] Like the imitative ray, affective contagion is self-spreading, automatic, and involuntary and functions according to a hypnotic action-at-a-distance with no discernable medium of contact. Affective contagions are manifested entirely in the force of encounter with events, independent of physical contact or scale. This is how small yet angry social confrontations can lead to widespread violence and how accidental events, like the death of a royal celebrity, can perhaps trigger large-scale contagious overspills of unforeseen mass hysteria.[138] Similarly, sizeable media-fueled epidemics of social vulnerability, fear, anxiety, and panic can be ignited by large-scale mediated events like 9/11 or relatively small events like recent outbreaks of a few cases of bird flu or swine fever, amplified out of all contexts by the media, further demonstrating the multiscalar nature of social contagion.

Thrift's affective reading of the imitative ray again provides further insight into Tarde's political economy, transforming the radiation of desire into a propensity or imitative momentum and, in doing so, interestingly rethinking the phenomenon of financial contagion. Yet, differing from Tarde, these aperiodic outbreaks of economic turmoil are not considered mere accidents. On the contrary, Thrift contends that Tarde maybe mistook the wildfire spreading of contagion to be capricious and accidental (a point of debate to which I return at various points in this book). He notes instead how, on one hand, there is a "tendency-cum-attraction" and, on the other, an "innate inclination" of those market traders who get caught up in the contagious flows of information cascades, herding decisions, and bubble building. A Tardean combination of a cultural attraction to the marketplace and a biologically hardwired inclination toward risk produces a "disposition to behave in a certain way which is only partly in the control of the agent."[139]

Fourth, then, and turning last to the issue of the networked economy, we find in Tarde an alternative to the friction-free commerce model made popular in the discourse of business enterprise, in the shape of an epidemiological atmosphere that can be affectively primed, or premediated, so that imitative momentum can be anticipated and purposefully spread. These are indeed viral atmospheres of the order of the wasp–orchid assemblage, in which corporations and politicians increasingly deploy the magnetic pull of mediated fascinations, intoxicating glories, and celebrity narratives so that small events can be encouraged to become bigger contagious overspills.

Here we see the production of what Thrift refers to as new "worlds," in which "semiconscious action can be put up for sale."[140] These viral atmospheres are increasingly evident in the opportunities online consumers have to share their intimacies, obsessions, and desires with producers. I have already briefly discussed how this functions with regard to the desire for friendship in social media, but an online business enterprise like Amazon, for example, makes this process far clearer. Amazon works by capturing and exploiting a wider range of consumer desires and obsessions. By turning previous purchases into new windows of opportunity, Amazon encourages shoppers to create wish lists, matching desirable purchases to comparable products and maximizing imitation–suggestibility by drawing attention to others who also share similar obsessions. Amazon is typical of a new business model of the network age Thrift describes as having the capacity to "catch" the nearby desire of someone just like us, which works alongside older methods of mass attraction, such as the affective charge of celebrity, to "spark" desires for associated products.[141] Indeed, the methods used to predict, measure, and exploit imitative rays are becoming ever more complex and neurologically invasive.

The viral atmosphere marks the point at which the conscious thought of the self "arises from an unconscious imitation of others."[142] It is at this location that human susceptibility becomes assimilated in the Tardean desiring machine. To maintain the virality of the atmosphere, though, the business enterprise requires the mostly unconscious mutuality or emotional investment of the infected consumer to guarantee that the affective contagion is passed on. As follows, affectively primed and premediated atmospheres must allow for these emotional investments to be freely made so that feelings become "increasingly available to be worked on and cultivated."[143] The network is the perfect tool, it seems, for propagating these sentimental attachments with brands since "through the internet and various mobile technologies, it becomes possible to rapidly feed information and recommendations to these populations, producing a means of trading on those susceptibilities that have been identified."[144] Networks permit a personalized dialogue with consumers so that "they feed back their reactions, both producing more informa-tion on their susceptibilities, and new triggers."[145]

Although Tarde anticipates a material world of subject creation, his materiality has, like Deleuze, an incorporeal materialist dimension to it. It is a concreteness made of virtuality, affective flows, rays, and the like. It is in this world of incorporeal passionate relations that a con-sumer's obsessive engagement with products and brands, as well as the slick empathetic performances of politicians, marks the increases and decreases of power implicated in "person-making."[146] Tarde's imitation– suggestibility becomes a mesmeric affective flow intended to steer the imitative inclinations of consumers and voters to predetermined goals.

Tarde prefigured an epidemiological relationality in which things (caffeine, sentimental novels, pornographic works, and all manner of consumer goods) mix with emotions, moods, and affects[147]—an atmo-sphere awash with hormones, making people happy or sad, sympathetic or apathetic, and a space in which affects are significantly passed on or suggested to others. These worlds are a Tardean time–space through and through, which Thrift contends "continually questions itself," generating "new forms of interrelation" and activities and function-ing according to Tarde's action-at-a-distance and akin to mesmerism, hypnosis, telepathy, and mind reading. These epidemiological densities critically value the indirect over the direct, yet within the crisscrossing of associations, it is "increasingly clear that subconscious processes of imitation can be directed."[148]

Perhaps through the inventions of neuromarketing, we are just beginning to see a more thorough exploration of this epidemiological relation intended to better understand how affective flows can lead to purchase intent. Neuromarketers not only map the contagions themselves but delve into the constituents of the imitative rays of the consumer: the semiconscious flows of feeling and affect and their subsequent emotional, neurological, and physiological responses. New partnerships between the new media business enterprises, user experience designers, and neuroscientists use advanced technologies to measure facial expressions, eye movement, gesture, and body in relation to consumer enthusiasms, emotions, and moods. What was once "genetically encoded" and "neurally etched" into the thoughts, feelings, motivations, needs, and desires of the consumer now becomes, like this, "open to all kinds of operation," thus increasing the number of profitable flows.[149]

The tapping into what spreads, or hormonally swashes about in these viral atmospheres, follows, to some extent, a Tardean trajectory of biopower. In what we might call a trend toward the virality of network capitalism, there is certainly a distinct ramping up of the repetitious spread of affective contagion. The point of this exercise of biopower is to mesmerize the consumer (and voter) to such an extent that her susceptible porousness to the inventions of others, received mostly unawares, becomes an escalating point of vulnerability. The inseparability of the ever-circulating repetitions of mechanical desires and the often illusory sense that our choices and decisions belong to us, as Tarde had already contended, make the social a hypnotic state: "a dream of command and a dream of action" in which the somnambulist is "possessed by the illusion that their ideas, all of which have been suggested to them, are spontaneous."[150]

2

What Spreads? From Memes and Crowds to the Phantom Events of Desire and Belief

This chapter begins with the premise that what spreads through a social network is all too often attributed to two largely uncontested logics of resemblance and repetition. First, cultural contagion is assumed to correspond to a distinctive biologically determined unit of imitation. This is unquestionably a mechanistic virality analogically compared to the canonical imprint of genetic code. Second, what spreads is said to occur in a representational space of collective contamination in which individual persons who become part of a crowd tend toward thinking in the same mental images (real and imagined). Like this, the reasoned individual is seemingly overpowered by a neurotic mental state of unity unique to the crowd, which renders subjectivity vulnerable to further symbolic contagious encounters and entrainments.

In the first instance, analogous to genetic replication, the meme has indeed become more than a mere buzzword of the Internet age. It is a neo-Darwinian supposition perpetuated by academics, journalists, viral marketers, and software developers alike. The meme is, at its extreme, endemic to a claim that the Internet is the outcome of memetic units constructing a more efficient communicable environment in which to self-spread.[1] However, I argue that what is supposed to constitute the widely accepted unit of cultural imitation is in fact missing. Even though much literature emanating from memetics, computer science, and marketing has continued to acknowledge its universal application to cultural, digital, and biological contagion, efforts to locate the memetic unit have indeed floundered. This is because, I contend, what spreads cannot, beyond analogy, become unitized like a gene or, for that matter, be made concrete. What spreads has no *organized* unit or molar body. It is independent of a singular mechanism. The problem for memetics is the meme's dependence on an absent measurable evolutionary mechanism. Without this, the analogy of the meme–gene coupling simply collapses in on itself.

In the second instance, the discussion here follows a logical line linking the crowd theories introduced by Gustave Le Bon in the late nineteenth century to Freud's group psychology, and beyond to the social epidemiology popularized more recently by viral marketers. Le Bon in effect provides the flip side to the notion that the many are smarter than the few. Like this, and in sharp contrast to the collective intelligence thesis, Le Bon's *The Crowd* charts the intellectual erosion an individual experiences when encountering others. Yet, while there are many ostensible parallels to be made between Le Bon and Tarde's crowd theory, the hypnotic leadership Le Bon personified in *The Crowd* is a very different concept to the social relational forces that populate *The Laws of Imitation.* Unlike Tarde's diagram, in which the mostly unconscious tendency to pass on the influence of others is guided by a complex social theory of open-repetition, desire, and invention, Le Bon attributes social contagion to a *mechanism of collective hallucination.* A crowd, he tells us, "thinks in images."[2] Presenting a kind of inverted proto-psychoanalysis in the sense that visual representations are translated into collective dreams, Le Bon's crowd contagion becomes a neurotic suppression of the real events individuals experience once they become incorporated into the collective body.

Tarde's epidemiological diagram draws similar attention to a self-spreading tendency in crowds. Nonetheless, and significantly, the imitative ray, unlike the analogous meme or Le Bon's visual hallucinations, does not reduce social relation to a dumb medium for self-replicating hereditary codes or representations of the *Same.* To avoid following the contagion theories put forward by neo-Darwinists and Le Bon into their respective biological and sociological deterministic cul-de-sacs, *Virality* continues to point toward Tarde's cross-hybridist proto-assemblage theory. By doing so, it notes both the logic of

FIGURE 2.1. The YouTube viral video Lonelygirl15. Photograph by Jeff Ellis.

difference and repetition contained in Tarde's diagram and the important inseparability he affords to biological, psychosocial, and social phenomena. With particular regard to this latter diagrammatic feature, the discussion here contrasts Tarde's diagram with contagion theories that divide up real and imagined experiences into conscious and unconscious couplings.

Central to this discussion is a so-called viral video posted by Lonelygirl15 (see Figure 2.1). This example helps to distinguish contemporary network contagions from the mechanism-dependent presuppositions of both memetics and Le Bon's hallucinatory images. My intention here is to revisit Lonelygirl15, bringing in elements of the mechanism independence of Tarde's diagram, alongside Deleuze's notion of the *phantom event.* In this account, the unconscious tendency to pass on social influence is no longer regarded a vehicle for memes or mental representations, nor is it a proto-psychoanalytical storehouse in which the unconscious desires and dreams of the crowd are cut off from consciousness. In contrast, the unconscious becomes the *nonconscious*: a factory-like relation between the conscious and unconscious. This is a relation Deleuze contends connects the self-contained ego to the exteriority of the body and wherein the spreading of desire occurs not beneath consciousness but at the surface of social encounter.

Ripples in the Meme Pool

In 2006 a series of webcast blogs were uploaded to the video-sharing website YouTube. Set in the bedroom of an often-pouting teenager, Lonelygirl15 attracted the largest number of visitors to the file-sharing site since its creation the year before. It also triggered a wave of imitative video clips and feverish comments posted by fans of the blog. These comments, some of which are copied later, reveal a distinct lack of awareness on behalf of these fans concerning what would be later exposed as a hoax. Lonelygirl15 was an actress, and the video blog was designed to promote the work of a couple of budding Internet moviemakers. The video blog was apparently an example of what has become known as viral marketing. Indeed, drawing on an analogy between the contagiousness of this kind of Internet attraction and the propagation of biological viruses, marketers have enthusiastically embraced the term *viral* to explain how marketing messages can quickly spread through social networks mostly unawares. As one e-commerce consultant puts it,

> You have to admire the virus. He has a way of living in secrecy until he is so numerous that he wins by sheer weight of numbers. He piggybacks on other hosts and uses their resources to increase his tribe. And in the right environment, he grows exponentially. A virus don't [*sic*] even have to mate—he just replicates, again and again with geometrically increasing power, doubling with each iteration
>
> 1
> 11
> 1111
> 11111111
> 1111111111111111
> 11111111111111111111111111111111
> 1111111111111111111111111111111111111111111111
>
> In a few short generations, a virus population can explode.[3]

In marketing circles, this crude model of virality is not solely limited to the biological analogy. The tactics of the viral marketer were apparently inspired early on by the socially engineered Trojan trickery of thriving computer viruses like Melissa, which spread across the Internet in the late 1990s attached to seemingly harmless e-mails. To this effect, the Internet entrepreneur Esther Dyson claimed back in 1999 that while "most right-thinking people hear about *Melissa* the virus and shudder," there have been a "few politically incorrect marketers" thinking about how marketing messages might be attached to such a virus.[4] Nonetheless, the virality of marketing, like the computer virus itself, has more often than not been framed by a neo-Darwinian-derived gene–meme analogy.

It is indeed the assumed capacity of the virally encoded meme to hide its source, and make its contagion appear accidental, that has arguably appealed to the marketer. Like this, Trojanlike video virals are intended to seep into the collective consciousness of social media networks like YouTube and from there spread, person to person, like a memetic *thought contagion*.[5] A "good meme," we are told, is in fact "simple, provocative and infectious." It will roll off the tongue and stick in the mind so that it is remembered and passed on like a gene.[6] Indeed, being able to virally extend the meme through the collective mind of net consumers became part of an early and very desirable low-cost approach to contemporary online marketing. For companies "without a national advertising budget," spreading marketing messages via word of mouth (or mouse) is a form of "zero cost marketing."[7]

But just how viral is viral marketing? Well, by appealing to memetics, the marketing rhetoric lays claim to an engineered cultural virality dependent on the same mechanistic forces that determine "natural" evolution. Indeed, believe the hype, and it seems that viral marketers appear to have pulled off a marketing coup d'état. As the self-proclaimed idea-virus merchant Seth Godin argues, viral marketing practices shift the workload away from the marketer to the self-spreading virus and the networks it infects. Consequently, the memetically encoded virus circumnavigates the "tyranny" of transparently marketing to people who often resist being marketed to by tapping into the "invisible currents that run between and among consumers."[8] However, rather than answering this question negatively, I want to ask if this memetic escape from tyranny conceals a far more sophisticated and dictatorial manipulation of the online consumer's affective landscape. As Thrift convincingly argues, corporate attempts to cultivate relations with consumers are increasingly infused by contagions that endeavor to manipulate moods, promoting principally semiconscious identifications and commitments to products and brands.[9] This is a mode of virality that is not, arguably, well captured by the neo-Darwinist language of memes, which says "both something and nothing" about contagion theory. Indeed, by feeding culture into the logic of the memetic–genetic analogy, analysis has become "flattened . . . in ways which Tarde would never have allowed."[10] What is needed here is a probing of the validity of this overhyped claim to virality, that is, the assertion that social and cultural imitation can in reality be memetically encoded to make a marketing campaign, as Godin describes it, *go viral*. But beyond this probe, there is a need to bring into view, so to speak, a far more pervasive mode of contagion marketing that has emerged in recent years. Let's begin, though, with the memetic claim for an evolutionarily engineered virality.

In short, memetics is a neo-Darwinian account of the cultural evolution of ideas. Dating back to the 1930s, neo-Darwinism is the modern synthesis of Darwin's theory of natural selection and Mendel's empirical study of instructional mechanisms in biological inheritance. However, both social Darwinism and cultural evolutionism can be traced back to Herbert Spenser, who applied evolutionary theory to civilizations in Victorian times. The American psychologist James Baldwin similarly applied a theory of natural selection to the mind as early as 1909.[11] Yet it was Richard Dawkins who, in 1976, fleetingly introduced the idea of the meme in the closing chapter of his book *The Selfish Gene*. As Dawkins defines it:

> When you plant a fertile meme in my mind you literally parasitize my brain, turning it into a vehicle for the meme's propagation in just the same way that a virus may parasitize the genetic mechanism of a host cell.[12]

Dawkins's meme is a self-copying message system, regulated by the decision-making process of an evolutionary algorithm. Its mode of algorithmic propagation is characterized by an inheritance mechanism that (1) resists variations caused by environmental interaction and (2) achieves the widest prevalence dependent on its parasitical fitness as arbitrated by the evolutionary survival mechanism. Significantly, the meme is Dawkins's example of a special case of Universal Darwinian replication—a second replicator determined by a universal set of rules that compel it to fight for survival in the so-called *meme pool*.[13] In other words, the memetic code spreads by advantage using, for example, the video clip as a carrier or host to increase the viral contagiousness of the idea concealed within it. To illustrate this point, Dawkins points to the similarity between a population of minds and a computer network, arguing that the mind, like a computer running viral software, becomes an arbitrary vehicle or medium existing in a randomized evolutionary search space.[14] The memetic code attaches itself to these vehicles, seeking out others, which in turn play host to the most successful replicator programs. The medium, in this context, is reduced to a mysterious virus-friendly environment: a space that "obeys[s] a program of coded instructions."[15]

Many others followed Dawkins's notion that ideas spread like biological viruses. For example, Douglas Hofstadter's *Metamagical Themas* in 1985, Daniel Dennett's *Consciousness Explained* in 1991, Aaron Lynch's *Thought Contagion* in 1996, and Blackmore's *The Meme Machine* in 1999 all approach cultural contagion using the gene–meme analogy.[16] In fact, in the early 1990s, subjects as diverse as religion,[17] the cultural evolution of birdsong,[18] and adolescent sexual behavior[19] had all been subjected to memetic analysis. By the mid-1990s, the meme had its own ecology,[20] computational model,[21] and conceptual framework.[22] By spring 1997, meme theory became the central focus of an academic journal *(Journal of Memetics: Evolutionary Models of Information Transmission).*[23] The theory of the meme was during this period a contagion in itself!

Notably, Blackmore's approach to memetics is marked by her endeavor to bring rigor to Dawkins's analogical proposition and adheres closely to the concept of an exploitative replicator. Her account focuses on the readiness of a human mind to blindly accept a preprogrammed idea, which spreads in accordance to its own advantage and survival. Indeed, Blackmore adds a specified memetic unit of imitation. As she argues,

> When you imitate someone else, something is passed on. This "something" can then be passed on again, and again, and so take on a life of

its own. We might call this thing an idea, an instruction, a behavior, a piece of information . . . but if we are going to study it we shall need to give it a name. . . . Fortunately, there is a name. It is the meme.[24]

To further illustrate memetic imitation, Blackmore uses the example of catchy musical tunes.[25] A number of these tunes, for instance, a sequence of notes played on a piano, infect the listener's mind, using it as a vehicle to get to the meme pool, where tunes can then compete for survival. Once the evolutionary algorithm runs, all that follows happens at the expense of other, less contagious tunes. Competition is often fierce. As Blackmore proposes, there are more memes than vehicles. Like this, the mind that receives the tune becomes a tape machine that is always switched to record mode but only retains the best-coded meme. This notion of the mind as a dumb vehicle or tape recorder follows on from Dawkins's concept of the computer-like mind as a "sitting duck," waiting to be infected by a torrent of competing coded ideas.[26]

The deterministic mode in which the meme manipulates the medium is not restricted to its spread through the minds of a population. Indeed, the production of media technologies, embedded in genetic, artificial materials or linguistic forms, is considered as solely influenced by the running of the memetic evolutionary algorithm. This is a deterministic viewpoint echoed in Dennett's assumption that "a human mind is itself an artefact created when memes restructure a human brain in order to make it a better habitat for memes."[27] Blackmore goes on to similarly suggest that memetic selection is responsible for the evolution of artificial communication technologies such as radios, televisions, and the Internet.[28] The latter of these is understood to increasingly obey the logic of the survival-of-the-fittest mechanism and has therefore become a superefficient transmitter for memes. Like this, both Dennett and Blackmore make a claim for the universal explanatory power of the memetic algorithm, proposing that it produces media (biological and technological) that become progressively more evolved: more prosperous vehicles designed purely for the fecundity, longevity, and fidelity of further memes.

The autonomous mode of the meme code is enthusiastically employed by memeticians to challenge the causality afforded to a central designer.

Blackmore claims, for example, that the capacity of a transcendental god or the freewill of human beings to spread ideas and beliefs is an erroneous misunderstanding of cultural contagion:

> The evolutionary algorithm runs, and the evolutionary algorithm produces design. . . . The consciousness of a designer is not the causal factor. . . . Design comes about entirely from the playing out of the evolutionary algorithm.[29]

Following Dawkins's lead, a number of memetic studies focus on the memetic construction of human consciousness in the spreading of organized and cult religions. Here memetics perhaps usefully aims to deny religious claims to transcendental power, for example, via the propagation of a belief system dominated by dead ancestors and/or single or multiple gods. Like Tarde, this viewpoint exposes the powerful use of multiple apparitions and phantoms to galvanize belief and control it. The way in which a successful religion spreads, despite having to cope with resistant forces like violent persecution, is best achieved, according to Lynch, via *proselytising* transmission.[30] To put it another way, the meme code must extend beyond the verticalness of the family unit and broaden out horizontally into the wider community. The process of religious conversion—*go forth and preach the Gospel to all*—is given as an example of horizontal faith preserving in which advantage is driven by the successful dissemination of the meme virus.[31]

Memetics effectively crosses out both transcendental designer gods and the conscious self, defined by the agency of the human soul or freewill. It replaces these with an intriguing mode of filiative evolution that determines cultural propagation by way of an illusory consciousness state (the *selfplex*) structured around the "reality" of the *memeplex*.[32] Both the illusion of the self and the false claim to freewill are themselves due to memes that "get inside" the human physical system and "persuade" it that it has both a self and freewill to trick it into the further propagation of memes: "Memes have made us do it—because a 'self' aids their replication."[33]

Although meme theory poses a number of interesting questions concerning the causality awarded to nonnaturalistic designer gods and the freewill of human beings, its claim to a specific mode of universal contagion, organized around evolutionary determinism, is equally problematic. Generally speaking, the choice it poses between either Darwin or god is, as Keith Ansell Pearson argues, a "simple-minded" realization of the philosophical questions concerning evolution.[34] More specifically, though, I want to go on to propose five interrelated conceptual problems that challenge the meme as a theory of universal contagion. Each has the specific purpose of questioning the effectiveness of the asymmetric analogical relation established between, on one hand, the neo-Darwinist interpretations of "natural" laws and, on the other hand, the assumption that these laws then become the mark of contagious cultural environments.

The first problem facing memetics is that *the meme is missing.* As critics from within memetics have themselves argued, the memetic unit of imitation, unlike the gene, has yet to be located. This lack of substance seriously undermines the agency of what is intended to be a mechanism-dependent empirical tool that can trace and potentially predict cultural evolution. Writing in the online edition of the now defunct *Journal of Memetics,* Bruce Edmonds similarly argues that the "poverty of the gene–meme analogy" is in part due to the failure of its predictive powers. As he proposes,

> The fact is that the closer the work has been to the core of memetics, the less successful it has been. The central core, the meme–gene analogy, has not been a wellspring of models and studies which have provided "explanatory leverage" upon observed phenomena. Rather, it has been a short-lived fad whose effect has been to obscure more than it has been to enlighten. I am afraid that memetics, as an identifiable discipline, will not be widely missed.[35]

Indeed, the issue of the meme's lack of demonstrable material affect stresses the empirical problems the discipline faces. Unlike the nonsubstance analysis proposed in this book, which concerns the mechanism independence of assemblages, events, environments, and affect, memetics has, it seems, an empirical requirement for a material unit of measurement. Without the measurable substance of a unit, the precise rules of transmission and working parts of the mechanism of inheritance will arguably continue to trouble sociobiologists. Unlike typogenetics, which enables geneticists to reduce DNA to the manipulative code of nucleotides (A, G, C, and T), the lack of a precise memetic unit has become an open problem in memetics. As Dawkins confesses, the meme has yet to find its Crick and Watson.[36] There is no equivalent typomemetics that marketers can use to manipulate the imitation of ideas.

Second, despite claims that the meme traverses the nature–culture continuum, the exact functioning of evolutionary inheritance is still by and large contested. How can this mechanistic approach explain the universality of biological, social, and cultural contagion? This second problem orbits around two inheritance mechanisms that have been aligned to both biological evolution and cultural imitation. First, in the Lamarckian mechanism, codes interact with their environment. Blackmore has called this approach to inheritance *copying-the-product*. The composer teaches a tune to a musician, who then teaches it to another, and so on. Each time the composition is passed on, slight changes can be made to the feel or even the notation of the work. The idea of the tune will feed back on itself as it is transmitted through a network of players. This will evidently result in a very high mutation rate. Like a game of Chinese Whispers or the passing on of a chain letter, the end product may well become unrecognizable. However, in terms of both biological and cultural evolutionary inheritance, neo-Darwinists regard such low-fidelity invariance as unworkable.[37] For example, specific ideas would not spread very far if they mutated to such a high degree. The second inheritance mechanism, Dawkins argues, solves this problem. It refutes, at least in biological terms, the Lamarckian interaction and subsequent deterioration of hereditary lines. Weismannian inheritance mechanisms, favored by the neo-Darwinists, deny that environmental alterations to the product will be passed on since the entire process of transmission is based on a repetition of the primary replication instruction set, ad infinitum. Blackmore refers to this as *copying-the-instructions*. The composer's tune is passed down to musicians directly from the original notation of the score. The final product is determined by the persistence of memetic information, undergoing a random differential survival decision-making process. The best tunes survive!

For Blackmore, the difference between Lamarckian and Weismannian inheritance mechanisms equates to the difference between analog and digital codes. Indeed, the shift from analog to digital media communication technology is regarded as an evolutionary progression since it makes "memetic copying mechanisms more similar to [the more highly evolved] genetic one"[38] and therefore better conforms to Weismannian inheritance. This notion that the Internet is an ideal imitation medium clearly appeals to some aspects of Shannon's information model, in which the digital signal is designed to overcome environmental variance.[39] However, the convergence of information processes and the survival-of-the-fittest mechanism does not necessarily explain how variant invention functions in evolutionary processes and has been roundly criticized for assuming that it does. Saying that it is only the fittest that leave behind the largest numbers of descendants "is not too far from saying that those who survive, survive."[40] Similarly, Ansell Pearson argues that Dennett can "only think evolution in terms of logical possibility," albeit in a design space that just happens to be a mindless mechanism.[41] What is arguably missing from this design space is the potential to consider novelty and creative evolution. Lonelygirl15 is in fact a stark example of the novel potential that arises from digital cultural practices. As Figure 2.2 shows, the video was widely imitated but had distinct variations in each new "copy." The structuring of culture via Weismannian inheritance does not, it would seem, explain the practice of file sharing or the differential contagions it produces.[42]

Third, in memetics, the medium in which an idea is transmitted is typically dismissed as an inert channel through which the determining fitness algorithm is transmitted. But what makes social media passive to memetic infection? The problem here centers on the forced decoupling of the memetic code from the social environments it infects. This tendency to underestimate the medium of transmission has influenced viral marketers where going viral, it seems, is all about the careful structuring and seeding of the marketing message alone. Whether the message is a text, an image, or a video is of lesser importance since the medium is merely the "substance that the idea lives in."[43] However, returning again to Lonelygirl15, it is possible to argue that it is a message designed entirely around the cultural diversities of file-sharing practices. The message did

The Equinox

an Equinox celebration with my parents. Very exciting :) ... LG15 **lonelygirl15** equinox daniel danielbeast bibliomancy dad mom chartreuse ceremony ...

by **lonelygirl15** | 4 years ago | **532,496 views**

LonelyGirl15 Recap 7

Bree reunites with an old friend. She also reveals a startling secret about the Ceremony. Music: SD by DJ Lenin On The Moon (Trip Hop mix) by ...

by **LonelyGirl15Recaps** | 4 years ago | **27,318 views**

Where LonelyGirl15 is now

Just a collection of clips starring the actress who played LG15. Yeah, I know. It seems like everyone has a LG15 video; but hey! No matter how you ...

by **Hrei88** | 3 years ago | **4,875 views**

Lonelygirl15: Breaking News!!!

This is a clip I just recorded from 'Aljazeera Worldwide' - It turns out that purple monkey is actually an international terrorist. I must admit ...

by **randomjoe2006** | 4 years ago | **10,157 views**

TheHill88 Lost Footage Lonelygirl15 is a Fake

Caitlin gave me this original footage many months ago it is her original video Lonelygirl5 Is a Fake and I Turned 18. Well here it is in its ...

by **TheHill88Fans** | 4 years ago | **8,059 views**

Remembering Lonelygirl15 YouTube Orbit 28-365

Found an old blog post from October of 2006, right after I'd discovered YouTube and **Lonelygirl15**. Please leave a comment or video with your ...

by **illuminatta** | 8 months ago | **134 views**

An outsider's view of Lonelygirl15

Amy28's view of **Lonelygirl15**, the series.

by **betz28** | 2 years ago | **389 views**

Lonelygirl15 spoof [short version]

Lets make a light hearted **Lonelygirl15** spoof. That's Wendy doing what she does. The extended version will go live on Wednesday. Enjoy

by **swoozie06** | 4 years ago | **57,951 views**

The Angry News - Lonelygirl15 Takes Hollywood!

It's official, Jessica Rose, who plays Bree/**Lonelygirl15** has a Hollywood career! What YouTuber will be next? Today's news source: www.theage.com ...

by **AngryAussie** | 4 years ago | **5,205 views**

Lonelygirl15

LG15 slideshow Music: Lonelygirl - Dee Montreal

by **DeathstarPsycho** | 4 years ago | **5,440 views**

FIGURE 2.2. Just a few of the 8,420 YouTube search results for Lonelygirl15.

not, as memeticians and viral marketers argue, determine the medium. There is an interaction between code and environment, in which the circulation and interruption of productive flows exceed the causality of an evolutionary code. For example, the interactive capacity to "broadcast yourself" to the YouTube community in a nonlinear mode—responding and commenting on the webcast—suggests that the viral spreading of Lonelygirl15 was dependent on the file-sharing medium.

Fourth, there is, I suggest, a crudely made distinction between the "tyranny of selfish replicators" and the proposal that memes can be culturally engineered.[44] How can the meme be both omnipotent and manipulable? This last problem is particularly relevant to the claims made by viral marketers and begins with concerns about a contradictory relation between the blind watchmaker thesis and memetic engineering. In the former, there are no transcendental or conscious human designers, just algorithms and vehicles for memes. In the latter, human actors deliberately engineer the memes that promote, for example, fake healing and religious cults. Memetics makes something of a U-turn here by initially attributing the spread of an idea entirely to the running of an algorithm and, later, pointing to "clever tricks" evolved from experience and research but nevertheless comparable to marketing and propaganda and therefore "deliberately" applied to the spreading of ideas and making money.[45] This is an interesting volte-face considering that Blackmore's goal is ultimately to expose the illusionary paradox of the conscious self "in charge" and "responsible" for individual action in the face of a barrage of autonomous, self-propagating memes.[46] How can meme theory reconcile a self-imposed dichotomy between the *natural* tyrannies of selfish replicators and the *culturally* defined memetic engineering of the marketer? Perhaps it is the case that the paradox between what is real and what is imagined cannot be flattened. More significantly, as a theory of mass persuasion, memetics says very little about the politics of social power that is concealed in such a paradoxical relation.

Last, I want to approach the memetics that underpins viral marketing as an imperfect crime. It is important to note from the outset that most viral videos fail to have the impact of a Lonelygirl15. So despite the neo-Darwinian formulas proposed by marketing gurus, the process of actually "going viral," although desirable, seems to be a rare and often accidental event. This has prompted further academic skepticism concerning the claims of commercially applied memetics. Along these lines, Matthew Fuller and Andrew Goffey argue that despite the promise of the "efficacy of the circulation of anonymous affect," viral marketing "simply isn't viral enough."[47] So, while marketing experts claim that their technique shifts the burden of marketing labor onto the consumer, the distribution of the viral itself becomes "compromised by the endgame of *appropriation*."[48] As Goffey and Fuller put it,

> Viral marketing is an imperfect crime, because the identity of the criminal needs to be circulated along with the act itself. By pushing marketing into the realm of experiential communication, by attempting thereby to become part of the flow of material affect, virals move ever further away from strictly coded messages into the uncertain realm of pervasive communication.[49]

Like this, the example of Lonelygirl15 problematizes the viral marketer's claim to have control over a coded unit of cultural imitation that absolutely transcends the freewill of the consumer by obscuring its source and making appropriation seem accidental. As Godin claims, "while it may appear accidental, it's possible to dramatically increase the chances your idea-virus will catch on and spread."[50] In response to these claims, Goffey and Fuller propose that a necessary function of viral marketing is that the viral-event will, as they claim, ultimately have to reveal its source. This is the "imperfect crime,"[51] in which the illusion of the Trojan ultimately turns into a highly visible scam.

Yet, despite the limits of the hallucinatory duration of a video viral, questions still remain concerning how any level of illusory accidentality is sustained at all. While perhaps memetics fails to explain the induced reverie of the fans of Lonelygirl15, there is a discernable manipulation of the collective mind, which at very least passes through the semiconsciousness of the network. To be sure, on one hand, the negative responses posted on YouTube following the Lonelygirl15 scam support Goffey and Fuller's location of a potential flaw in the management of such hallucinatory events and accidents. Some visitors begrudgingly acknowledged being duped. Others claimed that although they went along with it, on reflection, they suspected a hoax all along. Conversely, though, for many of those caught up in the viral campaign, the end of the hallucination appears to have been marked by an emotional out-pouring of shock, sadness, confusion, disappointment, and disapproval, which, although seemingly contrary to the goals of marketing, suggests that a hypnotic force or affective charge is indeed apparent. One user in particular summed up the disappointment with a short posting:

LONELY GIRL BROKED [sic] MY HEART.

Other postings reveal a similar manipulation of mood apparent in the revelations that Lonelygirl15 was a hoax:

wow . . . thats messed up. . . . I honestly dont know what to think. . . . huh. .wow; seriously are these "scripwriters" that sad they have to cheat people to think that there watching something real i mean come on can u get more sad; holly fuck it was a friggen escapade! she REALLY will be a lonely girl who can take her seriously after this?; she'll always be known as a fake and a phoney baloney from now on; can some[one] pleeease tell me what this is all about?? why has she got fans, and why is she a fake? is she normal? some1 please tell me what she is trying to do! [52]

To some extent, then, these comments support the fatalistic imperfection of the viral crime. Nevertheless, although the claims of memetic illusion are evidently problematic, the fact that contagious hallucinations of this kind occur at all prompts further questions about the kind of affective relations in which real and imaginary events become paradoxically blurred in the minds of network users. The question still remains as to how these rare events are able to route around the collective conscious-ness and contaminate the consumer, mostly unawares.

Despite the many fault lines running through the meme project, it is nevertheless constructive to ask what can be extracted from this contagion theory and productively integrated into further theorization. In this context, Fuller has set out a fruitful reorientation of meme theory in which the potential of a localized and collectivist contagion can exist outside the constraints of the neo-Darwinian frame:[53]

Geared as it is to an appreciation of fitness, memetics . . . tends to
miss out on an opportunity to recognize or observe those memes
that die out, that do not replicate beyond a certain spatial or temporal territory.[54]

The ephemerality of an idea is indeed a compelling analytical source.
Unlike many other theories of the idea, it does not assemble global
edifices of immaterial meaning and ideology. There are no public or
private spheres of communication or structural apparatuses on which
ideas are crudely suspended. On the contrary, it is a conceptualization
that, Fuller argues, "sees the individual operator in culture as a nodal
point, not a totality."[55] The meme unit is therefore distinct from the
structuralist prefiguring of signification and meaning. In contrast, memetic analysis concentrates on node-to-node contagion occurring in
populations. As Fuller further argues, a localized memetics is far more
useful than a grand-scale theory of cultural evolution.

Moreover, to sidestep the limitations of the fitness algorithm, the
memetic unit should become inseparable from the involutive (not the
evolutive) vectors of environmental cultural replication. To achieve this,
Fuller's resuscitation of the meme requires an additional criterion that
might "generate it as an event."[56] *Monitorability* joins fidelity, fecundity,
and longevity as a memetic mode that could provide the much-desired
visibility of the memetic unit of imitation. Like this, Fuller's memetic
event cuts across scales, passes through environments, becomes blocked,
and generates or mutates.[57] Stripped of neo-Darwinian dogma, the
passage of the memetic event usefully provides a trace of the complex
media ecologies Fuller goes on to vividly explore. Nevertheless, can
this renewal manage to shake off the analogical foundation of memetics? This is an analogy that overwhelmingly imposes the effects of the
fitness algorithm on viral events, environments, and affects. So while
the meme promises marketers a tool that can be consciously guided by
individual persons, utilizing tricks of sex, fear, truth, altruism, and even
hypnotic sleep paralysis to covertly infect the vulnerable in society, the
social environment in the neo-Darwinian frame is always reduced to the
universal application of the survival mechanism. Indeed, the problem
with the meme is inherent to a theory of evolution that is imposed on
nearly every facet of human life. As Parisi contends, neo-Darwinism

has become "representative of all modes of organization of society, economy and politics," but significantly, its zoocentric doctrine has not at all engaged with the "biophysical, socio-cultural and techno-economic dynamics of evolution."[58]

The biologist Gabriel Dover argues that the product of the gene is not necessarily designed by a master evolutionary mechanism. It is more probable that it is shaped by a programless search space. In this topological space of genetic communication, it is the interaction that evolves, not the gene.[59] In the context of cultural contagion, then, the neo-Darwinian analogy can be seen to negate the creative potential of chance encounters between bodies, environment, events, and accidents in favor of a deterministic evolutionary code. Memetics treats social encounter as the passive passing on of a competing idea. By attributing this level of intentionality to the fidelity, fecundity, and longevity of the meme itself, the theory crudely consigns the by and large unconscious transmission of attitudes, expectancies, beliefs, compliance, imagination, attention, concentration, and distraction through social collectives to an insentient surrender to a self-seeking code.

Memetics is a theory that ultimately argues that the illusion of conscious freewill is attributable to a code. The hallucinogenic events of Lonelygirl15 therefore render the users of YouTube a dumb social medium through which the code replicates itself. The idea that such a mode of hypnosis might play a role in social contagion is certainly intriguing. However, by neglecting to include the mutuality of social encounters in processes of contagion, memetics arguably consigns the hypnotic qualities of social interaction to the same determinisms of the evolutionary algorithm. In contrast, I argue that hypnotic contagions have an inseparable relation to the social environment that exceeds code determinism.

Despite attempts to align Tarde to memetics, the excessive biological determinism of neo-Darwinian contagion theory can never be effectively reconciled within the Tardean diagram. In contrast, *Virality* firmly rejects the imposed "naturalness" of the gene–meme analogy wherein the biological *always* determines the social. As Brennan convincingly argues, the neo-Darwinist accounts of viral culture poorly frame the "urges and affects" of social beings as predetermined by birth and therefore part of the fate of the individual.[60] As she puts it:

The meme can be transmitted, but only through the birth of new human subjects, only as part of the genetic package that officially marshals the action in the development of the embryo.[61]

Virality is, in a similar sense, not tied to an evolutionary mechanism. The ontology of the Tardean–Deleuzian diagram needs to be alternatively rethought in terms of the machinic independence of relationality, which produces difference, not resemblance.

Viral Encounters with the Crowd

Le Bon's account of how hypnotic encounters with images trigger collective contagion includes features that are surprisingly comparable to those events experienced with Lonelygirl15. His crowd contagion is principally a psychological symptom of becoming collective. However, also contained in the logic of *The Crowd* is a considerable micro/macroreduction of the social insofar as becoming part of the crowd leads to the mental erosion of the individual's conscious personality. Mental unity thus exercises "a decisive influence over the mental life of the individual."[62] Once immersed in the crowd, an individual becomes paralyzed by its "magnetic influence." He becomes a hypnotized subject "slave" to all the "unconscious activities of his spinal cord, which the hypnotizer directs at will."[63] Like this, the individual not only loses his personality but freewill and discernment are lost too, along with feelings and thoughts that are all "bent in the direction determined by the hypnotizer."[64] So quite unlike Durkheim's macro/microreduction, the crowd does not come together to rid itself of social anomie but instead propagates a corrosive neurosis. *The Crowd* is a markedly conservative contagion theory after all, in which Le Bon warns of the contagious passions associated with prevailing democratic social movements that endangered the established order of nineteenth-century institutional power. Yet Le Bon's social theory does not altogether escape the molarity of organicism. Although the psychological crowd is a being very much formed out of "heterogeneous elements," it comes together precisely like the cells of living bodies do and displays, as a result, very different characteristics.[65]

Notwithstanding its overt racism and tendency to record rather than explain the contagiousness of crowds,[66] Le Bon's book was nevertheless an influential study. It played a prominent role in early mass persuasion theory[67] and supposedly informed both Hitler's and Mussolini's notions of crowd control and leadership in the 1930s. But it was Le Bon's ideas on how "mental unity" is supposed to work on the body and mind of the individual that not surprisingly influenced Freud's early study of group psychology. To be sure, a proto-psychoanalysis is evident in Le Bon's focus on the spreading of a dreamlike neurotic mechanism of representation. As Le Bon proposes, it is the "permanent repression of selfish impulses" in the crowd that distinguishes it from the free consciousness of the individual.[68] Freud made extensive use of this idea of group repression to probe the psychological source that unites the cells of the collective social body.[69]

In *The Crowd*, it is contagion that holds sway over the collective body, influencing the feelings, thoughts, and actions of every individual. As Le Bon goes on to argue,

> In a crowd every sentiment and act is contagious, and contagious to such a degree that an individual readily sacrifices his personal interest to the collective interest. This is an aptitude very contrary to his nature, and of which a man is scarcely capable, except when he makes part of a crowd.[70]

Contagion thus "intervenes to determine the manifestation in crowds of their special characteristics, and at the same time the trend they are to take."[71] However, Le Bon makes contagion only "an effect of hypnosis."[72] The hypnotic source of contagion is a "special state" in which conscious individuals fall into the hands of a hypnotizer. This is how personalities vanish and the discernment of the suggestible feelings and actions of others becomes diminished. Ultimately, the attentions of the constituent individuals are bent in the direction solely determined by the hypnotizer. Indeed, like many of his contemporaries, including Tarde, Le Bon was greatly influenced by experiments with hypnosis at the time. But as Freud pointed out, the exact source of the points of fascination that hold sway over *The Crowd* needs to be teased out of the vagueness of Le Bon's account. The answer he found is very much couched in the Freudian interpretation of the somnambulist state. The hypnotic-leader is in effect the unconscious that leads *The Crowd*.

The concept of hypnotic leadership in *The Crowd* "accords great power to the image as an organizer of crowd responses."[73] This is an unconscious unity that significantly thinks in images, or more precisely, dreams of images that get passed on.[74] Indeed, unlike Tarde, Le Bon attributes "magnetic influences" to a mechanism that passes from images to those immersed in the social order of the crowd. Like this, crowd control is generally defined by a mechanism of mass hallucination. This is a power relation established between the hypotizer and the hypnotized individual that renders the latter unconscious and therefore made vulnerable to the magnetism of images. For Freud, this mechanism of the mass hallucination of images is a fantasy in the sense that it falls under the logic of the psychology of unfulfilled neuroses. *The Crowd* is the neurotic guided by a "psychological reality" or "hysterical symptom" rather than the "repetition of real experience":[75]

> The sense of guilt [of the neurotic crowd is] an obsessional neurosis based upon the fact of an evil intention which was never carried out. Indeed, just as in dreams and in hypnosis, in the mental operations of a group the function for testing the reality of things falls into the background in comparison with the strength of wishes with their affective cathexis.[76]

This dream of images is an outpouring of the representational contents of a repressed collective unconscious. It is possible to see why the 1930s fascist movements may well have been energized by *The Crowd* and potentially developed their visual style of propaganda around Le Bon's image-hypnosis premise. As Freud points out, unlike the discerning intellect of the individual, *The Crowd* is excited by excessive stimuli. Significantly, these are not sensitivities to empathic or compassionate appeals to others but relate to two kinds of obsessive attention to (1) heroes, violence, and brute force and (2) morality, devotion, or abnegation to a cause.[77] Here we observe the cultivation of a blind love not directed at the intellect but operating through appeals to violent and conservative feelings that contaminate the thoughts and actions of an obedient, herdlike crowd. Moreover, and as all fascist movements seem to realize, the lovelorn crowd is in desperate need of a master to love. The persuasion machine just needs to make the leader the visual point of fascination.

Indeed, Le Bon provides early examples of contagions sparked by images, which, he proposes, help to explain how a mechanism of hallucination functions. These include the spreading of contagious ideas often triggered by events that could not possibly be observed by all, if indeed by anyone at all, except by way of a hallucination but that are passed on regardless. He reasons that despite not having direct visual or physical contact with a causal event, for example, a crusader experiencing the vision of St. George as it "appeared" on the walls of Jerusalem,[78] the anticipating mind of the crowd would nevertheless psychologically absorb the hallucination and pass it on. To put it another way, contagion can be ignited by events imagined to be real by the crowd. This is perhaps how the ensuing image-event becomes a hallucinogenic phantasm that passes through the collective unconsciousness.

Le Bon provides a further example of the functioning of his mechanism of hallucination, which, to some extent, reverberates with the events of Lonelygirl15:

> The frigate, the *Belle Poule,* was cruising in the open sea for the purpose of finding the cruiser *Le Berceau,* from which she had been separated by a violent storm. It was broad daylight and in full sunshine. Suddenly the watch signaled a disabled vessel; the crew looked in the direction signaled, and every one, officers and sailors, clearly perceived a raft covered with men towed by boats which were displaying signals of distress. Yet this was nothing more than a collective hallucination. Admiral Desfosses lowered a boat to go to the rescue of the wrecked sailors. On nearing the object sighted, the sailors and officers on board the boat saw "masses of men in motion, stretching out their hands, and heard the dull and confused noise of a great number of voices." When the object was reached those in the boat found themselves simply and solely in the presence of a few branches of trees covered with leaves that had been swept out from the neighboring coast. Before evidence so palpable the hallucination vanished.[79]

The duration of the events of *Belle Poule* are, according to Le Bon, dependent on the extent to which delirium is sustained in the mind of the crowd. What was once mentally heterogeneous becomes submerged in the homogenous psychology of the crowd. The passage of the hallucinatory image-event is therefore determined by the unity of the collective mind: the "sameness" or averaging out implied by the cellular structure of mental unity.

The Crowd has since been roundly demonized in contemporary sociological studies—and for good reason perhaps. Many of the ideas Le Bon uses seem to have been plagiarized from Tarde and given a rather sinister contextual twist. *The Crowd* is after all an aristocratic expression of fear against the rise of democratic movements in the nineteenth century. Nevertheless, it is possible to relocate parts of this straw man of contagion theory away from organicism, Freud, and fascism. It must be noted that although *The Crowd* could be "modified by slow hereditary accumulations," it is neither perfectly aligned to the elementary social Darwinism developed by Spencer[80] nor straightforwardly embedded in the homogeneity of a proto-psychoanalytical notion of mental unity. Akin to a nineteenth-century Malcolm Gladwell, perhaps, Le Bon's social epidemiology interestingly draws on a shorthand version of contemporary science, using it to point to a tendency in humans to imitate each other as a way to explain, for example, the propagation of fashionable ideas. He continues:

> Imitation is a necessity for him. . . . It is this necessity that makes the influence of what is called fashion so powerful. Whether in the matter of opinions, ideas, literary manifestations, or merely of dress, how many persons are bold enough to run counter to the fashion? It is by examples not by arguments that crowds are guided. At every period there exists a small number of individualities which react upon the remainder and are imitated by the unconscious mass.[81]

Anticipating Gladwell's popularization of the physics of epidemiology in *The Tipping Point*, Le Bon notes the significant role promiscuous individuals play in the spreading of fads and innovations throughout society. Furthermore, his notion of the evolution of the collective seems to similarly owe more to an evolving nineteenth-century understanding of chemistry and emergence than it does to an analogical account of the averaging out of cells in an organism. Although the coming together of the individual cells of the collective body constitutes its living form and characteristics, in the aggregate of the crowd, "there is in no sort a summing-up of or an average struck between its elements":

> What really takes place is a combination followed by the creation of new characteristics, just as in chemistry certain elements, when brought into contact—bases and acids, for example—combine to form a new body possessing properties quite different from those of the bodies that have served to form it.[82]

Concerned as it is with how the molecular becomes molar, these transformations of heterogeneous cells into the collective body are evidently of interest to this study. So, although *The Crowd* has been portrayed (by those keen to prove the wisdom of collectives) as a dystopian vision,[83] and is very much tied to Le Bon's recurrent fear of the mutating social and political incoherence of nineteenth-century Europe, it makes a useful distinction between two kinds of propagating ideas. These two ideas spread through the crowd, influencing the political and cultural stability, and instabilities, of the age.[84] The first idea is classed as the *fundamental* idea through which great stability is brought to the environment, heredity, and public opinion. The second class of idea, however, is the *accidental* passing on of ideas that are very much "of the moment." Typical of the conservative political stance of Le Bon's analysis, these latter "transitory ideas" appear to be eroding the solidity of the former fundamental ideas of mainstream politics and religion. Yet, in one noteworthy paragraph, Le Bon compares the tension between fundamental and transitory ideas to the way in which the solid volume of water in a stream is agitated on its surface by the small and ever-changing waves.[85] In other words, he points to a social aggregation in which a tension exists between the influential flow of small ideas and the big institutional norms that underpin the social organic structure. Of course, this is again a far simpler notion of countercontagion than that explained by Tarde's processes of assimilation. Nevertheless, for an analysis otherwise intent on retaining organic order formed in the traditions of the past, Le Bon allows a glimpse into the chaotic force of encounter at work in the social environment in which ideas spread.

The Crowd suggests a production of subjectivity that is informed as much by the indirectness of accidents and events as it is by the organic structuring of norms. The play between stability and instability is again evocative of the signature of chaos borrowed by the likes of Gladwell and others currently promoting epidemiology as a way to grasp how ostensibly unpredictable small events in social networks can be transformed into large-scale events. So while Le Bon argues that an external hypnotizer can exploit the contagious idea to determine future events, he also manages to introduce a sense of the vulnerability of the social environment to the forces of encounter. The contagious crowd is in itself a corrosive force, wearing away the identity of both the individual and the larger social unities that structure individualism. In sharp contrast to the contagion-friendly passive medium of Dawkins's population of minds, Le Bon asks, "is it not the genius of crowds that has furnished the thousands of grains of dust forming the soil in which [ideas] have sprung up?"[86] In doing so, he further recognizes that the "environment, circumstances, and events represent the social suggestions of the moment."[87] Although Le Bon hints that accidental environments "may have a considerable influence,"[88] he provides but a trace of the complex imitative ecologies of desire and invention proposed by Tarde. The real poverty of *The Crowd,* though, is its failure to explain why the hidden motives of the crowd persist beyond saying that they fall under the magnetic influence of hypnotic images.

The Affective Turn

Brennan's theory of affective transmission provides an interesting starting place by which to disentangle viral encounters from both memetics and Le Bon's proto-psychoanalysis of the crowd. Although unusual in its omission of Tarde, this account of the rise and fall and rise again of crowd theory offers an intense probing and resuscitation of nineteenth-century notions of contagion. It begins by clearing away the ambiguities of Le Bon's explanation of how contagion spreads through crowds primarily via visual means and instead links social epidemics to biochemical and neurological factors. Contagion, for Brennan, is equal to entrainment, which is "a simple affective transfer" discerned by porous individuals in rooms and other social atmospheres of encounter.[89] The important point is that transmission does not originate in the evolutionarily determined and biologically hardwired drives of the individuals that compose the crowd. On the contrary, the affective transfer is always, from the outset, *social*. Despite the prevalent "prejudice concerning the biological and the social" and the "belief in [a subject's] self-containment" that replaced the early social scientists' interest in how collectives respond to each other, the biological and the social are irrevocably blended together.[90] Contagion spreads from person to person via the multisensory affective social atmospheres before it passes through the skin of each individual.

It is significant that Brennan singles out Le Bon's tendency toward a visual explanation for the mass psychosis of the crowd. Effectively, it is a porous inclination of the collective to hallucinogenic delusions that defines Le Bon's notion of social agency as more generally stupid together than it is discerning when alone. However, Brennan infers that Le Bon's concentration on sight as the main mechanism of contagion prefigures the more problematic shift in the twentieth century toward ocularcentric cognitive social models in which affective communication takes place between individuals whose affects are self-contained: one individual has the affect, other individuals *see it,* or sometimes hear it, then they drum it up within themselves, and ad infinitum, the affect spreads.[91] Like this, the separating power of sight not only functions in the Cartesian sense to detach human subjects from the world of objects they inhabit but makes individuals discrete from one another. However, as Brennan convincingly argues, "images and mimesis explain some of it, but olfactory and auditory entrainment offer more comprehensive explanations" of what constitutes social influence.[92] She goes on from this point to introduce an array of rhythmic means whereby one person's affects can be linked to another, like the spread of identification that results not from self-contained psychologies but from multisensory affective contagions: "now I am feeling your nervousness," "we are both yawning."[93] Significantly, for Brennan, as it is here, affective contagion is a "profoundly social thing."[94]

Mechanism Dependence/Independence

The failure of memeticists to locate a unit of imitation equivalent to the gene questions the validity of a universality founded on the strict analogical coupling of evolutionary theory and cultural practices. Similarly,

The Crowd reduces contagion to a hallucinatory mechanism: a mental unity that dreams in images. My aim here is to therefore disentangle contagion theory from the mechanistic limitations imposed on it by these two representational approaches. Clearly any attempt to move beyond the space of representation prompts the question, what kind of universality is *Virality* forwarding? To put it another way, what connects cascading financial instabilities, global pandemics of social influence, snowballing desires, and the actions of computer virus writers? The answer again points to an assemblage theory of Tarde's diagram. There is, as such, a need to reconsider unification and universality in at least two ways. That is, unity needs to be grasped in the affective charge of the event spaces of Tarde's diagram and a concept of universality understood as the distribution of singularities in an assemblage.

To begin with, Tardean contagions are established in complex intersection points that bring physical, biological, cultural, and political phenomena into social relation with each other. The imitative ray is not consequently reducible to a unit. It is not intrinsic or essential. Radiation is an *insubstantial* or *inessential* relationality. To explain how this might work, it is useful to refer to a distinction made between the *relations of interiority* in essentialist accounts and the *relations of exteriority* of assemblage theory.[95] In the former, essentialist identities are formed around the resemblance of component parts and their relation to a homogeneous whole. In the latter, any degree of resemblance between a small component of one assemblage and a larger unity is not guaranteed in the processes of heterogeneous emergence and historical differentiation. Regarded in this way, the open exteriority of a machinic assemblage contrasts sharply with the interiority of a closed mechanism. The social assemblage is, as such, "a synthesis of the properties of a whole not reducible to its parts."[96] Nonetheless, although a social assemblage is not a seamless whole, its component parts may have the capacity (or not) to become connected, or detached, and affect other assemblages.[97] Assemblages do not therefore come together via analogy. There are no representational mirrors held up between nature, culture, and technology. Assemblage relationality is a process of contagion and contamination of component parts.[98]

Second, then, assemblages are "individual singularities," yet the "possibilities open to them at any given time are constrained by a distribution of universal singularities."[99] It is indeed the distribution of singularities that constitutes the diagram of the assemblage. The key to understanding universal contagion is, for that reason, being able to grasp the significance of the sensitivity assemblages have to this distribution. The notion that what becomes whole is due to the spreading of singularities enables a radical rethinking of what might appear to be an ostensibly oppositional relation between singularity and universality. Understood as part and parcel of a departure from the closed Euclidian spaces of representation, the singularity flags the influence of Riemann geometry on Deleuzian ontology. The singularity is grasped, as such, in a topological diagramming of tendencies or a space of possibilities that does not take the reified categorizations of collective or individual representations as defining social entities. The singularity is not a given body; rather, it is a topological constraint, or degree of freedom, that is yet to come.

Here the resonance between Tarde's diagram and assemblage theory becomes even more evident. In both, singularities of habitual repetitions and special replicators sustain routine [and recurrent] associations.[100] They are indeed the base of all action. A singularity in this sense determines the long-term tendencies of topological relation. Like the imitative ray, it is not a person, or a body, but the cocausal relations of social multiplicity. It may be crudely located as somewhere in between a node and an edge in a network topology, insofar that a nodal point constrains or liberates the relational edges, and without an edge, a node ceases to be social. However, dynamic singularities are not just nodal attractors or linkages. They are in Riemann's terms also recurrent in topological forms as saddle points, foci, and rare centers. Significantly, though, the singularity is a tendency, but it does not lead to a final mechanistic state of unity or stability.

The social multiplicity of Tarde's diagram can be further contrasted with the mental unity of the crowd insofar as the latter is regarded as "passive," easily led, and "susceptible to external manipulation," while the former is leaderless and acts on the basis of what it has in common rather than based on the imposition of identity or unity.[101] Counter to Le Bon's crowd, the commonness of singularities implies the potential to influence the coming together, dissolution, or bifurcation of an assemblage. The universality of contagion needs to be understood, like this, as independent of unifying mechanisms and analyzed accordingly through the relationalities and associations established between singularities.

Two Kinds of Crowd

Despite their apparent similarities, Tarde and Le Bon are at variance with each other. Significantly, whereas the mental unity of *The Crowd* divides up real and psychological experiences, respectively, into individual–collective and conscious–unconscious couplings, Tarde's diagram is nonunifying and therefore traces the relations between forces that traverse the spatiotemporal confines of such pairings. Indeed, before going on to think through the mechanism independence of imitative radiation, it is perhaps important to position both Tarde and Le Bon as alternative *forefathers* of contagion theory. This certainly becomes apparent in at least three areas that warrant further attention. First, they both seem to be at the base of two distinct theoretical lines of influence characterized by Le Bon's direct link to Freud's psychoanalysis and Tarde's role in Deleuzian ontology. Second, both present conflicting ideas about the role contagion plays in social movements such as those rare and exceptional outbreaks of democracy. Here it is possible to see how, unlike Le Bon's conservative concerns for the stability of the old aristocratic order, Tarde introduces a novel media theory that considers both the potential and improbability of rare moments of democratic contagion. Last, there are two very different notions of hypnotic power at work in *The Crowd* and Tarde's diagram. The former falls back on a direct representational means of control, while the latter speaks of indirect subrepresentational and reciprocal magnetisms.

At the outset, there is this distinctive fork in the theoretical lines of flight extending from Le Bon and Tarde. There is a notable proto-psychoanalytical division setup in *The Crowd* between, on one hand, the real conscious experience of the individual and, on the other, the dreaming of the unconscious crowd. In contrast, Tarde's trajectory becomes apparent in very different attempts to understand the dream of action evident in social encounter. Through the lenses of assemblage theory, post-Fordist analysis of labor, Thrift's creation of worlds of infection, and Crary's making of the attentive subject, he becomes more than a mere footnote to contemporary thinking on subjectivation.

Second, and before further distinguishing between Tarde's and Le Bon's approaches to emergent democratic movements, there are ostensible resemblances to note. For example, their analyses of nineteenth-century crowds similarly link the credulity of urban collectives to the contagions of new embryonic forms of social democracy. Tarde argues that the voice of public opinion increasingly becomes the authority whose example is copied, while traditional and expert opinion wanes.[102] The rise of the mass mediation of public opinion could indeed act to subjugate the individual to the group. Like this, Tarde observed the relationship established between the popular press and public opinion, which "mobilized passions and deeply divided the French" during the infamous Dreyfus affair.[103] It was the almost unavoidable collective "obsession" with the "seductive agitations" of the newly animated nineteenth-century media society, which he contended drew the attention of the crowd toward negative racist contagions and posed a threat to the new democracies. So, whereas Le Bon was concerned with the threats posed to established hierarchies by what he regarded as the negative contagious spreading of democracy in the late 1800s, Tarde, later on in his career, became a stalwart defender of democracy and committed himself as a Dreyfus supporter.

Significantly, then, it was not through the proliferation of mass media that Tarde's contagious forces of democratic encounter would most gainfully spread. To be sure, he was exceedingly skeptical about the "magical charm" of this new emerging environment, with its continual supply of fresh sights and renewed conversations. It was these recently animated urban environments that would provide a point of fascination for "concentrated attention, of passive and vivid imagination."[104] Yet, unlike Le Bon's account of the hypnotic power of images, Tarde's somnambulist becomes feverishly absorbed in the "noise and movement of the streets, the display of shop-windows, and the wild and unbridled rush of existence," which "affect" people like "magnetic passes."[105] Increases in urban affectivity simply exaggerate social life.

What spreads for Tarde is not, as Le Bon would have it, an effect of unconscious hypnosis but is rather due entirely to the force of imitative encounters with events that elicit a kind of hypnotic social medium. This is to some extent akin to a chain letter, wherein subjectivity becomes embedded in relationality. Like this, Tarde questioned the social medium of his day. "Suppose a somnambulist should imitate his medium to the point of becoming a medium himself," he asked. From thereon he magnetizes "a third person, who, in turn, would imitate him, and so on, indefinitely."[106] Mostly these magnetizations flow through the asymmetrical terraces of social influence that connect the self to the other in social life, but magnetization can become part of an exceptional mutual relation. For the most part, then, the imitative ray flows through the terraces from those with social prestige in the direction of those who merely copy. Nevertheless, there are "rare moments" when that tumbledown effect becomes exhausted and the "movement down the scale" is transformed into an "inverse movement." It is such moments that Tarde regards as democratic, that is, when "millions of men collectively fascinate and tyrannize over their quondam mediums."[107]

Although recognizing the role of terraces in maintaining social status, it is the mutuality established between hypnotizer and a hypnotized subject that underpins the social power relations in Tarde's diagram. Indeed, whereas Le Bon's contagious crowd is without doubt an irresponsible agitator, Tarde's force of imitative encounter becomes the very locus of the emergence of the dream of social action. In *The Laws of Imitation,* the gullibility of the crowd is not a given as such. On the contrary, the relation between magnetizer and magnetized is not preformed but emerges from reciprocal magnetizations. To be sure, the relation between magnetizer and magnetized is unquestionably one sided, but there remains an exceptional tension between attractor and attracted in processes of magnetization. As a consequence, "the magnetizer does not need to lie or terrorize to secure the blind belief and the passive obedience of his magnetized subject."[108] It is through the magnetized somnambulist himself that "a certain potential force of belief and desire" flows. The force of desire always seeks expression in belief. All the magnetizer need do is "open the necessary outlet to this force."[109]

Last, for Tarde, and distinct from Le Bon, the force of hypnotic encounter is a nonrepresentational mediation. He explains the similarity of millions of people not as the result of a unifying fantasy founded on image-events alone. The society of imitation instead brings the repetitions of subrepresentative matter into relation with each other. Tarde's imitative rays are, as such, caught up in the ever-increasing maelstrom of "constant communication,"[110] full of waves, currents, conductors, and assimilators that propagate the imitative flows from person to person. The somnambulist's dream of action is not constrained to a social category but becomes part of a contagious assemblage in which people "unconsciously and involuntarily reflect the opinion of others," allowing actions to be suggested to them as "initiations of ideas or acts."[111]

The Phantom Event

Before concluding, I want to persist with this notion that contagion theory has two trajectories. Herein both Tarde and Le Bon can be viewed through the lenses of schizoid analysis, which further breaks down the proto-psychoanalytical mechanisms of the crowd. What this analysis reveals is a very different understanding of the relational coupling of conscious and unconscious states. As Deleuze and Guattari argue, "Freud tried to approach crowd phenomena from the point of view of the unconscious, but he did not see clearly, he did not see that the unconscious itself was fundamentally a crowd." He was indeed "myopic and hard of hearing" insofar as he misunderstood the crowd to be an individual. Schizoid analysis, conversely, does not "mistake the buzz and shove of the crowd for daddy's voice."[112] Here we see just how far Le Bon's theoretical line is from Tarde's. The hypnotic authority of Daddy's voice is grasped by schizoid analysis as symptomatic of the psychoanalyst's predisposition to repress the desiring machine by locking it away *inside* the representational space of the unconscious. In the mental unification of the unconscious crowd, Le Bon's individual is as such caught up in "repression" and "selfish impulses."[113] The crowd either becomes, like this, (1) a weapon of subjugation wielded to reproduce unconscious imitations necessary for the preservation of a mental unity–dominated by family relations or (2) a suppression of the amoral desires or dangerous overspills of affective contagion that threaten the stability of society as a whole. Like this, Le Bon's crowd contagion *acts on* the social, forcing it to reproduce a unified collective mind. In this light, it is interesting to note how Mussolini was intrigued by what Le Bon had to say about crowd control and how it related to the fascist's need to transform the irrational and conservative delusions of the crowd into a revolutionary force. Like Le Bon, Mussolini understood that not only is the mass a servile flock that needs a master but its multiplicity must become magnetized by the prestigious image of this master.[114]

For Deleuze and Guattari, it is, however, Canetti's analysis of packs that provides a specific antidote to the molar magnetism of singularities. Canetti proposes that the social aggregate *as a whole* can be "interpenetrated" by a pack mentality in which "each member is alone even in the company of others."[115] Yet, when brought into relation with each other, the contagious overspills of the schizoid desiring machine can function to contaminate the repressive forms of an Oedipalized crowd. Indeed, opposed to the unconscious embedded in this Oedipalized collective representation is Deleuze and Guattari's factory-like productions of the schizoid, which trace a continuum between consciousness and unconsciousness. Certainly, unlike Le Bon and Freud, the schizoid unconscious is not a symbolic repression. Instead, it reproduces consciousness by way of desire. This is not at all like the thermodynamic engines that populate the industrial factory of Freud's unconsciousness. Whereas Freud's unconscious is "full of machines that grind and stop in various rhythms, beating out and recording their drive like printing presses,"[116] the schizoid factory is a circuitry of networked cerebral motion relays: recursive loops of incorporeal contagious events that reproduce consciousness. It is a neurological unconscious that connects to the surface of the body.

The notion of the schizoid factory helps move *Virality* beyond the Oedipalized opposition between conscious and unconscious states to what Massumi similarly calls the *nonconscious*.[117] Here "it is only as a local force that the properly human is registered, becomes conscious (operationally present)." However, once immersed in the machinic universe—the "felt reality of relation"—the human becomes the unconscious of relationality.[118] Conscious freewill and intent are exchanged for a series of circuitous relay motions. Unlike the individual subsumed into the mental unity of the unconscious crowd, the "individual body" is "always-already plugged into a collectivity."[119] In the schizoid factory, conscious and unconscious agencies are in concert with each other. To put it another way, Daddy's voice is displaced by an ego that is in constant communication with the force of encounter with events.

As an alternative to the mechanism dependence of both the meme and Le Bon's delusional fantasy, Deleuze points to how the tendency to pass on hallucinatory contagions can be grasped as a phantom-event.[120] Significantly, phantom-events are results, or effects, of actions and passions, not their Oedipal representation. The phantasm is paradoxically without a body but is nevertheless a material thing (an incorporeal materiality). It becomes detached from its causes, spreads itself at the surface, and gets passed on, as such, from surface to surface. This is not the point at which affect turns into fantasy but rather where the ego opens itself to the surface.

In the phantom-events of *Belle Poule* and Lonelygirl15, a relation is established between social corporeality (bodies) and the incorporeal event (imitative encounter). This is not a hypnotic paralysis resolved solely in the depths of a repressed mental unity or the hardwiring of evolutionary memetic encoding but rather an event that affects the surface. As Deleuze puts it, "[the phantom-event's] topological property is to bring 'its' internal and external sides into contact, in order for them to unfold onto a single side."[121] At the surface, the hallucinatory event disengages from its source and spreads itself. Like this, phantom-events are surface effects that can appear as spontaneously intersecting simulacra like the figure of a giant or a mountain range that materializes in the ephemeral formations of clouds in the sky.[122] Similar to the floating branches and leaves of *Le Berceau,* a religious apparition, or the sudden appearance of a pouting teenager on YouTube, these surface effects can, albeit briefly, become detached from direct experience and autonomously spread their affective charge. Indeed, it is the magnetized subject's distance from the phantom-event that makes it prone to variable appearances of the real and the imagined. This is the logic of sense apparent in the spreading of chain letters, Trojan viruses, and contagious false rumors. These are not simply preprogrammed units of imitation but emergent forces of contagion in the social field that function according to an action-at-a-distance. The phantom-event is a surplus, or excess, of the nonconscious. It contaminates the somnambulist, who is caught somewhere in the loop between the imaginary and the real events she encounters and believes in.

Conclusion

The problem for viral marketers, it would seem, is that contagion appears to be all but out of control. Even if they manage to attract the attention of a few influential and promiscuous YouTube visitors, how long will it be before the hallucination is revealed as what Goffey and Fuller refer to as the imperfection of the viral marketing crime? In other words, how long can their viruses stay in the loop between the imaginary and the real before these "accidents" are exposed as mere clouds in the sky? The chaotic rhythm of contagious encounter is indeed easy to observe but not so easy to control. Certainly, unlike the assumed substance of the memetic unit, the incorporeal material of affective contagion has a distinct ungraspability.

There has nevertheless been a recent shift in such marketing fads away from the predominance of the meme toward a focus on networks, collective psychologies, and the relation between emotions and cognition. Like this, Thrift observes a Tardean trajectory in corporate and political strategies intent on gradually "build[ing] up small changes into something significant without a guiding hand." This includes the creation and management, at-a-distance, of active epidemiological spaces, in which affective contagions can be more readily produced, engineered, and traded.[123] Like Stanley Milgram, perhaps, studying the contagions of 1960s urban spaces, marketers are looking to readily steer contagion and magnetize the imitative radiations of the desiring machine by affectively priming encounters at the microrelational level so that fresh points of fascination can be cultivated and nursed to fruition. These attractions make a hypnotic appeal to the moods, emotions, and feelings that guide attentiveness and influence purchase intent. In these new media nurseries, marketers bide their time like Milgram, keep their distance, and wait for the viral events to unfold. Nevertheless, with enough added affect, absorption, hormonal stimulus, intoxicating glory, love, and celebrity worship, the attention of the somnambulist will eventually be drawn to this or that decision point.

3

What Diagram? Toward a Political Economy of Desire and Contagion

It is Deleuze's reading of Foucault that stresses the ontological importance of locating the appropriate abstract diagram to grasp the forces of social power relations.[1] The most suitable diagram can both exercise a force (or many forces of relation) on the social field and display these relations between forces that determine concrete features apparent in the field. Today the ubiquitous diagram of social power is, it would seem, the network, and the force of relation is increasingly understood in terms of epidemics and contagions represented by network graphs. In recent years, indeed, the nodes and edges of the network space have become the focus of many attempts to diagram universal forces of contagion and register them as endemic to a general trend toward an ever-present network power.[2]

Nevertheless, despite its prevalence, a number of ontological limitations regarding the network diagram require attention here. For example, for Galloway and Thacker, there is a notable dissatisfaction with the graph theories used to model contagion in network science. It is argued that they tend to attribute an unfettered and apolitical naturalness to what are considered to be asymmetrical spaces of network power.[3] Certainly a crude line is all too often drawn between the democratically linked network and one-to-many power relations of hierarchical structures. As a result, many-to-many relations are frequently misconstrued as prerequisites for assembling democratic political and economic spaces.

The focus on the equally distributed physics of the network space often ignores, as such, the capacity for a network to become a tyranny as constraining as any hierarchical chain of command.

The limitations of the network diagram are further heightened by the spatial homogeneity it exercises on a relational ontology tending toward the occasional and chaotic overflow of aperiodic events. This is a critique of the network form not only emanating from Deleuzian ontology. It is a concern echoed, to some extent, by contagion theorists working within network science who openly acknowledge that geometric network spaces, standardized by nodes and edges, tend to freeze out the temporality of the event.[4] In social theory, too, this is a problem similarly located in actor networks, where despite awarding equal agency to objects, there is a tendency to counteract the intensity and sudden movements of events by sustaining effectivity and steady accumulation in the network diagram.[5]

To assimilate the intensity of contagious events into an appropriate abstract diagram, the discussion here looks beyond the geometric relations of nodes and edges. By way of examples of recent financial contagions, the Tardean diagrammatic trajectory is more readily traced to a topological event than it is to the feverish excitement surrounding the network economy. Like this, the economy is reconceived as a topological space without measurement but nonetheless with affective capacities. That is to say, the economy is a continuous movement of financial transactions and commodity consumption involving the simultaneous constraint and exploitation of a rare tendency for the seemingly predicable repetitions of market value and mood to effervesce and capriciously burst out.

On one hand, uncontained financial contagion is understood here as an immeasurable chaotic force of relation. This force arises from the mostly unconscious desires of a relatively small group of traders whose speculative transactions trigger the inflation of bubbles of market value and sentiment in the capitalist economy. This is a microrelational force of encounter generated by the few that aperiodically ruptures the global economy with devastating outcomes for the many. On the other hand, though, attention turns to attempts by business enterprises and network scientists to potentialize what appear to be comparable microrelational tendencies at work in the marketplace of commodity consumption. The intention, it would seem, is clearly not to constrain contagion but to cultivate, nurse, and prime small worlds of infection to exploit the spreading of social influence from the few to the many and thus make small contagions, relating to fashions, brands, and products, spill over into much wider (and more profitable) epidemics of desire.

As this Tardean trajectory is traced through these two kinds of eco-nomic containment and exploitation, an important question becomes apparent, that is, whether the events of Tarde's diagram are indeed an unpredictable and uncontrollable chaos at the center of the capitalist machine, or whether economists, marketers, and politicians alike can exercise these contagious *accidents of influence?* As Thrift points out, Tarde may well have overestimated the accidentalness of contagion and negated to grasp the capacity for increasingly mediated encounters of imitation-suggestibility to be "consciously and carefully steered."[6] Despite the efforts of network scientists to tap into the accidents of influence, the answer to this question is not, I suggest, exclusively located in the diagram of network power but pertains to what has been termed the *networkability of the event.*[7] While acknowledging that what spreads through the economy is, of course, influenced by the networking of financial information, and that post–big bang electronic circuits have clearly played a major role in speeding up and automating speculative trading and contagious spillovers, the networkability of the event, and the affective contagions it triggers, is not wholly reducible to a distrib-uted form of digital capitalism. "The medium of communication [of the event] is not the technology."[8] It is rather the event's movability, displacement, communicability, and relationality that require attention.

The diagrammatic logic of what Parikka has called elsewhere a *viral capitalism,* which evolves through its accidents,[9] is similarly grasped here in terms of a kind of Tardean economic bubble theory, that is to say, a repetition of periodic events that sustains enough topological surface tension to retain the stability of market value and sentiment, until the liquid skeleton of the bubble becomes inflated to the point where it is fit to burst outward as a contagious overspill of event-spaces.

Constraining Financial Contagion

Van Dijk contends that universal contagion is a pressing concern for the age of networks. Increased contact means new threats, and he readily identifies a range of contagious pressures emerging from seemingly intrinsic topological instabilities. Like this, contagion universally contaminates physical, technological, and cultural network spaces, speeding up the transmission of political and economic vulnerabilities. International airports function as hubs for spreading biological viruses like HIV and SARS. Technological networks become similarly volatile to the destructive potential of digital contagions. The spread of cultural and political conformity, rumor, fads, fashions, gossip, and hype—enhanced by the rapidity and extensity of digital networks—threatens to destabilize social order. Yet it is perhaps Van Dijk's reference to the volatility of stocks and currency markets to financial contagion that poses the greatest threat to the economy of network capitalism. Indeed, it is conceivably the case that financial contagion points to the partial failure of network capitalism to predict and contain anomalous shocks, generally of its own making. As recent events in the global economy have revealed, the abuse of financial instruments designed to spread profitable risk also propagates perilous contagions triggered by uninhibited greed, hesitation, and panic. Monetary institutions are so interwoven that bad moods, as well as bad practices, can become a threat to all.

There is, of course, politics in the economy. In the decades preceding the credit crunch and the ensuing frenzied age of austerity cuts, economists tried to explain how small, rare, and nonperiodic events shock an economy, triggering market panic to spread chaotically from country to country. Research funded by the International Monetary Fund and the World Bank focused on complex cross-country transmissions of shocks and spillovers passing through the expanding meshwork of financial, trade, and political links that connect the global market.[10] The European Exchange Rate Mechanism crisis in the early 1990s, for example, not only affected Europe but also spread to emerging markets in the Middle East and Africa. The Mexican crisis affected Latin America and Asia. The Russian crisis affected Eastern Europe and Brazil. However, despite the deployment of a variety of contagion models intended to map trader decision-making patterns, herding instincts, and network cascades, the failure of crisis indicators and the irregularity and reversals of unforeseen financial flows have frustrated efforts to find a rigorous predictive tool.

In the intervening time, while a fresh financial bubble was beginning to build around the U.S. housing market in the mid-2000s, the containment of unanticipated contagion moved closer to the center of international political policy. Politicians appear to have sought to deflect attention away from (or ignore) the dysfunctionalities of network capitalism, pointing toward new threats posed from outside its boundaries. Typical of this distracting rhetoric, and on the eve of the invasion of Iraq in 2003, former British prime minister Tony Blair warned the capitalist world that because its "stock markets and economies rise and fall together," it was "ever more interdependent." The key to prosperity, he contended, was all about defending against new insecurities that "spread like contagion." Significantly, Blair suggested that the current threat to economic stability was not like that posed in the 1930s. The threat today is from new "begetters of chaos" in the shape of tyrannical regimes with weapons of mass destruction and extreme terrorist groups.[11]

While the events of 9/11 certainly did disturb market equilibrium for a time,[12] financial contagion is not, however, inexorably the result of external threats to capitalist economic order. The recent chaos reeked by subprime contagion originated not from the interventions of "villainous" rogue states but from the desires and inventions of the marketplace itself. The spreading of toxic debt began as a chaos lingering at the superhub of network capitalism. It was a U.S.-born speculative bubble (and eventual contagious spillover) intimately coupled to the selling of Trojanlike financial products, the naive bullish mood of the market, and the cynical greed of the global banking sector. It is indeed a contagion that has since spread beyond the contaminating testosterone-fueled practices of a small number of so-called casino traders. The contagion has become a mental health problem requiring the administering of antidepressants to try to dull the pain of double-dip recession, politicized austerity, and worthlessness.[13]

The credit crunch has exploded a myth of network capitalism; that is, despite the hype concerning the special empowerments bestowed on consumers with ready access to value chains like stock market trading, the network has developed into a flawed medium for value exchange. Networks are not, and never have been, democratic spaces for economic activity. They have become highly promiscuous vectors for risk-driven increases in market value, which, on rare, nonperiodic occasions, develop into anomalous speculative bubbles that build and build until they inevitably burst. As follows, the problem of financial contagion has reintroduced old questions concerning the assumption that the self-interest of the market *always knows best.* The rationality of *Homo Economicus,* combined as it is today with an algorithmic logic that powers up the mostly autonomous transactions of digitally encoded value on a network, is not guided by smart decision making, it seems. Decisions are prone to an emotional disposition toward rumor, risk, hazard, anxiety, and panic that affects the rise and fall of value much like the outbreak of tulipomania did back in the 1600s. The persistence of this imperfection raises a puzzling question for market capitalism. That is to say, if nearly all professional traders agree that there is a bubble present in the economy, why is the bubble actively encouraged to build until it reaches a point where it overspills into crisis? It would seem that in times of crisis, the rational and the irrational are fixed in paradoxical relation to each other.

Of course, many scenarios might explain the bubble phenomenon, but the interwovenness of so-called smart decision making and bullish sentiment appears to be fairly significant in terms of understanding how the mood and value of the market become interrelated. One recent financial study, for example, interestingly approaches the market bubble phenomenon by pointing to the destructive interactions between humans acting as smart traders and an automated sentiment trader programmed to make bullish, irrational decisions.[14] The human smart traders begin, as expected, by front running the sentiment traders: they buy up stocks before prices begin to rise. Nonetheless, the smart traders decide to delay taking advantage of price differentials because of an apparent tendency to believe that more profit can be made from the arbitrage of price errors than by selling in periods of market equilibrium. As the resulting bubble starts to build, the decision-making processes of the smart traders tend to veer ever more toward uncertainty. No one knows whether to sell or hold off until prices hit their ceiling. Subsequently, prolonged greed and hesitation continue to inflate the bubble, leading to aggressive short selling only when the bubble finally begins to burst.

The problem of fluctuating value and market mood becomes ever apparent in the difference between Durkheim's and Tarde's approaches to political economy. Although perhaps never truly considered a serious political economist, insofar as he understood the economy as just one of many other determining social facts, Durkheim's theory of anomie is never too far away from debates concerning the damaging fallout of financial crisis.[15] In times of economic disaster, when individuals go bust and become unemployed, or indeed, periods of boom, in which entrenched social power and wealth grow out of proportion, Durkheim contends that the affected anomic actors need to recommence their "moral education." The outcome of which is that they either learn greater self-control, and thus fit back into the equilibrium of the collective consciousness (the "soul" or *l'ame collective*) that influences the consciousness of the individual,[16] or drift further toward a state of anomie, ultimately committing the anomic act of suicide.[17]

Perhaps Durkheim has a point. It would seem that financial crisis and suicide do go hand in hand. Certainly recent news reports frequently compare the cataclysmic events of the Great Depression in the 1930s to the credit crunch. But what would have the positivistic Durkheim made of such a comparison? To begin with, the popular notion that the Great Depression sparked a suicide epidemic among investors who made financial losses in Manhattan on October 29, 1929, is, it appears, another myth. Although a very small number of high-profile, and widely reported, cases gave the impression of an epidemic, the suicide rate was in fact higher in the summer before the Wall Street crash than it was shortly after.[18] It is more likely that the banker will live on to collect his next bonus than develop greater self-control! Whatever his fate, the subsequent rise in long-term unemployment following the 1930s crash, and the social problems associated with it, did more concretely correspond to a rise in the suicide rate.[19] In the credit crunch, too, a similar overhyping of investment banker suicide is masking a mostly ignored link between recession, antidepressant use, and potential suicide.

In contrast to Durkheim's anomic focus on the postbubble casualties (and causalities) of financial contagion, the Tardean diagram points directly to the processes of the bubble phenomenon. The trader is once again the mostly unconscious somnambulist convinced that his actions are his own. Nevertheless, he is mired in the "interplay" between, on one hand, a dream of rational freewill and, on the other, an irrational relation to the affects, desires, beliefs, and sentiments of others.[20] Decisions are not therefore entirely embedded in the self-contained cognition of economic man, but as Borch contends, judgments become embedded in the flow of social inventions that connect self and others to objects of desire (tulips, dot-com shares, or subprime mortgage investments). Like this, subjectivity in the marketplace becomes caught up in the bubble-building event and its eventual overspill. The trader is but a magnetized subject whose role in the event exceeds that of an interacting person merely following the influence of market leaders. Traders are so mesmerized by their desire for the riches, commodities, and prices infecting their moods and inflating the speculative bubble that they become the imitated and erroneous examples in a social medium of contagion. In other words, speculative bubbles are codetermined by the unfettered desire to accumulate riches, hesitations, and the social inventions designed to appropriate these desires and propagate them as risk. But as the erroneous decisions cascade through the networks that connect banking institutions to the many, the anomaly of the bubble becomes concretized in a mode distinctly different from the downward pressure of Durkheim's collective consciousness (the error-correcting force of anomie). The mostly unconscious collective associations that trigger Tardean contagions flow down the mountainous terracing that constitutes the society of imitation to become the depressing actualization of a politically motivated postbubble world of deficit reduction.

Compared by Thrift to the spread of an addictive behavior, like tobacco consumption, the impetus of financial contagion combines the necessary flows of money (and information related to it) with "a series of conversations fuelled by hormones reacting within a mediated environment."[21] Financial contagions thus operate on both economic and affective "psychological" registers. As Tarde contends in *Psychological Economy,*

> The peaks and troughs of values in the stock market, unlike the oscillations of a barometer, could not even remotely be explained without

considering their psychological causes: fits of hope or discouragement in the public, the propagation of a good or bad sensational story in the minds of speculators.[22]

The spreading of these *felt* responses to market forces of affect is the stuff political economy has long hinted at, but never truly explained, albeit as some ill-defined *natural* force of animal spirit—that is, until one reads Tarde. As Thrift points out, with Tarde, there is no secreting "under abstractions such as credit, service and work, the sensations and feelings underlying them."[23] What spreads through financial networks is a mixture of "confidence, fear, 'irrational' exuberance, bad faith, corruption, confidence, [and] a sense of fairness."[24] Moreover, it is significantly the moods of speculators that affect the market and market value, in turn, that affects the mood of speculators. Consequently, the billions of transactions of risk and return flowing through modern economic networks are reproduced in mutual compositions of hormonal splashes of testosterone and cortisol (the moods of speculators) and the financial flows in the marketplace.[25] It is indeed this relation of mutual influence that has a momentum of its own, a vital force, a propelling vigor that can, dependent on certain triggers, travel rapidly from the minutely small investment to the very big recession.

Potentializing Small Worlds of Infection

How the small becomes big has developed into a major interest of network science and a second wave of viral marketing enterprises endeavoring to increase commodity consumption. Along these lines, I want to expand on the Tardean trajectory Thrift traces in contemporary capitalism, pointing to a present-day epidemiological diagram that is redefining the business practices of a burgeoning network business. Many of these new digital enterprises look to exploit new windows of opportunity by hooking up the microrelational flows of the consumer to emotionally persuasive purchase environments. Like this, the priming of consumer mood and flows of social influence produce new affective relations between people, products, and brands, which can be cultivated and purposefully steered.

There are already a number of network science, popular business, and management books that provide evidence of this trajectory. Significantly, though, these books should not be misunderstood as providing a valuable Tardean critique of viral capitalism. On the contrary, as Thrift points out, "they usually come laden with hyperbole in the manner of many management books."[26] Nonetheless, this is not to say that they do not have a "grip." Behind the marketing puff and faddish management lingo are a growing number of "practical experiments" that produce "prescriptions that work,"

> not least, of course, because they begin to change how the world is thought to turn up—through a combination of rhetoric, new technologies and practical short-cuts—all against a background of a capitalism which is increasingly rooted in the exercise of biopower.[27]

Thrift draws particular attention in this respect to Duncan Watts's *Six Degrees: The Science of a Connected Age,* a book that "bears some relation to Tarde's work."[28] In addition to Watts, though, Albert-Laszlo Barabási's *Linked: How Everything Is Connected to Everything Else and What It Means for Business, Science, and Everyday Life* and the popular business, science, and medicine journalist Malcolm Gladwell's business best seller *The Tipping Point: How Little Things Can Make a Big Difference* need to be noted as similar endeavors to locate (and sell on) the potential of networked virality.

Significantly, research into human interactions with biological and digital viruses feeds directly into the epidemiological diagramming of social influence and becomes regurgitated in the new science of networks and its various business offshoots.[29] This is a universal virus that has, it seems, informed a decidedly general understanding of epidemic spreading said to occur across a range of networks. However, despite the tendency toward universality, the diagrams presented do not go uncontested. To be sure, there is a dispute over the question of what actually sparks a network epidemic and how controllable or accidental they are. On one hand, an established epidemiological approach points to the predicable "stickiness" of so-called influentials: a few promiscuous elites who pass on trends to less significant others. On the other hand, though, powerful computer simulations of contagion suggest a new research focus on the accidental and unpredictable environmental factors at play in the pass-on power of consumer influence.

Despite their differences, these two strands of epidemiology can be traced back to a distinctly social rather than medical research program. Both are inspired by Milgram's Boston experiment from the 1960s, in which he famously set out to better understand how people are connected to each other in the world by passing on letters addressed to a stockbroker friend of his living in Boston to randomly selected people in Omaha, Nebraska.[30] Given the assumedly random set of social nodes that connect the wilderness of Nebraska to the urban sprawl of Boston, it was perhaps reasonable to assume that Milgram's letters might never make it to their intended destination point. However, they did, remarkably passing through fewer hands than anticipated. Although it is important to note that Milgram's early conception of what has become known as a *small world network* (or *six degree phenomenon*) does not directly infer epidemic spreading, the unique social clustering it implies has inspired others to consider how the spreading of things in general might pertain to a universal logic that is not exclusively random.

The concept of the influential features strongly in Gladwell's endeavor to sell on the idea of social epidemiology to marketers. As follows, he manages to blend Milgram's Boston experiment with a crude rendition of epidemic threshold theory.[31] In short, threshold theory argues that an epidemic spreads via a few highly promiscuous and infected nodes whose influences can spill over into the network, eventually breaching a tipping (or threshold) point at which the number of infected nodes outlives the number of uninfected nodes. Gladwell argues that tipping points can be breached when small world clusters form around the social relations of a promiscuous few. He illustrates this idea by comparing the spread of syphilis by promiscuous crack cocaine addicts in poor neighborhoods in Baltimore to a flourishing craze for hush puppies spread by influential trendsetters attending fashionable clubs in New York.[32] Suede shoes and syphilis spread to the many, Gladwell claims, "like a virus" following their appropriation by a small but influential group. This is a rare but seemingly maneuverable imitative propensity for small influences to capriciously build into larger trends. Like this, the appearance of crack cocaine in one part of Baltimore brought a relatively small number of people into the area in search of the drug who would also engage in risky sexual behavior associated with crack use. The drug-fueled syphilitic diaspora coincided with other small events such as the reduction in the number of medical personnel working in sexually transmitted disease (STD) clinics and the demolition of a few downtown public housing projects, notorious for crime, drugs, and STDs. In effect, Gladwell's social epidemiology encompasses the larger crime waves that resonate out from these small events. The breaking of a single window in such neighborhoods can, for example, lead to more broken windows, a potential break in, and a vandalized building, before a wave of similar events spreads to the entire city.[33] With its deceptive air of simplicity, it is perhaps not surprising that Gladwell's influence on marketing circles has been "enormously seductive."[34] The notion that a few connected people can trigger big trends is considered to be the very premise of viral and word-of-mouth campaigns.

Two authors frequently associated with what might be regarded as a new epidemiological paradigm in the study of social influence and conformity (and similarly exporting it to the business enterprise) are Watts and Barabási. While also trying to get to grips with fad contagions by comparing them to biological and digital viral outbreaks, Barabási ushered in a new approach by blending Milgram's small world phenomena with more recent scale-free epidemiological models.[35] Based on studies of electronic networks in the late 1990s, scale-free networks present a topological architecture in which stability and instability, order and randomness, and robustness and fragility are in paradoxical mixture with each other. Using this idea, Barabási draws attention to how the epidemic persistence of the Love Bug computer virus undermines both the tenets of threshold theory and the predictability of the influential.[36] Citing a research paper published a year after it was first noted that the Love Bug presented a mystery to threshold modeling, he points to a "new epidemiological framework" marked by the absence of a threshold and its associated critical behavior.[37] Simply put, in scale-free networks, any promiscuous computer in a hub is enough to create an epidemic. Because it is likely to be unprotected and connected to so many other computers in a network, it will eventually spread a virus to another computer without the appropriate virus protection. The Internet is prone to the spreading and the persistence of infections, no matter how low their virulence.

The scale-free network presents a challenge to an old paradigm of network science grounded in the randomness of connectivity. To be sure, before the late 1990s, the complex network theory underpinning contagion modeling, including those used to track computer viruses using threshold theory, had been dominated by the work carried out by Erdos and Renyi in the late 1950s.[38] In simple terms, the random model defines complex networks as homogenously mixed or *democratically* linked: each node has an equally probable chance of having the same amount of links. However, after analyzing the distribution of links across a large sample of web pages, a complex mapping emerged, exhibiting a strange, skewed topological consistency. The fractal patterning of the scale-free network prompted one author to contrast the physical democracy of random networks with a far from random *aristocratic* connectivity.[39] Although randomness and chance are factors in the growth of the topologies of both the World Wide Web and the Internet, there is also a dynamic "organization" of nodes and edges. Distinct from the equilibrium state of random networks, scale-free networks follow an approximate 80–20 rule, in which, as already stated, a few rich or promiscuous nodes continue to get richer (approximately 20 percent of the nodes have 80 percent of the links).

Through the application of graph theory, it has been established that rather than the well-proportioned bell curve graph produced by the average distribution of links in a random network, the topologies of these electronic networks demonstrate a power law. This law is evident in nonperiodic, open systems in which small perturbations, like the economic shocks discussed earlier, can send a system into a new configuration or phase transition, triggering unforeseen events and introducing alternative states. The decaying tail of a power law on a graph denotes that many small events "coexist with a few very large ones" or "highly linked anomalies."[40] As Barabási illustrates,

If the heights of an imaginary planet's inhabitants followed a power law distribution, most creatures would be really short. But nobody would be surprised to see occasionally a-hundred feet-tall monster . . .

in fact among six billion inhabitants there would be at least one over 8,000 feet tall.[41]

The scale-free model suggests a topological tendency toward undemocratic virality produced in the encounters between a network's architecture and its users. It traces emergent vulnerable fractal patterns of clustered connectivity (see Figure 3.1). Unlike the frozen relations apparent in the random network model, the nodes and edges of a scale-free network are not given—they grow. Starting with a smaller number of nodes and developing links over time, older nodes in the network become vulnerable hubs or clusters. Although clearly constrained to a network space, the fractallike growth of the scale-free network provides a rare glimpse into the events of an epidemic. It demonstrates, at very least, how emergent physical branching structures can become sensitive over time to events conditioned by the force of social encounters.

One factor hypothetically driving this tendency toward undemocratic virality is a process Barabási terms *preferential attachment*.[42] The web has no central design: "it evolves from the individual actions of millions of users."[43] Yet many connections seem to be made to established nodes, as is the case when, Barabási contends, web designers, more often than not, make links to the most popular search engines. Preferential attachment resonates well with Milgram's notion of social proof, insofar as individuals tend to herd in the direction of the most popular sites. As the results of Milgram's experiment with skyward looking actors suggested, the propensity to imitate seems to correlate with the growing number of other people looking up at the sky.

Watts's Milgram-inspired six degrees also addresses the question of how social conformity spreads on a network. Referring to the herding and cascade theories used by economists to explain how financial bubbles and panic selling develop, he recounts observations of how individuals, sometimes provided with imperfect information, tend to act in accordance with those around them, contrary to the quality or accuracy of the instructions received. Social conformity is, as such, highly sensitive to the externality of information received from others, which can, on rare occasions, cascade out from a series of small binary

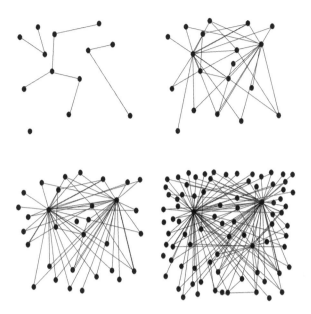

FIGURE 3.1. A scale-free network grows.

decisions (yes–no) at the local level of individual imitation toward a momentous global overspill. Watts argues that although the effervescence of smart trading and bullish sentiment can (and does) exist in prolonged periods of market equilibrium, it is relatively small and unpredictable events that shock an economic system into crisis. This leads in turn to value investors joining hands with trend followers in a "chain of fools" comparable to the delusions of tulipomania. It is this seemingly intrinsic mania within collective decision-making processes that steers the market toward anomalous bubble building and eventual outbursts of financial catastrophe.[44]

Importantly, and in sharp contrast to the theory of the influential, Watts suggests that cascading decisions materialize from a mostly accidental force of encounter with events. Conceding that while most "network analysts have tended to treat [networks] as the frozen embodiment of those forces,"[45] he infers that such spaces are in fact *events in passage* marked by the absence of any grand plan. As he puts it, "small events percolate through obscure places by happenstance and random encounters." These events can trigger "a multitude of individual decisions ... yet aggregating somehow into a momentous event unanticipated by anyone."[46] Like Barabási, then, Watts alludes to a viral susceptibility at the heart of the global emergence of collective decision making, but rather than rely on social proof to explain clustering, he points to the unconscious impulses of traders, which circumnavigate conscious individual volition and act as codeterminants in the tendency to cascade. While neither entirely rational nor irrational, the mania of the collective decision making draws attention to how an individual becomes connected to a network via a force of encounter manifested in events outside the control of an individual subject.

The potential for this new epidemiological paradigm to be exported to the business enterprise became more visible in 2007 when Watts moved to Yahoo! as a principal research scientist modeling consumer pass-on power by endeavoring to trigger contagious cascades in virtual simulations of networked worlds. Again, unlike the predictabilities assumed in the theory of Gladwell's influentials, Watts's research seems to point more readily to the happenstance of events befalling a susceptible (and for that reason) more infectable social network. This means that it is not solely influentials who trigger contagion; rather, it is triggered by anybody connected to the network, dependent on her stumbling into chance encounters. As Watts puts it, "if society is ready to embrace a trend, almost anyone can start one—and if it isn't, then almost no one can." To succeed with a new product, it is not simply "a matter of finding the perfect hipster to infect," he continues. It is "more a matter of gauging the public's mood."[47] It is not therefore so much the viral stickiness of brands or the infected consumers that matter to marketers as it is the *infectability* of the affective atmospheres in which consumption takes place. This suggests an accidental theory of influence, in which, as expected, contagion is unpredictable, but the capriciousness of the mood of the marketplace is not necessarily beyond the grip of the marketer.

Business enterprises are already looking to produce atmospheres ripe for epidemics to persist by "inducing particular habits of buying."[48] Books like *The Tipping Point, Linked,* and *Six Degrees* have, as such, contributed, in good measure, to the gradual unpacking of the social and biological relations a consumer has to the circulation of commodities and cultural practices. Going beyond mere analogy, these books intend to sell marketers a deeper understanding of how social influence and conformity spread according to the network diagram. In what might be regarded as a further extension of the economy of the imitative ray, or an exercise of biopower aimed at influencing feelings, behavior, and thought by appealing to mood, we see how the epidemiological diagram is reaching further and further into the space of affective flows.

The age of networks has provided a technological infrastructure for the mapping of more than the flows of friction-free commerce. It provides a map for tracing the flows of money in relation to consumer data regarding enthusiasms, emotions, and moods. The virality of the network is thus more than a space in which digitized capital roams without restraint. It is fast becoming the site of production of what Thrift refers to as "worlds," in which epidemics of influence can endure and become measurable, thus increasing the amount of profitable flows.[49] The generation of these worlds or "atmospherics," in which imitative rays are readily transmitted, becomes central to a suggestion that Tardean accidents can indeed be engineered. What might appear to be "genetically encoded" and "neurally etched" into the moods, desires, and imitations of the consumer become "open to all kinds of operation."[50]

Two Kinds of Desire

To grasp how the accidents of contagion might be purposefully steered, it is necessary to initially return to Tarde's distinction between two kinds of contagious desire at work in the political economy. To recap, in the first instance, an organism's survival needs to become interwoven with the repetitious and mechanical habits of day-to-day social events: the *periodic* desires to eat, drink, and clothe oneself, for example. However, when such desires become economically appropriated by social invention, they can, on rare occasions, become special *nonperiodic* desire-events, taking on an imitative and spontaneous life of their own as passionate interests, fashions, trends, and fads. We might say that desire-events are triggered by both social encounter and a biologically hardwired craving for things that organic life seems to aspire toward passionately, and socially imitate, mostly unaware of the mesmeric and magnetic attraction they generate. It is indeed on these occasions that the intensity of passionate interests magnetizes the self–other relation, building rare anomalous bubbles of influence and overspill.

The economy may appear to be a "logical arrangement" of events, organized around transcendent superstructures or natural laws, but the backdrop by which desire becomes appropriated by social invention is, according to Tarde, merely "capricious and accidental."[51] Yet it is the relational forces of accidental contagion apparent in financial transactions and commodity exchange that seem to guide the magnetized subject, raising the question concerning just how exploitable these forces of infrarelation may indeed become. Most unlike the political economy of *Homo Economicus,* who is supposed to be driven by an uncontaminated desire to possess wealth and a talent for judging the comparative efficacy of means for obtaining it, the infrarelations of Tarde's diagram circumvent such self-contained reasoning.[52] Like this, economic man is exposed to the capricious radiations of imitation-suggestibility, which spread via the absorbent and mostly unconscious relation traders establish between self and other. To be sure, it is the infrarelation that becomes exploitable, not the infected bodies it passes through. The spreading of financial crisis and cascading consumer conformity certainly reveals how embedded people become in the flows of spontaneous desire-events that potentially relate everyone to everybody and everything.

Today, as Thrift reminds us, the "reach and complexity [of imitation-suggestibility] has expanded inordinately since Tarde's time."[53] This is an expansion of the flows of imitative rays that has corresponded with the growth of an economy driven by new sociotechnical platforms. Vast electronic networks and automated modes of trading increase the fluidity (and rapidity) of financial information. Contagion is thrust forward through the imitative meshwork of financial media via discursive utterances and subrepresentational flows of affect. As follows, Tarde's diagram presents an alternative to the Milgram-inspired theory of the herd. The flows of financial information that feed into the cognitive decisions of speculators are accompanied by indirect appeals to noncognitive bodily and neuronal receptors. Herding is not therefore merely a product of the rational (or irrational) processing of social proof or preference but becomes dependent on the propensity of a visceral mode of affect to contaminate ostensibly calculated decisions. Along these lines, a Tardean herd "depends for its momentum on the swash and swirl of affect"—a collectivity of hesitant indecision linked to the riskiness of speculation that allows "prices to be continuously made and unmade, liquidity to be maintained and profits to be made—until market sentiment turns and panic, caused by a flight to safety by investors."[54]

Exceeding the measurable network space, then, the Tardean diagram places subjectivation amid "a complex blend and interplay of . . . purposeful behavior and affection, desire, [and] emotions . . . usually associated with the 'irrationality' of crowds."[55] In other words, the reception of spontaneous money flows occurs somewhere in between a perhaps illusory sense of freewill and mostly unconscious desire. The virality of money thus links persons, flows of desire, and collective identities to the value of the currency they possess.[56] But more than this, the spreading of financial crisis not only relates a person to the desires of others but also makes it almost impossible to dissociate the subject from the flows of money to which he connects. Here the lessons from the 1930s *are* relevant today. The combined mesmeric flow of affect and the rise and fall of value are as interwoven now as they were then. Borch draws attention, as such, to Canetti's crowd analysis of the inflation crisis in pre–World War II Germany, which illustrates how the emotional lives of those connected to the flow of money become affected.[57] Canetti further highlights how the self-spreading autonomy of recession can be politically exploited to discriminate against certain communities and stir up racially motivated hatred. It is the increasing "humiliation," Canetti argues, caused by rising inflation [that] makes the person as "worthless" as the money she has in her pocket and leaves her, as such, seeking someone to blame for her plight.[58]

A Question Concerning Accidents

Tarde's accidents of contagion are similarly compared to the potential spreading of the glory of fame. In what amounts to a nineteenth-century equivalent of celebrity worship, he contends that fame begins in small deferential social groups, before it becomes more widely dispersed into a public that "does not know its hero personally" but nevertheless feels the same "fanatical, impassioned and devoted admiration."[59] This jump from the respect of the few to the emotionally charged adulation of the many, experienced *at-a-distance*, is, however, explicitly linked by Tarde to the spontaneity of an encounter with complex currents of imitation. One person's fame is, it would appear, an accidental unfolding of the events of his eventual glory—a point Tarde reinforces in *Economic Psychology* when he argues,

> One can see ... what is accidental about glory. Given equal natural genius, a man will or will not encounter ingenious ideas, depending on whether the elements of these ideas are or are not brought to him by the intersecting currents of imitation. And, given an equal ingeniousness of discovered ideas, they will make him illustrious or obscure depending on whether they do or do not encounter a public which desires them and is disposed to welcome.[60]

Although this account resourcefully points to an infectable desiring population as a necessary prerequisite for epidemics of influence, it also draws attention to a particular criticism of how Tarde contends with the accidentality of what spreads. As Thrift points out, he may well have overestimated the accidentalness of contagion and neglected to fully understand the capacity for increasingly mediated encounters of imitation-suggestibility to be "consciously and carefully steered."[61] While Tarde successfully grasps "the power of imitative processes in the mediated environments" of his time, he tended to "see these mediated processes [as currents pushing up against each other in a fluid dynamics] spreading like wildfire, like mobs ... all but accidental."[62]

Tarde conceivably overlooked the capacity of present-day corporate and political agencies to affectively prime the public mood and guide accidental contagions. How, for instance, today's PR strategists endeavor to set the context (paint the right mood) to capture the accidents and events of desire, and make populations more readily infectious, is perhaps amiss in the original diagram. Yet modern-day consumption of brands, products, and political campaigns takes place in "an ever-growing multiplicity and difference of celebrities and notorieties buoyed up by persistent media attention."[63] Celebrity encounter is a prerequisite force of an increasingly mediated desiring machine that marketers and

politicians compete with each other to plug in to. This is an epidemiological diagram redefined by "a potent combination of technology and
genre, imitation and hormone."[64] The key to marketing success today,
it would appear, comprises a process of subjectivation (or reproduction
of infrasubjectivity) akin to the wasp–orchid assemblage. Counterfeit
experiences are readily primed to capture desire and imitation and pass
them on to others in, for example, the inventions of celebrity hype.

There seem to be two diagrammatic possibilities to consider here. The
first regards the diagram as Tarde deemed it: as all but accidental. The
social somnambulist is merely an unconscious conduit through which
the capricious currents of imitation flow. What spreads either catches
on or simply dies, depending on the chance encounter with the logical
contests and oppositions of imitative radiation. The second option is
not, however, as straightforwardly nonaccidental as is perhaps inferred
earlier. On the contrary, it stresses how the unfolding of spontaneous
events can be captured, measured, primed, and organized, even made
to look like an accident of chance encounter, to dip below conscious
awareness and become more readily absorbed into the neurological
unconsciousness of the consumer. Indeed, despite the overemphasis
on the capricious nature of contagion, a Tardean analysis hints at a
novel understanding of how the forces emitted from the encounter
with events might be tapped into and, to some extent, guided. Accordingly, the forces of relation in the epidemiological diagram function
in circumstances where (1) a clear purpose is not a necessity and (2)
there is no discernable contact with the other. This is a by and large
subjectless social relation, explained by Tarde using a vibratory theory
of the social that resonates outward without a set goal in mind and
functions as an action-at-a-distance. This leads Borch to argue that
Tarde's imitation-suggestibility "need not refer to human interaction"
at all.[65] It describes instead a "mechanics of sociality" emerging from
relations humans have with the hypnotizing objects and tendencies they
encounter. Moreover, this relation is not necessarily, as viral marketers
might anticipate, a momentum decisively guided by a network of charismatic influentials (financial leaders or trendsetters). This relationality
is indeed very different from the passing on of an information virus
through a network of promiscuous individuals. In contrast to viral

models of this kind, the repetitive movement of the imitative ray has a life of its own. It is an indirect mesmerism that flows viscerally *below* consciousness rather than linking cognitive processes by way of direct interaction.

Returning to Tarde's two kinds of desire, we see that while the first is a repetitious refrain of events related to specific needs, the contagiousness of the second spreads according to the logic of propensity that exceeds purpose.[66] The political and economic manipulation of this second kind of desire-event requires an intervention into the indirect and spontaneous forces of the epidemiological diagram—*the tendency to build anomalous bubbles.* This marks a distinct shift away from the rational decisions of economic man, guided by his need for wealth and equilibrium, toward a "prolonged action of imitation": a social medium that opens to a collective dream (or nightmare) couched in instability.[67] What is required here, then, is a topological diagram that does not freeze the forces of imitative encounter into geometric spaces but instead points to the immeasurable spatiotemporality of accidents and events. The diagram must grasp their movability, displacement, communicability, and relationality. *What is needed is a theory of accidents and events.*

The Networkability of the Desire-Event: What Can a Virus Do?

When approaching the theory of accidents, a relational diagram that cannot conceivably be ignored is the one put forward by Paul Virilio. Virilio argues that given the technological speedup of events, like those driven by the exponential growth of electronic networks, what becomes important are no longer the encounters with technological objects in isolation but rather the accidents that are hidden within these objects. As he puts it more fully,

> The occurrence of the accident is being denied. This is the result of the hype which always goes together with technological objects.... This hype in favor of technology dismisses its negative aspects.... But from the moment that the absolute velocity of electromagnetic waves is put to use, the potential of the accident is no longer local, but general.... When an event takes place somewhere today, the possibility arises that it might destroy everything.[68]

In fact, for Virilio, the accident of the network age is the computer virus.[69] As those readers already familiar with the development of this particular problem will recognize, the virus is indeed part of a long history of undecidable paradoxes, glitches, crashes, and security flaws that have befallen the binary logic of computer technology.[70] To grasp these accidents, Virilio introduces the philosophical terms of his *riddle of technology*.[71] His intention is to decelerate the emergence of the contemporary accident in an ever more technologically dependent world by inverting the classic metaphysical Aristotelian substance–accident dichotomy. The accident thus becomes the necessary and the substance (the technology) the relative and contingent. The digital virus is, like a shipwreck or plane crash, understood as integral to the technology from which it came: an *accident of substance.* It is, accordingly, the invention of the network that "provokes" the accident because the potential to break down preexisted, *pre-force,* in the substance of its invention.[72] There is, as a result, a pressing need to slow down the rapidity of events determined by technological progress, once considered as "successive, but now simultaneously, cannoning into one another."[73] Certainly the riddle of technology interestingly brings the accidents of the network to the foreground rather than ushering them away to some dubious backdrop of endless technological progress. Yet, by linking the chance event of the virus in such a linear way to outright catastrophe, is not Virilio's substance thinking at risk of preguessing the "fateful mark of finitude" and therefore negating the potential unfolding of the accident? Like this, Virilio perhaps misses an important question: *what can a virus do?*

In sharp contrast to Virilio's negative substance thinking, Tarde's epidemiological diagram (and its subsequent merging into Deleuze's ontology) points more readily toward an *insubstantial* space of affirmative accidents and topological events. Consider the seemingly purposeless meandering of open repetitions, collisions, and adaptations, like a drop of red wine poured into the ocean or a child's laughter spreading through a crowd, as vibratory forces emitting from indirect encounters as an alternative to the pre-force of Virilio's invention. Tarde's accidental contagions are not hidden within substances as such but radiate outward from the accident of encounter. Like Virilio, substance is not the most important factor of a Tardean diagram (if indeed it matters at all), but accidents and events are differently understood in terms of the incorporeal materiality established in relations between bodies in passage.

Another way of grasping the ontology at work here is to take up A. N. Whitehead's suggestion that "actual occasions" (events) are taken "together," insofar as each occasion becomes a process in passage.[74] Along these lines, the selection of each event is removed from the substance thinker's filtering out of what is important and what is accidental and is replaced with "diversities of function" that appear on one level of relation.[75] According to Whitehead, this "same level" is where the grandest and most trivial of entities reside together. In contrast to substance thinking, Deleuze similarly adopts Whitehead to argue that the question concerning what is essential (and what is nonessential) should be entirely reframed within the *inessential*: a multiplicity, or a "distribution of singular and regular, distinctive and ordinary points" in a topology. By doing so, he effectively "remove[s] essences and . . . substitute[s] events in their place . . . as jets of singularities."[76]

Similarly addressing the problematic distinction between substance and accident, Pierre Levy notes Whitehead's insistence that the final terms of philosophical analysis exist only in the event. The "configuration of trends, forces and constraints" (the virtual) becomes resolved, Levy suggests, in the event (the actual).[77] The event in this sense is a molecular substance, and the substance is a molar event, or the two perhaps are a mixture or transitional aspect of phenomena. Indeed, it is with a degree of uncertainty that Levy asks an understandable question of Whitehead's denial of the role of durable substances: why is it that we can sense the durable qualities of objects, a stone, for example, which at least appears to be concrete? Is that not the substance or the essence of a thing? Levy recalls how Whitehead answered this problem by describing the experience of durable things as "nothing more than the appearance of a [coordinated] *society of events*."[78] The body of matter is therefore not *in itself*, but as Bertrand Russell wonderfully grasps it, matter is always relational and "resolved into a series of events":

> An event does not persist and move, like the traditional piece of matter; it merely exists for its little moment and then ceases. A piece of matter will thus be resolved into a series of events. Just as, in the

old view, an extended body was composed of a number of particles, so, now each particle, being extended in time, must be regarded as composed of what we may call "event-particles." The whole series of these events makes up the whole history of the particle, and the particle is regarded as being its history, not some metaphysical entity to which the events happen.[79]

Again, unlike substance thinking, and its focus on immutable essential components like particles and cells (or memetic units of imitation *goddamnit!*), which determine form, an event philosophy moves away from the primacy of inner components to the relative uncertainty of forces of encounter that compose the body in passage. As Foucault proposes subsequently, materiality is founded on the notion that the *nature of the body* is formed around a succession of incorporeal events:

> The event is not of the order of bodies. Yet is in no way immaterial; it is on a level with materiality that it takes effect; it has its locus and consists in the relation, coexistence, dispersion, intersection, accumulation, and selection of material elements.... Suffice to say that the philosophy of the event should move in the paradoxical direction of a materialism of the incorporeal.[80]

This does not mean that an event is simply the introduction of movement into matter. Incorporeal materialism is not a simple dualism between material–immaterial. It defines instead a relation between what is seemingly actual or *extensive* and the "underlying" virtual and *intensive* processes that lead to extension. Extensions may be considered as surfaces, regions, zones, or territories, compared to intensities, which are "underneath," like plates, folds, and the process of becoming folded.[81] Intensity is nonmetric, like a topological space. Extension is a metric property, like an architectural structure or geometric network. But importantly, extensions do not have immutable essences or finite states. What is significant here are the procedural actions that motivate change and movement, in intensive time and spatial environments.[82] This is an ontological diagram in which events become dispersed. The focus of analysis therefore shifts away from purpose, predictability, and measurable regularity toward the registering of dynamic and variable change: *from static bodies* to *bodies in passage.*

Accepting the body in passage thesis is tantamount to "accepting the paradox that there is an incorporeal dimension *of the body.*"[83] However, it is important that the insubstantial relations established between the body and events (body–event) are not misconstrued as the disappearance of the body. The incorporeal relation itself becomes an analytical tool by which it is possible to trace the movement and changes of a body in passage. The process of *incorporeal transformation* thus becomes central to Deleuze's notion of body–event relationality. The incorporeal transformation of an extension signifies, as such, two things. On one hand, "an eternal object . . . remains the same over the succession of moments," while on the other, "a passage . . . or a flux" continuously ensures that the object gains and loses molecules.[84] The body–event relation therefore occurs at both the perceptible "unification" or repetition of matter and the imperceptible subatomic level of differentiated matter.

Looking at Tarde's diagram from this ontological perspective adds a further topological layer to the distinction he makes between periodic and nonperiodic events (a distinction incidentally already made in chaos theory). On one hand, periodic events are moments of stability or resemblance, like Levy's molar event of substance, or a repetition of a predictable, coexisting, and amassed society of related desire-events. They are also moments of sustained belief, assurance, and security. This is, Tarde contends, the object of desire: to strive toward the stability of belief. On the other hand, though, aperiodic events (molecular events) complicate predictability and introduce variation. In the process of becoming big, molarity loses energy. Belief, assurance, and security lose their propelling vigor. Precise calculation becomes problematic in chaotic forces. However, intensive spatial conditions introduce a *creative potential* that does not preexist the emergence of the event. The spatial conditions of the repetitious event are in effect its potential for newness and anomaly.[85]

The accidents of contagion are not regarded in this topological diagram, as Virilio would have it, as the accidental inverse of substance. Accidents are instead set free or constrained by the historical potentiality of the force of encounter with events. Even when the environment tends to fix chance, these periodic fixtures of repetition are prone to rare molecular fluxes. Repetition is always open to the variation of resemblance. Therefore it is important not to approach a diagram as a body that is *already made* but alternatively to begin with the emergent repetition and intensive fluxes of what is *being made.* It is useful, like this, to conceive of a Tardean diagrammatic relation in terms of a body's *infinitive encounter* with events—to consider it in terms of the event's movability from intensity to extensity, and how the incorporeal transformation of the event can be carried over, or materially translated, into different modes of communicability.[86] It is this *networkability of the event* (the topological movement from one space to another) that enables such translations to occur, moving from one medium to another, at a point when bodies are discernibly distant from each other yet come into relation. Events can, as Massumi points out, be "catapulted" into "the inexhaustible complexity" and "indefinite circuit of reproduction and systematic variation" in any other media context, defining "each unique encounter's conditions of emergence."[87]

Significantly, then, it is not the network technology itself that distributes the repetition and contagion of desire-events. The network is "the relationality of that which it distributes . . . the passing-on of the event."[88] The networkability of the event is "what connects coding to coding, codification to codification." With every repetition comes the "ebb and flow of potentialization and containment."[89]

The notion that the marketplace functions as an epidemiological diagram is, of course, nothing new. In times of financial crisis, stories of viral capitalism are everywhere. But it is Massumi's event analysis that draws particular attention to the virality of perhaps the most successful event transmission of all, that is, money. The virality of the money-event becomes apparent in the way it can "piggyback every intervallic body without exception."[90] Viral money is certainly the only event that manages to negotiate almost all event spaces, demonstrating viral capitalism's capacity to arrive late and absorb and extract the surplus value from nearly everything, even objects once considered worthless.[91] Money becomes the "ultimate capture . . . of the movement of the event itself."[92]

Toward a Political Economy of Contagion and Repetition

It is not surprising, perhaps, to discover that network business enterprises are learning from the behavior of the virus. Capitalism has, after all, been associated with viral diseases, piggybacking parasites, and even blood-sucking vampires throughout its history. But is this capitulation to the universality of the virus, as some seem to understand it, intrinsic to the logic of the network, or does it suggest a different kind of diagrammatic relation? Well, as earlier, it is important when choosing the appropriate diagram not to confuse immutable essences with the event. The events of virality (the forces of relation) are not, as such, intended to be frozen out by the nodes and edges of the network. The topological relationality of Tarde's epidemiological diagram exceeds these static geometric spaces. Virality refers instead to a universal virus that indeed predates the fever of the network age. At the very least, it has been a constant of capitalism, as Parikka well argues, from the self-spreading mass replication of the mundane objects of the Fordist factory model to the post-Fordist parasites to the variegated commodities of a networked Empire.[93] To be sure, capital is not immobile, and although the excitement of the digital network age continuously draws our attention to the increasing dynamism of repetition and contagion, the diagram it forwards may inhibit our understanding of the forces of abstraction that push small, periodic repetitions to outbursts of monstrous aperiodic contagion.

At this juncture, it is perhaps necessary to follow Tarde's diagram more closely, which is, after all, less about universal contagion than it is about the universality of difference and repetition. Repetition is the *base of all action.* Tarde thus substitutes the *production of riches* with the primacy of *economic repetition.*[94] Like this, economic contagion is more readily conceived of in the topological logic of the bubble phenomenon. This is not merely a network space but a continuous buildup of events *fit to burst.* The periodic events of the first kind of desire are understood as the repetitive propagation of similar desires, labors, and judgments. The distribution of riches is nothing more than the "effect of an imitative repetition" of these three resemblances and their subsequent "reciprocal radiation by exchange."[95] The universal repetition of periodic events thus becomes the multiplication of resemblances, while the rare nonperiodic building of bubbles exposes the openness of universal repetition to variation and anomaly.

Conclusion

Tarde's work is in fact full of references to the outbursts and overspills of repetitious events. Not just the bursting of financial contagions and fashion imitations but also philosophic, religious, and social ideas, love, faith, and enthusiasm or rebellious social envy, pride, hatred, and so on. From time to time, epidemics of repentance burst out, as do the passion for politics and the sentiment of patriotism (love of nation). As Tarde puts it, on these rare occasions, "invention will burst its bounds and cause itself to be imitated outside."[96] This is not a diagram constrained to a stable society of events. It is the potential, through an encounter with other events, to become a self-spreading and contagious imitation-radiation.

It is, of course, more than likely that the process by which a periodic repetition becomes an exceptional outburst of contagion is amplified in various ways by communications technology. There is, as such, a rhythmic refrain of mediation implicated in the subjectivation of the somnabulist, in which conversations, feelings, and moods are connected to, and sped up by, networks of all kinds, including television and the Internet. This is plain to see in recent discussions concerning the role social media plays in the contagions of social protests and potential uprisings related to financial crisis and repressive dictatorships. Félix Guattari has already, like this, considered the captive relation social movements have to media ecologies derived from a "perceptual fascination" bordering on the hypnotic.[97] The events of Tiananmen Square were, he claims, driven in part by the students' fascination with Western media.[98] Although they had the slogans of democratization within their sights, it was a contagious affective charge, Guattari contends, that pulsed through this movement, surpassing mere ideological demands. Their drive for emancipation collided with a desire for a "whole lifestyle, collective ethic and conception of social relations," resulting in the large-scale student-led movements. Comparable in many ways to the repetitive refrains Canetti locates in the imitative ritual dances, percussive rhythms, and chants that pull together archaic crowds, Guattari's captive relation with media fixes subjectivities in front of the luminous screens, embedding them in a topology of relations. But eventually, the repetition gives way to a functional space, allowing for the adaptation and variation of further events that spill over into the event-space on the streets. The more recent events in Tahrir Square in Egypt are evidently an expression, in part, of the opening up of the event-space of revolution.

The extent to which the potential of revolutionary contagion can be steered toward these event-spaces leads this discussion back to the notion that spontaneous collective moods can indeed be primed and guided toward specific goals. This is perhaps the latent exercising of an affecting biopower over an increasingly connected population: the functioning of an indirect action-at-a-distance that readies emotional experiences, making them more susceptible to the contagions of others, harnessing their capacity to affect (and to be affected), and organizing social belief and action without a discernable medium of contact.

4

From Terror Contagion to the Virality of Love

This chapter continues to the question how virality might be purposely (and deceivingly) steered through the accidentality of Tarde's epidemiological social space. It endeavors, as such, to identify and unravel the pretexts underscoring two communication stratagems.[1] The first, *immunologic*, involves the spreading of fear relating to encounters between a knowable self and an unknown nonself to justify, among other things, the intensification of security measures. The second is grasped through the concept of *viral love*. This is a deceptive joyful encounter that seems to be ever more deployed in the affectively charged arenas of corporate and political persuasion. The first stratagem combines discursive practices and prediscursive registers to spread fear concerning the threat posed by digital contagion and the "cultural plagues" of Islamic terror far and wide. Together these threats are characteristic of a social power relation that controls by way of using fear to fascinate beliefs and guide social action toward some specified goal. Yet, rather than typically approach viruses and terror through the conventional lenses of a communication theory concentrated on language, ideology, and myth making, the focus here shifts to explore their role in contemporary exercises of biopower. That is to say, fear mongering is not simply encoded into messages and conveyed through meaningful media channels. Efforts to persuade involve what Thrift has called "premediation,"[2] which in this context requires the potentialization of feelings and readying of moods to prepare the way for contagion.

The second stratagem intervenes in the assumption that populations are controlled by fear alone. Despite frequent epidemics of panic and terror, it is contagions of hope, faith, and, more significantly perhaps, love that Tarde contends are far more catching.[3] Indeed, following a more recent political conception of love, viruses and terror are reassessed, and the analytical focus shifts to the role joyful encounters play in exerting a power without fear.

Stratagem 1: Immunologic

The immunologic stratagem has two parts. The first is explained here by way of registering the efforts made by the antivirus (AV) industry to counter the computer virus writing scene (VX). Both AV and VX have been complicit in a discursive and prediscursive immunological conflict that associates digital contagion with anxieties concerning biological contamination. This decidedly asymmetrical conflict involves the stirring up of a kind of *misotramontanism* (a fear of the other) that is endemic to an entrepreneurial endeavor to sell more security via appeals to insecurity as well as being inserted into the materiality of AV software systems. Indeed, immunological conflict is more than a rhetorical war of words intended to "legitimize" the immunity (and integrity) of a discursively designated self pitted against a hostile nonself. It also features in the software infrastructures that organize the network space. Clearly language plays a major role. As Sean Cubitt eloquently puts it, the "metaphor of contagion is at once to presume the integrity of the cell" and therefore legitimatize "a counter-attack based on maintaining that integrity and limiting, if not destroying, the virus's ability to mutate."[4] Nonetheless, these linguistic associations have become more concretely embedded in the logic of future network conflict. The persuasive force of this logic is not fixed or limited by linguistic representations but is transformed by the discursive *events of language* that order the contents of the assemblages to which they relate. Unlike a linguistic representation, then, the immunological binaries of self and nonself operate as an incorporeal transformation via expressions "inserted into" contents, that is, not represented but delimited, anticipated, moved back, slowed down or sped up, separated or combined.[5] As follows, the second part of the immunologic stratagem cunningly positions a wide range of new network threats at the center of further anxieties concerning the lack of an assignable enemy. Like the War on Viruses, then, the deceptions of the War on Terror exemplify how the heightening of fears associated with a transmittable and infectious *unknown* enemy becomes endemic to the subterfuge of a progressively more indiscriminate network security paradigm.

The Computer Virus Problem

The dramatic escalation of the computer virus problem in the late 1980s is often discursively traced back to the innovations of the so-called Bulgarian Virus Factory.[6] In particular, one as yet unidentified VX, working under the pseudonym of the "Dark Avenger," widely distributed a mutation engine that enabled viruses to avoid detection and spread to Europe and the United States. Appearing as it did at the latter end of the Cold War, this small group of VX provided the West with a perfect opportunity to discursively assemble what Parikka well describes as a *new dark digital continent*: a space to replace the fading evil faces of communism.[7] With their ominous heavy metal aliases and mutating viral codes like Anthrax and Leech, the VX from Sofia perhaps all too easily lent themselves to the fearsome discursive formations of Ronald Reagan's triumphant war on the Evil Empire. Indeed, the biological analogies and metaphors of digital contagion conveniently slotted into a Western discourse intent on legitimizing the development of intruder detection systems. Moreover, they have also provided an expedient and unidentifiable enemy that could be readily assimilated into a more general stratagem of network security.

Along similar lines, the cultural anthropologist Stefan Helmreich has argued that the rhetorical portrayal of the VX as a pathological "counter-cultural class" hides a deeper articulation of an immunologic discourse deployed in ideological conflict.[8] The biological analogies adopted by computer security experts in the 1980s, he contends, help to justify measures of decontamination against a wide range of threats such as computer viruses, acts of crime, espionage, vandalism, threats to market stability, and, more recently, terrorism. What Helmreich pinpoints is how the "natural" immunological defense of the biological organism is metaphorically (and ideologically) transferred over to the "body" of the computer network or nation-state to "image" it as "beleaguered" or a "community under threat from within and without." This enables the further exploitation of "culturally specific worries about contamination," which "come to structure the way computer [and other security] professionals think about and respond to threats." In other words, Helmreich sees how the "importation of biological language into discourses about digital technology" stimulates anxieties concerning the integrity of the organic body. This allows security rhetoric "to lean on the authority of natural sciences" so that "bodies, nations, and economies can be articulated in the idiom of organic nature."[9]

However, although the following brief history of the computer virus problem highlights the rhetoricalness of the immunologic stratagem, it also exposes a deception that seems to exceed ideological conflict. The computer virus problem arises instead from out of the happenstance events of computer science, beginning with a "legitimized" interest in virality and a subsequent struggle to control its "illegitimate" overspill. Indeed, alongside other notorious outbreaks of digital contagion occurring in the late 1980s, including the Morris worm in the United States, the Bulgarian VX certainly helped to justify organizations like the Computer Emergency Response Team (CERT) set up in 1988 to police the rapidly expanding capitalist network infrastructure. CERT argued for the mass introduction of intruder technology as a key component of defensive strategies against a range of "illegitimate" practices.[10] Yet, while the headlines of *The New York Times* screamed "Bulgarians Linked to Computer Virus," it is important to note that the early empirical development of digital contagion initially grew out of the once acceptable fascination of Western mathematicians and computer scientists for artificial life.

Commencing during a period of time Tiziana Terranova well describes as the biological turn in computing, digital contagion can be traced back to John von Neumann's influential theories concerning digital reproduction back in the 1940s.[11] Von Neumann applied ideas borrowed from evolutionary theory to computable cellular automata. He imagined, as such, a point at which a complexity threshold would be breached, followed by an explosion of variety, novelty, and surprise in computing, as it had already done in nature.[12] These early mathematical manipulations of cellular automata went on to influence experiments carried out in the 1970s by the Cambridge mathematician John Conway. Conway's Game of Life presented a series of simple mathematical rules, drawing on fairly crude laws of survival, death, and birth, repetitiously applied to a collection of cells to produce self-replicating and exotic patterns.

In the early 1980s, the popular science magazine *Scientific American* reported on the virallike behaviors of Conway's life game and, in a series of subsequent articles, discussed Von Neumann's influence on earlier experiments in the 1960s. The magazine pointed to other life games, like Darwin and Core War, which were played out by programmers working on the computer systems at Bell Labs and Xerox's Palo Alto Research Center.[13] Indeed, by 1984, what had initially been regarded as a legitimate pursuit for computer programmers gradually began to unfold, almost overnight, into a situation the computer scientist and author of the *Scientific American* articles A. K. Dewdney regarded as a far more sinister turn of events:

> When the column about *Core War* appeared last May, it had not oc-
> curred to me how serious a topic I was raising. My descriptions of
> machine-language programs, moving about in memory and trying
> to destroy each other, struck a resonant chord. According to many
> readers, whose stories I shall tell, there are abundant examples of
> worms, viruses and other software creatures living in every conceivable
> computing environment. Some of the possibilities are so horrifying
> that I hesitate to set them down at all.[14]

Also published in 1984, Fred Cohen's doctoral paper made the first formal link between these early games of digital self-replication and the potential for widespread epidemics of viruses and wormlike computer programs.[15] Cohen's PhD work links the evolutionary behavior of the computer virus to both Von Neumann's cellular automata and neo-Darwinist accounts of the selfish gene. From that point forward, the resemblances Cohen established between the biologically derived gene and self-replicating computer code preceded a raft of popular and academic accounts of the virus problem. Many of these made use of further analogical and metaphorical associations between cells and computers, the capacity of genetic and binary code to replicate, and the ability of both to evolve and, significantly, *do harm*.[16] Although most of the biological analogies employed were considered imprecise, and tended to overgeneralize the concepts of information, replication, and system,[17] their application captured the attention of both the mass media and entrepreneurial computer specialists alert to the commercial potential of the virus problem.

In the early 1990s, the analogies and metaphors of immunological intrusion detection became a part of both the rhetorical and practical inventions of the AV industry.[18] At IBM's Thomas J. Watson Research Center, for example, early AV practices were defined by a *microscopic* level of the immunological analogy involving reactive cycles of detection, in which "the focus of hundreds of researchers" was simply to "dissect and try to kill off the dozens of new viruses written every month."[19] The costly nature of these practices prompted the industry to develop semiautomated processes, including misuse and anomaly detection and integrity and heuristic checking. Although human researchers were still employed to categorize new viruses in terms of behavior and the identification of particular viral signatures embedded in the code, AV software was designed to automatically recognize known viral strings and check for changes to files and the activities typical of infective code. Nonetheless, automated immunology encountered certain technical flaws, particularly in misuse detection, where virus scanners match incoming viral signatures (so-called digital footprints) to lists of known viruses. In fact, whether or not they are automated, such comparisons can only be made with viral code already dissected by a researcher and made known to the vendor before updates can be passed on to the end user. In technical terms, this method produces a low rate of false positives but cannot recognize novel attacks, therefore leading to high rates of false negatives.[20] In the vast transitive flows of information sharing on a network, the continuous identification of what is known is difficult to differentiate from what is unknown. Such a distinction requires the constant updating of viral signature lists.

Similarly, the detection of the unknown proved problematic for a range of new AV products branded as anomaly detection and integrity checking (systems that look for suspected changes to a file) and as heuristic virus checking (systems that differentiate between viruses and nonviruses). The problem here is that the differentiation made between virus and nonvirus is, like any other code, not always decidable. Like this, the computer virus is a modern-day liar paradox that tests the incompleteness of binary logic.[21] It follows that although anomaly detection can identify novel attacks, it can also register a large number of false positives. There is, as such, a heady mixture of fuzzy programming relating to known, unknown, self, nonself, and "dangerous" others. The frequency of false negatives and positives made by anomaly checkers thus makes them unstable and costly in terms of maintaining information flow. In some cases, the automation process will need to be halted and checked by a researcher to confirm if the change is in fact malicious. Even if antivirus software can be effective against *known* viral code, or recognizable "malicious" changes to code, new viruses (new unknowns) will inevitably exploit a security hole or new feature of an existing program. These gaps in security act as new replication vectors, and more often than not, VX endeavor to subvert a new set of rules by introducing mutating code that can circumvent or even disable detection.

It is at the so-called *macroscopic level* of the immunological analogy that IBM's AV researchers claim to have been "inspired" by the fully automated human immune system (HIS).[22] In the late 1990s, IBM thus developed the Intrusion Detection System (IDS), a "signature-extraction method" loosely analogous to what the researchers themselves regarded as an outmoded theory of the HIS.[23] Nonetheless, although the subsequent automation of anomaly detection clearly helped to reduce labor costs and increase the speed of detection, it generally applies the same flawed logic evident in the microscopic analogy. Despite a few added features, like a decoy device and a link to a database of viral signatures, the IDS product merely automates the mundane tasks originally carried on at the microscopic level.

Significantly, the development of these proprietary intruder systems needs to be seen alongside a considerable torrent of marketing hyperbole, which obscures the objectives of the immunological stratagem emerging at the end of the 1990s. Amid the media panic surrounding the impending doom of the Y2K computer bug, IBM rebranded IDS the Digital Immune System (DIS) and marketed it through a licensing agreement with the leading AV vendor Symantec. In a timely press release, given the mass media interest in Y2K, an IBM spokesperson claimed that the licensing agreement between the two companies was a "first step toward a comprehensive system that can spread a global cure for a virus faster than the virus itself can spread."[24]

How to Spread Fear by Not Specifying Whom Your Enemy Is

These events help to illustrate how the immunologic stratagem is not merely an ideologically conceived deception. Its attempt to control the idiom by way of linguistic trickery is just one layer of far more concentrated discursive formation. In fact, as Foucault argues, discursive formations do not necessarily operate at the level of ideology at all.[25] There is, as such, a need to locate both the discursive and prediscursive forces that assemble the real practices of the virus problem. In contrast, then, to Helmreich's ideological approach, the analytical focus needs to shift away from the importation of language into discourse, toward the assembled components of this fearmongering stratagem. To begin with, immunology can be seen to permeate the very matter and functionality of network security. As follows, the binary filtering of immunological self and nonself exceeds abstract diagrammatic forces, becoming part of the concrete relations established between end users and the software they encounter. Again, in contrast to rhetorical analysis, what is acknowledged here is how the immunologic affects the concrete matter-functions of network culture, imposing the molar force of the organism on software designed to filter out viral anomalies.

Like this, the immunologic does more than represent the defense of the organic body via the importation of biological language. It concretely organizes these defenses in terms of organs or organisms, which ward off bodily threats according to the binary division of self and nonself. As follows, the IBM vision of a cybernetic model of society is part of a long tradition of immunological practice intended to manage the unknown threat. Immunologic stratagems of this kind can perhaps be traced back to Norbert Wiener's cybernetic social structures, in which an "organism is held together [by] resist[ing] the general stream of corruption and decay."[26] Since the late 1980s, though, the cybernetic organisms of the Internet have arguably evolved from Wiener's homeostatic organs into a spiraling culture of immunological responses continuously defining the self versus the nonself, while at the same time coming into increasingly "grating contact with one another."[27] Indeed, key to the immunologic stratagem is the growing significance of an unknown (and sometimes unwitting) threat to the unified body that functions on both a discursive and prediscursive plane. This unknown enemy is increasingly located as the source of contagion but is opportunely kept at a distance and cloaked in anonymity. The Bulgarian VX scene becomes, as such, just another example of unassignable adversaries of state power in the age of networks; that is, it is part of a demonstrative reorganization of the nation-state and its foes in terms of immunological rather than ideological conflict. The VX personify what Deleuze and Guattari regard as a state power that has "set its sights on a new type of enemy, no longer another state, or even a regime, but the unspecified enemy."[28] Along with cybercriminals, online activists, and network terrorists, the VX become a merged and mutating *whatever enemy* engaged in nebulous acts of material sabotage. The unassignability of this new enemy is indeed a recurrent theme of a contemporary epidemiological diagram inclusive of, but not restricted to, the Internet. It is also a recurring feature of a more generalized security stratagem that purposefully guides attention to the ever-expanding presence of an unknown epidemic threat that can spread to the unprotected user.

The unspecified enemy figures writ large in the immunology employed in the War on Terror too. As Robert Baer, a former CIA operative, contends, it is indeed becoming difficult to tell apart the virality of the network and those infected by it. Just "log on to the internet or visit a militant Islamic bookshop," he argues, "and within a few minutes you will find enough inspiration in CDs, ranting sermons, DVDs, for a hundred suicide bombs."[29] This epidemic flow of networked communication is redefined, accordingly, as a "deadly virus" that spreads radicalization far and wide by way of a somewhat mysterious, affecting connection with the societies it infects. Even old ways of doing communication (books and sermons) become entangled in this runaway viral assemblage, interwoven with fearsome biological analogies, medical metaphors, and the material resources and real practices of intruder detection. What these propagators of the War on Terror readily exploit is the same immunological logic applied in the War on Viruses. They, too, assume the legitimate integrity of the network infrastructure and seek to delineate, to a great extent, what you can and can't do in that space.[30]

Feeling Fear: A Communication Problem

There are distinct problems involved in understanding the unspecified enemy as part of a communication stratagem. To begin with, the strategy of using the unknown to organize network space exceeds the importation of biological language into discourse. Its function in organizing matter is far more concrete. Following the conventions of communication modeling, the expression of virality of this kind becomes an ungraspable noise that contaminates the binary opposites of the established sender–receiver paradigm, without prejudice. In the age of networks, senders and receivers (and information and meaning) both become susceptible to a rhizomatic transmission.[31] Recently, however, in network theory, the notion of *microbial contagion* has offered a refreshing alternative to the transmission model. Instead of understanding communication in terms of messages and channels, the microbe becomes synonymous with the network to which humans connect to communicate. Like this, it is the microbe that links up the individual nodes of the network, transforming them into a contagious collective social body.[32] Although positioning microbial contagion as a distinctly nonhuman affair, Eugene Thacker suggests an intriguing and perhaps purposefully indistinct human relation to it insofar as he draws our attention to how "we humans" *feel* about becoming infected.[33] The most apparent of these feelings is triggered by our contagious encounter with the unknown microbe, which tends to "elicit" the negative emotions of fear and anxiety.[34] As Thacker seems to infer, contagion is generally grasped within a medical discursive frame as a horrendous conflict between human and nonhuman agencies:

> Contagion and infection are more than mechanisms of antigen recognition and antibody response; they are, as our textbooks tell us, entire "wars" and "invasions" continuously fought on the battle lines of the human body.[35]

These are, it would appear, fears and anxieties induced by a sense of invasiveness of what spreads beyond the battle lines into nonbiological contexts. Reminiscent perhaps of Foucault's earlier observations on how the space of plagues and epidemics (like leprosy) opened up new disciplinary territories that would further exclude the nonhuman from the human world, this current exercise of biopower seems to carry forward discursive epidemiological power into new and as yet uncharted corners of social cartography.[36] To be sure, the emotional responses to these unwelcome (and unknowable) incursions by the microbe are increasingly exploited by the stratagems of network sovereignty—particularly with regard to the threat posed by the cultural and biological viruses of the terrorist cell.

There is, as Thacker argues elsewhere, an Agambenian *zone of indistinction,* or biopolitical continuum, at play in the rhetoric of the War on Terror that exceptionally merges the language used to describe the terrorist with that used to describe the microbial virus.[37] Like this, the unspecified enemy (the suicide bomber, in this case) becomes a part of a stratagem that aims to maintain and justify ongoing security measures in the absence of an identifiable assailant. The potential of the suicide terror attack becomes endemic to a social conflict in which the unknown is, as Paul Virilio argues, growing out of all proportion. It is, as follows, in the interest of the administrators of fear to intentionally prolong the duration of uncertainty over the origin of the next, and always anticipated, suicide attack.[38] The shock event of the terror attack is thus transformed into a continuous contagious rumor (or phantom-event) independent of reliable sources, allowing it to be both more effectively propagated and manipulated as something that is just about to occur. The War on Terror therefore plays on public fears concerning the potential of attack. The enemy remains advantageously unknown and always at hand to incite (and spread) further anxieties. This is a war, Thacker argues, that is indeed marked by a discursive "inability" in U.S. defense policy to distinguish between epidemics and war and emerging infectious disease and bioterrorism.[39] Discursive "exceptions of epidemics and war" form a strategic blending of biological warfare and bioterrorism: *one* emerging network threat to national security requiring U.S. defense policy to strategically manage uncertainty.

In future network conflict, the enemy will, it seems, become more ambiguous, less detectable, and identification will increasingly occur in the absence of intelligence or evidence. Intruder detection, we were told back in the 1990s, "will more likely occur only after an attack has begun."[40] But since 9/11 and the second invasion of Iraq, it seems that the assumptive and fuzzy equations of risk assessment have now become the basis of a new politics of fear and anticipation. So when the former U.S. secretary of defense Donald Rumsfeld, responding to questions from the press about the lack of evidence connecting Iraqi weapons of mass destruction with terrorists back in 2002, infamously made reference to known knowns, known unknowns, and unknown unknowns, he was clearly consulting the immunologic stratagem. In fact, the risk managers of the Internet go much further than Rumsfeld was prepared to go by not only differentiating between the fuzzy gradations of what is known and unknown but also acknowledging the uncontrollable quantities of the unknown yet to be exposed in an epidemic attack.[41] Both are nonetheless examples of how the stratagem seizes the potential of the unknowable anomaly as a means to spread belief in conflict and at the same time stabilize molar power structures.

Again, regarded as a problem for conventional communication modeling, it would appear that the stratagem not only questions the sender–receiver relation but further breaks open the semiotic structures of the encoder–decoder relation. It certainly confronts an ideological model of transmission based as it is on the spreading of false beliefs conjured up by images, words, meanings, and ideas. How does this old approach, which in effect divides up culture and nature, account for a communication stratagem that exploits a deeply felt social vulnerability to suggestion beyond resorting to a fuzzy state of false consciousness? It would seem that the emotional openness to repetitive and ever-converging transmissions of statements of this kind exceeds mere ideological productions of myth. Indeed, would not belief (and how it can spread) need to be reconsidered, *ahead of ideas,* as the bringing on of mostly insensible and unconscious responses intended to trigger deep-seated fears, anxieties, panic, and insecurity? Is this not a *neurological contamination* that exposes the mind to an entire valence (fearsome and joyful) of affective encounters that herald the idea?

To further deliberate on the affective encounters expressed in this first stratagem, I want to revisit three thinkers who help to frame an alternative communication theory founded on processes of contagion and contamination. The first (a cognitive scientist) focuses attention on a neurological understanding of how the political mind can be tapped and activated. The second presents a theory of affective transmission that rethinks the relation between culture and nature by removing the pretence of the divide that separates them and focuses instead on an *intersection point* at which what is socially encountered and biologically responded to meet. Finally, I return again to Tarde's epidemiological diagram, which similarly locates the spreading of desires and social invention somewhere in between volition and biologically motivated mechanical habits. Importantly, all three are advocates of a concept of social subjectivity that is not closed or self-contained but is instead open to the contagious affects of others. *This is subjectivity in the making.*

To begin with, I want to return to Lakoff's neurological understanding of a mostly unconscious political mind. Lakoff describes a mind made vulnerable to outside political manipulation through appeals to emotional markers, which can trigger feelings (including those related to infection) already contained in neurological bindings, or what he calls the *metaphorical frames* of the mind.[42] Following the prominent work of neuroscientist Antonio Damasio in the mid-1990s, as well as accepting the fairly recent mirror (or empathy) neuron hypothesis, Lakoff points to the absorbency of somatic markers, which can be persistently activated to provoke the right feelings and emotions, almost to order.[43] So, for example, following 9/11, the much-repeated video images of the Twin Towers falling played alongside rhythmic utterances of "Islam" and "extremism" evoke fear in the neural circuits of a mind that empathizes (shares in the feeling) with what it encounters via its sensory system.[44] Indeed, since 9/11, Lakoff claims that the War on Terror has evolved into neurological war, which presents "a misleading and destructive idea . . . introduced under conditions of trauma and then repeated so often that it is forever in your synapses."[45]

To fully grasp the relevance of the neurological unconscious to communication theory, we need first to register Damasio's contra-Cartesian (and Kantian) argument that our reasoning and decision-making processes are not as purely cognitive as we may think they are.

In fact, Damasio's somatic marker hypothesis persuasively argues that "emotions and feelings may not be intruders in the bastion of reason at all; they may be enmeshed in its networks."[46] Second, according to neuroscience, our understanding of how feelings get passed on need no longer be informed by an inexplicable empathic transmission. The location of so-called mirror neurons supposedly points to the brain processes behind the sharing of feelings and mood. Mirror neurons are said to be the equivalent of human-to-human wireless communication and have been linked to innate imitative human relations occurring between infants and adults.[47]

It is the porous volatility of the political mind to the feelings and suggestions of others (up close and mediated over distance) that leads to an important question for contagion theory: is it not what "we feel" about what spreads that becomes the most effectual contagion of all? If this is indeed the case, then the contagious encounter is not exclusively explained by the unique merging of linguistic terms strategically relating human to invasive nonhuman worlds but instead reveals a multisensory intersection point between what have traditionally been regarded by much of academia as separate social and biological domains. Arguably, unlike the horrors of the microbial metaphor, this force of contagious encounter is not at all biologically determined. The spreading of fear is instead an intermingling of affective social phenomena and hardwired biological responses that activate and adapt to each other.

At the very least, it might be said that such an appeal to cognitive neuroscience may help to provide a more graspable process by which infectable humans encounter the living horrors of the microbial world. Communication theory should, in any case, pay close attention to a similar neurological concentration apparent in political psychology, marketing, and product design, in which the affective priming of experience is fast becoming endemic to the study of social influence and methods of persuasion.[48] Accordingly, what spreads is understood to pass unconsciously through the skin into the viscerality of human experience, guiding automatic behavior before it moves *upstream* to the conscious reflective mind and dream of volition. Although the strategic convergence of the epidemic and suicide bomber can still be grasped, as Thacker puts it, in the "innovative ways" human beings have developed by which to "live through microbes,"[49] here we have a process, no less, that begins, for the most part, with a contaminating encounter with an event. It is the manifestation of affects in this encounter that move upstream, activating mostly unconscious feelings of horror, before they intersect with the downstream flows of a neural circuitry loaded with manipulable and biographical emotional content.

It is this seemingly ready-made yet highly absorbent and adaptable circuitry that, Lakoff claims, is tapped into by political strategists so that, for example, the repetition of the images and the utterances of the War on Terror reinforces and activates negative conservative neurological bindings rather than acting to challenge and change the way people think.[50] Significantly, for Lakoff, the idea that the political mind is openly vulnerable to suggestion in this way (and potentially prone to passing on such suggestions via neuronal transfers) confronts the unyielding artifice erected and maintained by the same Enlightenment aficionados Damasio identifies, that is, an abrupt separation between somatic experiences and the evolutionary hardwiring of a self-contained and rational mind. But as the subtitle of Lakoff's political mind thesis argues, "you can't understand 21st-Century American politics with an 18th-Century brain." It would seem that the Enlightenment artifice between contaminating emotion and pure reason disintegrates at the point where what is socially suggested, and biologically responded to, intersects: an encounter between upstream flows of affect and downstream biological responses.

In her analysis of the decline of nineteenth-century crowd theory, Teresa Brennan notes the ominous implications of what replaced it. The cognitive turn in the twentieth century not only reconcentrated enquiry on the rational minds of a self-contained individual but also bisected biological and sociological explanations of collective social interaction.[51] The theory of the self-contained individual stresses, as such, that it is an evolutionarily hardwired and conscious cognition that determines human agency rather than natural phenomena such as emotions, feelings, and affect. For Brennan, however, what spreads (affect) turns such a crude dichotomy on its head by significantly placing social encounter ahead of (or in mixture with) biological adaptation. Despite the prevalent "prejudice concerning the biological and the social" and the "belief in [a subject's] self-containment" that obsessed early social scientists' interest in how collectives respond to each other, Brennan argues that the biological and the social are irrevocably blended.[52] Contagion is, like this, "a simple affective transfer" discerned by permeable individuals in rooms and other affective atmospheres of encounter.[53] She compares it to entrainment, whereby a person's affects can contaminate another, pulling or pushing him along in rhythmic synchronization. Importantly, affective transmission does not originate in the biologically hardwired drives of the individual. To be sure, the porous self is nothing like the inward looking ego (only thinking of itself).[54] On the contrary, the affective transfer is always, from the outset, *social*. But this encounter is not social in the sense of the term accepted in mainstream sociological categorizations. The encounter comes from out there in the affective atmosphere and can, as such, spread from person to person, entering into the skin and *hacking* into the evolutionary drives.

There are distinct parallels here between Brennan's theory of affective transmission and Tarde's diagram. There are two kinds of interwoven desire at work in both. Imitation is indeed located at the intersection point between social and biological categories, as might be grasped when a crowd encounters a deadly enemy. Each person may instinctively feel fear as she encounters the sight of this terrifying foe. On direct encounter, then, perhaps it is the evolutionary hardwiring that fires first, as the fear-phobia triggers panic. But as part of a crowd, the encounter with *felt* fear is not necessarily a survival mechanism. To be sure, fears and anxieties take on an imitative momentum that spreads through the crowd as they flee from the impending violence. Panic in a crowd is, as Canetti argues, a "common collective experience" that can draw individuals into the flight of all, distributing danger and forcing direction.[55] Yet feeling the fear of others can be appropriated by social invention. Panic spreads by word of mouth, through mediated channels, and sometimes by way of the spreading of false rumors concerning the whereabouts of an unspecified enemy. The experience will become more indirect, as at the same time, each individual simultaneously seeks to fight his way out to the point of disintegration. Panic is self-destructive.

Significantly, though, such deceptions do not rely on negative transmissions of fear and anxiety alone. The infectable social mood is equally susceptible to affective contagions triggered by joyful encounters. Love contagions, or viral love, as I call it here, might even be regarded as a more infectious stratagem than fearmongering. As Brennan contends, love as an affect is very different to negative affects, which require an independent medium of transmission. Love, in contrast to fear, is both affect and the medium through which the affect travels.[56] Viral love is, in this sense, both virus and viral environment enfolded into one communicable space.

Whether viral love is in fact a more powerful contaminator than fear is not really the issue here. It is rather that love needs to be considered as a political concept. As Tarde claimed, the most ingenious and potent of political strategies appeals not to fear alone but also to the desire to love and be loved in return and to the potential to contagiously pass on those loving feelings to others to imitate. According to Tarde, it is the "power of belief and desire" of the "love and faith" of the somnambulist (a neurologically unconscious social subject by any other name) that produces "obedience and imitation."[57] Viral love may well be compared, as such, to a contagious social neurosis, or mass attention deficit disorder, but it is not feared like a microbial disease. Despite being mostly unconscious of its affects, the somnambulist is not controlled or panicked into submission by epidemics of fear but willingly engages with the faith and hope inspired by his joyful (and mesmeric) encounter with love. Social obedience is partially guided, then, by "unheard-of expenditures of love and of unsatisfied love at that."[58] Significantly, these investments in love made by religious and political institutions of power, Tarde claims, satisfy a "persistent need of loving and admiring," requiring the raising up of "new idols . . . from time to time."[59]

Stratagem 2: Viral Love

Love

Tarde clearly regarded love as a powerful political concept. In fact, in his science fiction–climate disaster novel *Underground Man,* published in 1905, he writes about the fate of the human race as it is forced to live beneath the surface of the earth when the sun begins to die. This catastrophic environmental event provokes social instabilities marked by a shift from social hierarchy to social harmony. As a consequence, love not only replaces the energy of the sun but becomes a major force of social power. Love becomes the very air that the Underground Man breathes. Not surprisingly, perhaps, humans soon become embroiled in a bloody conflict for this precious resourse. On one side, there are those who fight "to assert the freedom of love with its uncertain fecundity," and on the other, there are those who want to regulate it. In the "forced intimacy of a cave," Tarde writes, "there is no mean between warfare and love, between mutual slaughter or mutual embraces."[60] Love is war. It is also endemic to the "extra-logical" influences that underpin *The Laws of Imitation,* and by pointing to the desire to love as central to the exercise of power, Tarde similarly raises some very interesting questions concerning what is located between the "uncertain fecundity" of love and the tyrannies that seek to regulate its flow. Indeed, there seems to be a very thin line separating, on one hand, the spontaneity of a love that spreads freely and, on the other hand, a love that controls. There is "nothing more natural," Tarde states, "than that those who love each other should copy each other," but love-imitation is a distinctly asymmetrical relation insofar as it is the lover who by and large copies the beloved.[61]

There are indeed many interesting parallels between Tardean love and Michael Hardt's recent endeavor to make love a political concept. It is in effect via Hardt's lecture on the subject that I want to develop the idea that the virality of love becomes part and parcel of a second communication stratagem. This is because, like Tarde to some extent, Hardt makes a compelling case for rescuing love from a series of deceptive disguises. He traces it, as such, through a political journey from the repressions of religious, fascistic, and psychoanalytical love to the revolutionary potential of a *love of difference.* While exposing these former examples of love as grand-scale deceptions, Hardt tends to see the potential of revolutionary love as lost in a diluted form of romanticism. He grasps romantic love as a weakening of political power, which needs to be reignited as a more catching and joyful revolutionary encounter. My intention here is to sketch out the various ideas put forward in Hardt's lecture before going on to think them through in relation to how the stratagem of viral love operates as a political tactic in present-day network conflicts. Drawing once again on the joyful (and viral) encounters materialized in the wasp–orchid assemblage, what I go on to propose is a modified Tardean account of contagious love interwoven with political power and deception.

In an interview published in 2004, Hardt revealed that along with Antonio Negri, he had always wanted to make love a "properly political concept." To do so, though, he contended that the love needed to be expanded "beyond the limits of the couple," not only in terms of sexual and romantic love but also debunking the "psychoanalytic limits of coupling."[62] This interest was again picked up on in a series of lectures Hardt gave at the European Graduate School in 2007,[63] where he began by asking, why love? Why not use good old "commie" concepts (as Hardt puts it) like solidarity or comradeship? Well, for Hardt, love is integral to the Multitude project. Unlike solidarity, which is too rational and calculated, love is a social relation that goes beyond reason to mesh with the passions. Moreover, he contends that love is not a mere interaction between individuals, like comradeship, but has a "transformative capacity" in which people can lose themselves. Love in effect produces a "different relationship between reason and passions." But more than that, Hardt endeavors to think through ways in which the Multitude can exercise love to potentially resist the corruption and tyranny of the War on Terror. Like this, love becomes a revolutionary tool by which the Multitude will be enabled to spontaneously rule themselves.

Hardt's political love is both implicated in, and synonymous with, two kinds of democracy. There is, on one hand, the legitimate democracy of the Multitude. Love circulates here in a collective social space of "free interaction" that facilitates joyful encounters: a political notion of love that could challenge the illegitimacy of, on the other hand, a love gone bad. This second kind of corrupt democracy is exemplified by an "evil love" that destroys difference. It is the *love of the same* (same family, same race, same religion, and same nation). To some extent, then, Hardt's legitimate love is deployed to overcome distinct fault lines apparent in the Multitude project, namely, the limitations inherent in its embryonic account of the emergence of spontaneous and borderless self-rule. As Hardt concedes, for the people to become legitimately democratic, they might have to be lovingly remade. Resistance is not, however, realized in either an outright dictatorship of love or the free-flowing love of social multiplicity. Legitimate love is instead located in a space between spontaneity and dictatorship. This marks a departure from, on one hand, the nascent boundary-free notion of spontaneity and, on the other, Lenin's brand of dictatorial love, in which the postrevolutionary people are considered unprepared for spontaneous democracy and must therefore be *remade* to achieve it.[64] Such a legitimate kind of love can function, Hardt argues, "in [the] gap" between these two extremes. Yet, before entering into the no-man's land of love and exploring the transformative capacities that might exist there, it is necessary to look more closely at the various deceptions of a tyrannical expression of a love gone bad. Indeed, the trickery of love becomes apparent in at least five political arenas where the logic of a unifying force, which appears to have beneficial outcomes for those brought together in acts of love, nonetheless becomes a molar organization that destroys difference by obliterating the revolutionary potential of singularities.

First, Hardt points to the unifying forces of premodern religious love like that established in Christian and Judaic traditions. Religious love binds together communities of followers alongside the state powers to which it becomes aligned, producing enough like-minded preachers (and politicians) to propagate belief and remake the people as God's subjects. Religious love thus provides the facade behind which a love gone bad partakes in the destruction of difference. As follows, love of the same God encloses singularities within the union of heterosexual family values as sanctified under religious dogma as well as condemning the poor to become objects of charitable love. Indeed, although some Latin American liberation theologies have sought to encourage the love of God to grow out of these singularities (to see through the eyes of the poor, for example), they come into conflict with the Roman Catholic Church's steadfast resistance to any revolutionary visions that might empower the poor and endanger the state.[65]

The deceptions of the second kind of love gone bad become evident in psychoanalytical models of the family unit. At first glance, Oedipal love seems to be moving in a different direction from religious love. Freud certainly acknowledged that belief in God lacks tolerance for those who do not believe in God. "Even if it calls itself a religion of love," he argued, it "must be hard and unloving to those who do not belong to it."[66] But as Hardt points out, Oedipal love similarly locks the love of difference inside the same family unit. The Oedipalization of the family is indeed a stratagem of unification (or molarization) by way of repression. So although psychoanalytical and religious love is expressed at the polar opposites of inner psychosexual drives (Eros) and external, unconditional godly love (Agape), both function to unify and repress. As Hardt explains, on one hand, religious love functions under the true love of God as fixed by an asymmetric relation between Eros and Agape that can never be separated—Eros (love ascending *toward* God) is the love that directs man to Agape (the love that descends *from* God). Eros is, as such, effectively repressed by Agape. Freud's family love, on the other hand, is driven by sexual libido that unifies groups and society. In the Oedipal family, Agape is, as such, repressed by the biological drives of Eros.

The third deception of love similarly functions by bringing people together into family units to exert power over them. In this case, though, the organizational molar forces are not religious but provide evidence that the secular world is capable of making a love as bad as any fundamentalism. The nuclear heterosexual family has indeed become the bedrock on which the love of race and nation sits. The secular fascisms, racisms, and mass popularisms characteristic of 1930s Europe and beyond are an equally cruel corruption of the Multitude's capacity for free love. Like this, family love, as realized in Nazi policy, for example, continues as a central plank and guiding policy that functions as the germ cell of nation-states, reproducing the molarities of secular repression.[67]

The War on Terror is given as a fourth example of a contemporary illegitimate love of the same. The deception herein draws again on a love of God as well as on a poorly defined notion of democracy to justify violence against the other. The War on Terror conjures up a metaphysical enemy. As the first stratagem set out, epidemic terror has no need of a physical cause. It need not have anything do with global poverty or U.S. foreign policy in the Middle East. It is a miraculous threat and needs to be dealt with as such. With public opinion either mostly supportive of U.S. intervention in the affairs of Middle Eastern countries or grasping it as a strictly religious war intended to weaken and divide the Islamic world, there is an urgent need to determine a legitimate love.[68]

In the last political arena, love appears to be apolitical. Like this, love has become, Hardt argues, a *blind love,* particularly in the West, where it has dissolved into a "sentimentality" that lacks political efficacy. Love has been consigned, as such, to a powerless passion or sensation, denying its ontological capacity for productivity. Blind love is no longer a social act: it is something that just happens to someone. We fall in and out of love as passive beings. Nothing is learned. Nothing is practiced. The question concerning legitimacy therefore implicates a different kind of love that can overcome a love of same that propagates blind superstitions arising from the fear of the other. There is a need, as such, to consider how love may reenter into conscious thought and enable actions that change the relations we have with others. The power of the love of difference is not, in this sense, a power that reproduces unitary social bodies, like congregations, Oedipal families, or one nation under God, but instead increases the power to produce interplays between singularities.

To counter the molarizing forces of the love of the same and the descent of revolution into blind love, Hardt proposes rethinking love not as a passive passion but as a direct action of the passions. Legitimate love is approached by Hardt via a Spinozan love of joyful encounter, which provokes the capacity to think and act. He seeks an act of creative differentiation that re-creates singularities of love. He looks to mobilize the alterity of love, beginning with an intervention into the mostly straight ideologies of the family unit. The idea is to move love away from the centered heterosexual enclosures of "normative" behavior and rediscover a love of neighbor that is not limited to resemblances, identity, or closed spatial proximities. In place of centers, oppositions, and grids, love needs to function in open, continuous topological spaces that provide distributed pathways leading from the self to *all* others. Perhaps the most effective articulation of this kind of distributed love is not concerned with human love at all. As follows, assemblage theory brings in the transversal and phylogenetic love of the wasp–orchid assemblage, which explodes the love of the same by releasing singularities. Assemblage theory offers experimentations in love that deterritorialize the molar unities, producing novel and spontaneous assemblages. Hardt's no-man's land becomes, as such, a transformative power of love and reproduction. Like the fragility of a fractal shoreline that exists in the middle of the assemblages of the land and sea, sex can operate amid the assemblages of these two dictatorships. It is between free spontaneity and tough love that a space of joyful encounter might emerge and become a training ground for the production of subjectivities capable of reproducing the democracy of the Multitude.

It is nevertheless the deceptions at work in blind love that return this political conception to Tarde's diagram. For it is Tarde who exposes the power dynamic apparent in appeals made to these passionate obsessions. It is indeed a Tardean love that induces a kind of myopia that dissolves political action into sentimental fascinations and sensations that hold a mesmeric sway over social power relations. To be sure, although blind love appears to be something that *just happens* naturally to us, and is, as Hardt argues, increasingly relegated to the private realm, from a Tardean perspective, it is a force of relation that renders the public insensible to invasive affective contagions. It is at these volatile intersection points between biological and social encounter, where another contemporary site of struggle occurs, that social acts are ever more manipulated via the passions rather than direct appeals to reason. Beyond notions of the legitimacy and illegitimacy of love, then, the joyful encounter becomes a contested space with transformative capacities. Unlike Hardt's joyful encounters, in which collectives are consciously *directed* toward a legitimate form of democracy, Tarde's epidemiology infers a *nondirectional* space in which the porous self is contaminated by the contagions of the other. Love becomes a much imitated hypnotic force: a viral action-at-a-distance that works on and manipulates the feelings of those infected by it. The issue of control and resistance thus becomes increasingly coupled to the capacity of those infected to discern mostly indiscernible affects.

It is possible to see how Tarde's allusion to the affective flows of passion presents a differently orientated tyranny of blind love. He seems to offer more food for thought with regard to recent transitions in U.S. political power. On one hand, and resonating with Hardt's political concept of love, Tarde recognizes how religious love, transported via benevolent outpourings of sympathy and pity, conspires (or converges) with the power of the state. The modern state, he contends, could not exist without the proselytizing contagions of "all-conquering religion[s]."

Both religion and the state are "where the majority of elements are in agreement, and where almost everything proceeds from the same principles and converges towards the same ends."[69] The love of God may well be a much older concept than the love of nation, but the same imitative logic of proselytism applies when, as in the case of Bush and Blair's military intervention in the Middle East, faith justifies state violence.[70] On the other hand, though, the contagions of Obama's election seem to have initially shifted away from the microbial epidemics of fear and panic toward a short-lived joyful and empathic encounter. The promised closure of Guantánamo Bay symbolized much-needed change, yet, under the mesmeric sway of Obama-love, the violence in the Middle East has continued to surge.

So how can the concept of viral love help us think through a second communication stratagem and apply it to our examples of the wars on viruses and terror? First, in contrast to the rhetorical focus on fear, risk, and security used in the case of Bulgarian VX, I want to acknowledge what has been rather disparagingly referred to as the "pure nasty love of the wreckage."[71] Of course, what is now considered an illegitimate desire to wreck has been discursively appropriated by the inventions of network controllers and security enterprises, but this is a passion for vandalism that has nevertheless spread not so much as an ideological confrontation (sabotage) as a continuation of a fascination with digital virality expressed in the once legitimate work of von Neumann and those who followed him. Here I ask a question Tarde posed in *The Laws of Imitation,* that is, is not this fascination "a genuine neurosis, a kind of unconscious polarization of love and faith?"[72]

Second, I return to Obama-love and again see it through the lenses of *The Laws of Imitation.* Here Tarde's political concept of love involves the "subjective imitation of a recognised superior." The initial "obedience and trust" in that superior is at first founded on "devotion" and "loving admiration" but will eventually pass from love and admiration to "open contempt."[73] Notably, this process of imitation is regarded by Tarde as an irreversible passage of power that never passes back to the love and admiration of the one originally recognized as superior. To maintain power, it is therefore necessary to appeal to the imitator's "persistent need of loving and admiring" by hoisting up "new idols" to love.[74]

From the Dark Avenger to the Love Bug

The viral events that occurred in the old Soviet bloc during the 1980s point to a Tardean imitative social encounter between a small VX community in Bulgaria and the cloned and hacked U.S. computer technologies produced toward the latter end of the Cold War. Certainly this unique sociotechnical encounter between the East and the encroaching network economy of the West assembled the ideal medium for the propagation of the social inventions of the VX. The Bulgarian Virus Factory connected the ideas and sentiments of the VX to cloned computer hardware, hacked software, and clandestine links to the global network. Like this, the computer virus problem becomes inseparable from the spreading of a fascination and passionate interest in what viruses can do.

The unfolding of the computer virus problem is interestingly approached as such in a research paper presented at an AV conference in 1991. It begins by noting how "the whole of Bulgaria has turned into some kind of computer virus developing laboratory."[75] Schoolchildren, students, and programmers were all writing viruses and testing them in the wild. Indeed, Vesselin Bontchev's paper breaks from the usual focus on code detection methods to address a fundamentally social aspect of the computer virus problem. He argues that the inventions of the VX community were in part an outcome of the socioeconomic instabilities that swept through the Soviet bloc in the early 1980s. He pointed to how a largely disenfranchised generation in Bulgaria was fast becoming "a huge army of young and extremely qualified people," but these "computer wizards" were not actively involved in a recognized form of "economic life." Unlike the booming U.S. economy, for which a profitable digital economy was viable, Bulgaria's largely paper-based bureaucracies had little need for computer programmers. Bontchev argues that this small VX community, initially formed around clandestine access to computer equipment, was a consequence of the Bulgarian state's refusal to do business with the corporate West and instead encourage programmers to innovate using cloned hardware and hacked Western programs. "Bulgaria took the wrong decision in producing [cloned] computers and stealing programs," he claims, since these imitations (the result of the reverse engineering of hardware and software products from the West) "did nothing to stimulate the internal growth of a software industry." In short, although the Bulgarian state excluded itself from the capitalist-dominated digital revolution, these captivated Bulgarian programmers managed to hook up to the network by stealth.

Bontchev argues that when a Bulgarian programmer worked on a project, she did not treat it as labor but regarded it as more of a "kind of sport or entertainment." Contrary to the ongoing Cold War hysteria concerning iron curtain viruses, Bontchev finds little evidence to suggest that the virus problem started as a deliberate counterideological antagonism aimed at digital capitalism. Instead, a lack of willingness on behalf on the Bulgarian state legislator to take this fascination with viruses seriously seems to have inadvertently encouraged programmers to openly experiment with viral code as an entertaining cultural practice, challenging themselves, and others, to solve problems their viral innovations posed to the wider network. Moreover, unlike the United States, where it was financially feasible to hire a policing force, like CERT, to guard the network, a lack of funding in Bulgaria ensured that victims of the problem were not able to set up effective resistance or gain support from the state in the shape of appropriate laws to protect their property.[76]

Similarly, the economic instability in the region also helped to determine the production and social exchange of cloned computer equipment. The inexpensive Pravetz computer clones, made from copied parts of U.S.-made Apple II computers, provided programmers with the tools to produce viruses. Soviet factories built tens of thousands of Pravetz clones in the 1980s, beginning with the Pravetz 82, which was distributed to schools across Bulgaria and the socialist bloc as far as North Korea.[77] The encounter between the Bulgarian VX scene and the Pravetz is a novel reproductive encounter between social and technical assemblages comparable to Samuel Butler's *Book of Machines*. These cloned microcomputers were inseparable from the Bulgarian virus epidemic since they "were the first to show Bulgarian kids what strange new powers computers could give them."[78] The wide diffusion of the Pravetz clone and the programming know-how of the VX were indeed indissoluble and rapidly opened up new assemblage territories.

The trend for virus writing propagated through the network via impassioned conversations between groups similarly fascinated by how to effectively camouflage and reduce the size of infection mechanisms. Alongside the numerous technical discussions were emotional declarations regarding the entitlement to freely experiment with the adventures of code and much-repeated accounts of the intoxicating glories of successful attacks. To be sure, very much coupled to the spreading of the computer virus problem were the sociotechnical and transversal propagations of ideas and affects, bringing together the small groups that constituted these early nascent network communities and spreading their influence to form a much bigger VX assemblage. It was indeed the West itself, particularly the United States, that seems to have fascinated the Bulgarian VX the most. As one member of the community, the "Dark Avenger," puts it, "I think the idea of making a program that would travel on its own, and go to places its creator could never go, was the most interesting for me. The American government can stop me from going to the US, but they can't stop my virus."[79]

The new assemblage territories established between the VX and their Pravetz computers opened up even more when the first virus writing exchange bulletin board service (VX BBS) was set up on an Internet-linked server somewhere inside Bulgaria in 1990.[80] The invention of the VX BBS introduced a powerful distance-independent vector on which the computer virus problem could spread outside the Soviet bloc to the West. It acted as an epidemic hub for the global exchange of viral code and virus writing know-how as well as becoming a brand ambassador for VX bold enough to show off their skills under a cloak of anonymity. Programmers not only uploaded complete viral codes but exchanged technical notes on perfecting infection mechanisms and ready-made code templates, which would encourage others to copy viruses and use the polymorphic code encryption engines designed to help VX evade AV attempts to block viral attacks. The VX BBS also ensured that the dissemination of the emotive words and ideas posted on websites would affectively reinforce the reputations of VX and encourage new relations between the small assemblages of programmers to develop. Eventually, the inventions of the VX contagiously spread to other assemblages of like-minded coders, who, once linked to the VX BBS, could download and exchange examples of viral code and imitate their Bulgarian counterparts. Author and journalist David S. Bennahum well describes this digital contagion:

> [Viral] programs passed along in schools, offices, homes—from one disk to the next they carried the infection along, and in 1991, an international epidemic was diagnosed. One-hundred sixty documented Bulgarian viruses existed in the wild, and an estimated 10 percent of all infections in the United States came from Bulgaria.[81]

The spreading of the ideas and affects of the VX redefines the network space as in excess of the mere "passage of information."[82] Indeed, this trend stresses the affective capacity of a communication stratagem that propagates and appropriates the desires of the network user. In 2000, for example, a young computer science student from Manila put a failed college project proposal to the test using a fairly crude application of both the Visual Basic programming script and a social engineering technique using Trojanlike declarations of love to spread his e-mail worm. In the first instance, the Love Bug used the recipient's e-mail address book to send copies of itself to anyone listed there. These copies would appear to be sent from someone the recipient knew and would therefore propagate from address book to address book. Within hours, many variants (adapted versions of the infection mechanism propagated by others) also began to appear, the deluge alone widely reported as causing damages in excess of a billion dollars. In the second instance, though, the Love Bug only became contagious because it disguised its real objective to infect within the promises of a love letter written into the subject heading of the e-mail and its executable code. On opening the e-mail with the subject heading "I Love You," the user would then be persuaded to open up a file called LOVE-LETTER-FOR-YOU.TXT.vbs. Significantly, however, once detected, the Love Bug author did not announce that he was intent on dismantling the economic system that underpins the network. Instead, like the Bulgarian VX, he proclaimed that he was "a programmer" and that he wanted "to learn" and "to be creative" with code.[83]

Obama-Love

In contrast to the microbial contagions of the neo-Cons, and their appeal to the political unconscious through the cold, emotionless channels of advisors like Cheney and the fearmongering of Rumsfeld, Obama's campaign of hope and change managed to empathically tap into the infectable emotions of many U.S. voters. Indeed, empathy became the political tool of choice—a response to Bush's failure to connect with the public mood, particularly after Hurricane Katrina hit Louisiana. But Obama-love was also a contagion befitting the age of networks: the political shift in power from the G. W. Bush administration's spreading of fear via the repeated use of TV images of 9/11 to Obama's election campaign of hope and change propagated via Facebook and Flickr photos. From the outset, Obama's election campaign team made the best possible use of the intimate features of Web 2.0 applications to spread activism through joyful encounters experienced predominantly *at-a-distance.* At the height of Obama-love, more than seven million people connected themselves to Obama's Facebook page. On Facebook (see Figure 4.1), you can become Obama's friend (one of over 19 million to date). You can find out that he enjoys "basketball, writing, spending time w/ kids" and what his favorite music, books, and TV shows are. Activists who readily engaged in the campaign apparently did so spontaneously, arranging fund-raisers, parties, and gatherings "without any formal leadership from Obama headquarters."[84]

The fascination for the first black president propagated far beyond the country he was elected to serve. Among those signed up to his Facebook page are supporters from as far afield as Iran, Venezuela, Indonesia, Vietnam, India, Nigeria, Sierra Leone, and so on. In countries with limited media access, Obama-love spread via mobile phone, radio, T-shirts, posters, and even bumper stickers. But it was the Obama team's election-eve use of Flickr that perhaps best illustrates the extent to which the empathic virality of love could reach out to people,[85] for it signaled the new president's intention to sidestep the formality and distance of Cheney and Rumsfeld and instead intercept, through these networks, the affective flows of those voters disillusioned by the violence of the neo-Cons. Of course, Obama is a powerful orator, using rhetorical

FIGURE 4.1. Obama's Facebook page (2010).

skills as old as Aristotle, and that should never be underestimated, but the emotionally charged and intimate pictures of his family on the eve of his election spread through global media networks like a firestorm, painting a mood and stirring up a worldwide love contagion.

What is important to stress here, however, is not necessarily a dualistic relation between fear and love but a political element of communication that exceeds the semiotic realm of effect. Indeed, similar to the repeated TV images of the horror of 9/11, these are haptic images that quite literally reach out and *touch* the eye. One Flickr user's comments perfectly capture the empathic transmission of love flowing from these images: "I love this shot. You can feel the butterflies in their stomachs as they are watching the returns."[86]

The events leading to the election of the first black U.S. president were certainly marked by a global outpouring of love. In this sense, Obama-love seemed to attune itself to the positive flows of the love of difference. As Negri suggested shortly after Obama's election, behind this great victory may well be traces of the great struggle of the multitude, certainly in terms of its positive role in the globalization of the issue of race.[87] Yet viral love can be capricious too. Whether Obama can truly live up to the expectations of Hardt and Negri's Multitude project and deliver the spontaneous democracy it desires is, of course, highly questionable. Perhaps the short-lived virality of this example of a love of difference has already been subsumed into the dictatorial counterforces of the love of the same. As I write, Obama's contagion is seemingly oscillating uncontrollably between unrequited love and a love gone bad. The assassination of Osama bin Laden may have well sustained the admiration for a while, but with no end to the War on Terror in sight, the joyful encounter will perhaps subside once again. We may already be witnessing the irreversible passage of power that Tarde contends never passes back to an imitation of love, only contempt.

Conclusion

The political concept of viral love draws attention to the potential priming of joyful encounters to affect mood as well as raising questions concerning the extent to which the somnambulist can come under the control of corporate and political hypnotists. Like this, contagion theory needs to grasp what spreads as entering through the skin into the neural unconscious that relates the porous self to the other (and all other things). The affective contagion of viral love restresses, as such, the "involuntary precognitive nature" of what is passed-on.[88] Again, this is not an exclusively biological or social contagion, as traditionally understood. What spreads passes right through this artifice into the atmosphere of affect. Significantly, too, what spreads has the capacity to capriciously infect the entire valence of negative and positive affect. What spreads can, in other words, be either a fearful or joyful encounter. These are indeed adaptive contagions that trigger empathic transmissions of affect and imitative entrainment. As Brennan elegantly puts it, "my affect, if it comes across to you, alters your anatomical makeup for good or ill."[89]

5

Tardean Hypnosis: Capture and Escape in the Age of Contagion

Tarde's social somnambulism is a mesmerized subjectivity in the making. It is defined by an inseparable and insensible relation established between mechanical habit and a dream of volition. The somnambulist is caught up, as such, in a feverish dream of command and a dream of action in which he is "possessed by the illusion that [his] ideas, all of which have been suggested to [him], are spontaneous."[1] This hypnotic dream state renders subjectivities open to suggestibility, drawing them into an imitative social medium, making them the example that is copied and passed on—and potentially made more predictable and docile in the process. This is a trajectory of the Tardean diagram that is traced in this chapter from urban crowds to the network age, where today, absorption and persuasion have become the watchwords of new business enterprises intent on capturing the mostly unconscious pass-on power of consumers and putting it to work. This trajectory necessitates the thinking up of new ways in which such exercises of biopower can be discerned, resisted, or escaped or the potential for revolutionary countercontagion can be actualized.

Important to understanding Tarde's approach to social power are his ideas about hypnosis. Differing from Le Bon's notion of the image as the leader–hypnotist, he points toward a reciprocal biosocial relation between a hypnotizer and hypnotized subjectivities. But Tardean hypnotism not only blurs the distinction between leaders and followers;

it also questions notions of individual freewill and collective action in terms of what is knowingly and spontaneously attended to, responded to, and passed on. Tarde's dream of action emphasizes, as such, the significance of unconscious association, suggesting a social vulnerability to contagious affect.

Return of the Skyward Looking People

A number of recent studies of social network behavior have tended to follow Milgram's influence, viewing contagion in terms of herding or information cascades and stressing the significance of a *hardwired* proclivity of human beings to follow the lead of others.[2] Some of these studies point to how, for example, the building of speculative economic bubbles or the spreading of fashion and fads conforms (rationally or irrationally) to social proof.[3] Other popular accounts have similarly attributed the biologically hardwired brain to distinctly rational snap judgments (or rapid cognitions) that help an individual make sense of the world and relate to others without the interference of emotions.[4] Indeed, Milgram's focus on the guiding motivations of internal agentic states on an individual's decision-making processes can be seen as part of a more general cognitive turn in the twentieth century. Like this, the study of crowd behavior moved away from the collective actions of the many to focus on individual volition. In contrast to late-nineteenth-century crowd theories, which ascribed imitative behavior to collective manias and indiscernible processes of mass hypnosis, Milgram's imitative agent is linked to conformity and obedience by way of a built-in disposition to obey.[5] His experiments linking social conformity to authority and compliance can nonetheless be understood as symptomatic of Tarde's diagram of hypnotic social encounter. By way of setting up fake encounters, not only did Milgram manipulate the involuntary responses his experiment induced in the crowd, but he also seems to have tapped into a mesmeric imitative tendency—what Thrift has recently called an imitative momentum[6]—which spreads exponentially through urban social space without a guiding hand.

Milgram's contagion research in the 1960s exposed a mesmeric imitative encounter that could be socially engineered. That is to say, by planting skyward looking actors in the urban space of Manhattan, he in effect

primed the street corner with a counterfeit fascination that guided the
attention of the crowd toward a defined goal. Milgram's agentic subjects
and their hardwired tendency to imitate are clearly very different from
the inseparable self–other relations of Tarde's diagram, but the question
of what happens when Milgram, the great social hypnotist, is removed
from the streets of Manhattan is very much a Tardean problem. How,
without this leader of imitative subjects, do we account for a force that
seemingly steers the awareness (and intent) of those who encounter
its vital impetus?

One answer to this question, as Le Bon argued, is to link such contagious forces to the hypnotic order of the image. But what brings a
crowd together amounts to more than merely *thinking in images*. This
is because the imitative encounter exceeds the representational spaces
of the crowd, extending deeply into nonrepresentational relations experienced via feelings and affective capacities. *Virality* presents, as such,
an abstract diagram of contagion that considers how social singularities
are assembled in relation to each other in the grip of discursive semiotic
regimes (e.g., the metaphor of contagion) but also includes presocial
affective processes of contagion. There is, indeed, a significant blurring
of discursive formations and prediscursive flows in this diagram. On
one hand, contagious social assembly occurs by way of the constraining
intervention of immunological statements and metaphors of contagion.
These future network conflicts concretely divide up self from a conveniently unspecified nonself. On the other hand, though, discursive
power becomes blended with the magnetic sway of prediscursive and
subrepresentational flows, providing a propelling vigor that can bring
desires together, bolster belief, and potentialize social singularities in
revolutionary relation to each other. To grasp the imitative ray in this
mode, Tarde's trajectory needs to be followed into the present day, in
which both capitalist enterprises seem committed to exploiting its force
and the potential for revolutionary contagion is still on the horizon.

The so-called neuromarketer closely follows Tarde in this respect,
priming consumer purchase intent by way of exploiting the mostly
spontaneous and unconscious neurological absorption of affect. Neuromarketing practices point to how aperiodic desires can be appropriated
by social invention, transformed into the object of desire (the desire

to believe), and become imitated and sold on for profit. Like Tarde, to some extent, then, the neuromarketer cuts through the nature–culture artifice to tap into the dream of action. For Tarde, though, the docile body of the somnambulist was capriciously steered toward his judgments via the mostly *accidental* forces of imitative encounter. This is in contrast to the neuromarketer, who, more like Milgram perhaps, purposely attempts to capture the fascinations of the unconscious social medium, guiding attention to affectively primed encounters in which shared feelings and beliefs can be traded.[7]

The removal of the subject–hypnotist from contagious encounters of this kind nevertheless necessitates the resuscitation of Tarde's leaderless force of suggestibility expressing itself in, for example, imitative postures, gestures, languages, beliefs, and potential revolution.[8] This is a seemingly rudderless social action but one that nonetheless openly intervenes in the duality between freewill and dreams. To repeat the mantra of the Tardean diagram, there is no "*absolute separation . . . between the voluntary and the involuntary . . . between the conscious and the unconscious.*"[9] It is indeed at these intersection points that an absorbable vulnerability to contagious affect is actualized.

The concept of the imitative ray can be applied to a range of seemingly innocuous contagious encounters like those experienced between yawning or laughing people or the spreading of impulsive fads. But given recent events in the Middle East, we see how it also relates to widespread outbreaks of anger, disaffection, political violence, and revolution. Indeed, these events are a timely reminder of how sudden shocks to a social system can develop into a spontaneous epidemic, which, on very rare occasions, overwhelms firmly entrenched power institutions. There are, of course, parallels here to Le Bon's concerns with the threat revolutionary contagion posed to nineteenth-century aristocratic orders in Europe. Le Bon understood democratic crowd contagion to be guided by a dangerous unified mental inclination toward images that could subordinate freewill, pervert truth, and provoke revolutionary acts of violence. It was in fact the mass hallucination of such images through the unconscious crowd that became the mechanism of Le Bon's hypnotic contagion.

Today institutional power is once again under threat from similar democratic movements. Not surprisingly, then, revolutionary contagion is discursively attributed to the metaphor of contagion, that is, the metaphysical representation of a fearsome disease invading the boundaries of the nation-state, necessitating an immunological response. As the Yemeni president Ali Abdullah Saleh contended amid the spreading of protests to Yemen in 2011, the "virus" of revolution "is not part of our heritage or the culture . . . it's a virus that came from [the *outside*] Tunisia to Egypt."[10] Nevertheless, it is the irrepressible prediscursive transmission of affective contagion, and the volatility of the self–other relation to its force, that seems to give impetus to the revolutionary contagion. Beyond the immunological rhetoric, these Middle Eastern dictators recognize that it is not simply the case that the infectious idea of revolution spreads from the outside to the inside; rather, the transmission of affect spreads *throughout* the population. As Saleh conceded, before turning his guns on his own people, it is "the scent of the fever" of rebellion that is far more catching.

In recent media reports on the events in the Middle East, much revolutionary agency has been afforded to the smart mobs of social media. In the numerous accounts of blogging activists and Facebook rebellion, it seems the emergence of a distributed cognition or collective intelligence enhances Milgram's small world network, bringing people together in the pursuit of democracy. But it is perhaps imprudent to see these technological objects as somehow independent of the channeling of uninhibited anger regarding decades of economic poverty. To begin with, the often overstated role of Twitter and Facebook in these uprisings does not explain why revolutions in the past have occurred without access to electronic networks. Moreover, such naive technological determinism does not at all grasp why some authoritarian regimes in countries with ready access to social media can stem contagious revolution, while others cannot. Authoritarian regimes can (and do) close down communications—the impact of which needs to be better understood during periods of revolutionary contagion.

The potential manipulation of the dream of action does nevertheless draw attention to how social inventions, like social media, can appropriate desires in ways that Tarde once considered mostly capricious. Despite the overexcitement surrounding their revolutionary properties, it is equally rash to completely disregard the democratic features of Twitter or Facebook. Social media can speed up and intensify the crowd's desire to fight oppressors by encouraging them to share images of burning martyrs and downtown riots, which quickly spread affective contagions from region to region. This is a Tardean network in which affective contagion is "boosted and extended by all manner of technologies."[11]

The Technological Unconscious

Despite the assumed potential of electronic networks to escape unifying power structures and foster the new empowerments of a multiple social subject, network spaces can also provide the flip side of the desire for spontaneous democratic rule. The network distribution of affect is indeed regarded as an ever more "planned" expansion of a new kind of *technological unconscious.*[12] The proliferation of this insentient mode of relationality is marked to some extent by a shift from a dial-up culture to an age of permanent connectivity. The distinction between being offline and online is now a redundant concept. Today the end user is always online, *even when he is asleep.*[13] Marketing surveillance systems increasingly know who users are, where they are, and what they are doing, and based on transactions and behavioral reporting, they can approximate where they might be going. Online web analytics, for example, trace mouse moves, clicks, and keystrokes, which assume a high percentage of correlation between cursor movement and user attention. Similarly, the data mined from all kinds of transactions are fed into databases, and the extracted patterns are used to bring about future intentions by way of suggestion: *Customers who bought this also bought this... Explore similar items.* This is a somnambulistic space increasingly colonized by an unseen and ubiquitous computing (ubicomp), which pervades, organizes, and intensifies the open-ended repetitions of turbocapitalism. The Internet of things is the reinvention of the online experience embedded with radio frequency identification chips (RFID) and global positioning systems. It is from within this saturated software environment that the tragedy of interactive media unfolds in the sense that any freedoms awarded to the end user become overshadowed by a subjectivation in which bodies unconsciously trigger events. The technological unconscious is, as Thrift similarly puts it, a "bending of bodies-with-environments to a specific set of addresses without the benefit of any cognitive inputs." The outcome of this intensified addressing system is a readying of a "prepersonal substrate" from which "guaranteed correlations, assured encounters, and therefore unconsidered anticipations" can grow.[14]

The pervasiveness of the technological unconscious must not, however, be misconstrued as a psychoanalytical structuring of mediated power relations. Like Tarde's dream of action, it differs from a long tradition of Freudian media theory. Along these lines, Galloway and Thacker describe the network unconscious by substituting Freud's interpretation of subliminal dreams for a narcoleptic "liminal space":[15]

> Recall the basic premise of Freud's *Interpretation of Dreams*: Although one may consciously choose to go to sleep, what happens within sleep is largely the domain of the unconscious. Consider the reverse: You unconsciously fall asleep, but in that liminal space, you are the master of reality. Or, combine the two: You accidentally fall asleep, and then automatically begin to generate image, text, narrative.[16]

Certainly, unlike Freud's somnambulist, who is a zombie running via remote control, the narcoleptic end user enters into the technological unconsciousness infused by the "dreaming" of the algorithm. Like surrealist automatic writing, the consumption of the network is automatically generated and distributed while users and their computers are sleeping.

Evil media similarly ponders what constitutes the unconsciousness of software culture by associating it with "contemporary media practices of trickery, deception, and manipulation."[17] Like this, the persuasion-management of the end user occurs via an array of sophist techniques, cropping up like a mesmerizing flow that intercepts points of intersection between cognitive attention and noncognitive inattention. As Fuller and Goffey put it,

> The end-user has only finite resources for attention. She will slip up sooner or later. . . . A keen interest in the many points at which fatigue, overwork, and stress make her inattentive is invaluable. In attention economies, where the premium is placed on capturing the

eye, the ear, the imagination, the time of individuals... it is in the lapses of vigilant, conscious, rationality that the real gains are made.[18]

There are unambiguous links here to Crary's Tardean-influenced thesis, that is to say, modern distraction is not a disruption of stable or natural kinds of attention but a constitutive element of the many attempts to produce attentiveness in human subjects.[19] This hypnotic steering of subjectivity toward defined goals operates according to a "principle of narrow attentiveness and exclusion."[20] It is not the case that the end user "cannot do or think" but how even "rational subjects" are often "outstripped by events."[21] There are discursive formations at work here, such as those adhered to by software designers and digital marketers, but what directs the attention of the end user does so in composition with noncognitive states of inattentiveness, distraction, and reverie. As Crary puts it,

> For every mutation in the construction of attentiveness there are parallel shifts in the shape of inattention, distraction, and states of "absentmindedness." New thresholds continually emerge at which an institutionally competent attentiveness veers into something vagrant, unfocused, something folded back against itself.[22]

The consumer of evil media lives in a flimsy prison cell: a "world of captures" in which power operates not primarily by "repressing, suppressing or oppressing" but by "inciting, seducing, producing, and even creating."[23] The end user becomes, as such, a prisoner of techniques of capture derived from routinization and habituation and inflows of contagious-suggestibility. Like this, evil media studies recognizes the predisposition of digital culture to capitalize on the inattentiveness of the somnambulist. This is a model of the technological unconscious in which inattentiveness becomes an invaluable commodity in the end game of persuasion: part of an *inattention economy.*

The hypnotics of the network can also be thought of as primary relations established in prediscursive environments, in which bodily, affective, and presymbolic dimensions expose a tendency to crowd together. Prediscursive environments are evidenced in dynamic topological

clusters like those provoked by the magnetizing forces of social fascination. Changes in the stance of a docile body drawn toward a point
of fascination occur by way of hypnotic orientation, resulting from
autonomic hormonal and muscular responses to the animations of the
environment. It is through such affective movements and reflexes that the
imitative momentum becomes contagiously transferred between people.
"We know how credulous and docile the hypnotic subject becomes,"
Tarde contends. What is "suggested to him becomes incarnated in him."
It penetrates him before it "expresses itself in his posture or gesture or
speech."[24] It is the absorption of affect that produces the movement of
bodies in prediscursive spaces, comparable to "schools of fish briefly
stabilized by particular spaces, temporary solidifications which pulse
with particular affects."[25]

Significantly, though, it is not the case that discursive formations
simply disappear from these bodily movements, reflexes, and contagious
transmissions. On the contrary, discourse is transmitted along with the
prediscursive emergences of faces and stances.[26] There is nonetheless an
analytical requirement to map the changes in connectivities of prediscursive spaces and explore contemporary Tardean mediascapes, like the
Internet, which Thrift argues "act as new kinds of neural pathways . . .
forging new reflexes."[27]

If the hypnotic contagions of the nineteenth-century crowd were
mostly accidental, then there is a growing sense today that the inventions of biopower can exploit the accident and bring about a more
manipulable *mesmerism gone bad*.[28] This is particularly evident in the
recent inventions of corporate and political enterprises. Indeed, seen
against a backdrop of cognitive disengagement, populations seem to
be rarely turned on by a politics of "intellect and reasoning," preferring
instead a form of mediation that "appeals to the heart, passion, [and]
emotional imagination."[29] Corporate and political power increasingly
engages with populations through noncognitive communication channels, resonating with waves of networked affect, in which "obsessive and
compulsive" engagement becomes more traceable and manipulable.[30]
Thrift's reinvention of Tarde's social somnambulism is characterized,
as such, by volatility to a force of influence ever more powered by affective automatisms.[31]

Such invention is, of course, nothing new. Canetti's dancers serve as a conspicuous example of a primitive social invention that functions according to the Tardean diagram. The dream of action of the dancer is powered by a tendency to imitate the affects of others and is given impetus, so to speak, by the fascinations and intoxicating glories that exert a magnetic pull on those who come into contact with its invention. This is because the dancer appropriates desire, infecting subjectivities, and encouraging social clustering around the event of the dance. Just as Canetti's premodern crowd, on hearing and seeing music and dance, joins in and remains fixed within the neighborhood, today, the millions of consumers who cluster around Lady Gaga or Barak Obama on Twitter or Facebook perhaps do so in part because of a similar tendency to become fascinated by intoxicating glories.

Rosalind D. Williams sees Tarde an early analyst of this type of consumer culture. She marks the investment made in "dream worlds" intended to harness small flows of desire and builds them into a much bigger semiconscious reverie, leading to the purposive mass consumption of commodities.[32] In these dream worlds, the "mind of the individual [becomes] part of an endless social network which in turn contributes to that network in a dynamic relation of role-setting and role-following."[33] Although the hypnotic medium that brings these minds together does not appear to have a subject-leader, it is, nonetheless, constrained by ongoing social relations. Decisions are not, as such, embedded in people, or in their voluntary exchanges with others, but in the very networks to which they connect. It is, like this, the network relation that leads the way. As Borch puts it,

> Suggestion need not refer to human interaction but can instead describe a sociality which is built on the relationship between humans and objects. Rather than a hypnotizing subject, that is, we may identify a hypnotizing object, tendency etc.[34]

The power of influence an economy exerts on a population exceeds the charismatic magnetisms of political or financial leaders and pertains instead to the hypnotic draw of the events of the market itself. In other words, it is the action-at-a-distance of the market relation that magnetizes assemblages of desire in which people, commodities, and prices circulate and contaminate. Importantly, this account of capitalism is rooted neither in the rationale goals of economic man nor in any kind of transcendent superstructure. It is rather a viral capitalism driven by a "logic of propensity rather than purpose."[35] It is a political economy of imitative momentum determined by an unrestrained fascination for the merchandise of the marketplace and the sentiments that persist as a consequence.

The Mutuality of Hypnotic Contagion

A strange duality springs from Le Bon's proto-psychoanalytical division of individual–crowd. According to Le Bon, the mental unity of the crowd absorbs the individual into the suggestibility of the many. This is a unification of the group-mind defined by a diminishing individual intellect and collective susceptibility to group-based illusions. *The Crowd* presents, as such, a group psychology that erroneously separates individual consciousness from repressed unconscious states. Here Deleuze's phantom-event provides a far more compelling and productive in-between state, which can be linked to Tarde's dream of action in novel ways. The phantom-event replaces the repressed unconscious mind of Le Bon's crowd with a factory-like relation established between social singularities and the sometimes illusory events they encounter. This is arguably a combination of an epidemiological and neurological inner psyche, which has a distinctly schizoid rather than Oedipal relation to consciousness.[36] Along these lines, Tarde's diagram can be remapped onto Deleuze and Guattari's intervention into the molar organization of society according to Oedipal mechanisms, processes, and structures.[37] The authority of the psychoanalyst subject-hypnotist (Daddy's voice) becomes endemic to a predisposition to repress the social unconscious of the desiring machine. From Le Bon to Freud, then, the crowd is caught in the repression of selfish impulses. In the wrong hands, crowd psychology can in fact be wielded as a weapon against social singularities, forcing them to reproduce a unified collective mind and transforming its irrational and conservative delusions into a predicable and deadly social force.

In contrast, Tardean hypnosis draws attention to the inseparability of

conscious and unconscious states. Like this, it provides an understanding of how the relation between a magnetizing force and magnetized
subject functions as an action-at-a-distance. To begin with, as Rae Beth
Gordon points out, Tarde speaks of a "more or less" unconscious desire
to imitate: an unconscious state in which the hypnotized somnambulist can perhaps already read the mind of the hypnotizer;[38] that is, the
unconscious state is never completely controlled by the hypnotizer or
the crowd. On the contrary, the somnambulist "incarnates" intensive
imitative radiations, which control arm and leg movements, poses,
gestures, and language by way of suggestion. As Gordon claims, Tarde's
somnambulism is a composition of automatic physiological reflexes and
a conscious desire to imitate.[39] This is a nonconscious state, or nonstate,
more akin to vigilambulism, in which the hypnotized subject commits to
unconscious acts in the full light of the woken state.[40] In sharp contrast
to the psychoanalyst's endeavor to act on the altered state of those *under*
hypnosis, inducing trances, involuntary group swaying, and distortions
of perception and memory, the nonstate requires compliance to suggestibility. This entails social transmissions involving the sharing of
instructions between hypnotizer and hypnotized and reciprocal strategies
designed to bring about the desired effects of hypnosis. In instances of
group hypnosis, for example, the nonstate mode suggests a greater level
of autonomous affect running between the hypnotizer and the hypnotized. How crowds become susceptible to hypnotic events depends not
so much on techniques of hypnotic mass paralysis and repression as it
does on complex exchanges, the proximity of operators, the filtering of
information, unexpected connections, associations, modes of compliance, and even the mutual faking of outcomes.[41]

It is important to note that while Le Bon's crowd theory focuses on a
gullible, and even stupid, social aggregation, Tarde's notion of hypnotic
obedience reveals a complex reciprocal relationship in which subjects are
not simply controlled by deep-seated fears and phobias but also tend to
copy (on the surface) those whom they love or at least empathize with.
It is this mutuality established between hypnotizer and a hypnotized
subject that seems to underpin Tardean social power relations and social
reproduction in general. So the stupidity of the crowd is not preformed
but emerges from a decidedly one-sided mutual magnetization of a

loving subject.[42] It is indeed through the allusion made here to the potential forces of belief and desire (and other passions and sentiments) that we begin to fully grasp Tarde's notion of hypnotic social power. This is not simply a case of one subject's domination over another. The roles of hypnotizer and hypnotized become blurred in the indirectness of Tarde's social epidemiology. Control is not by fear alone. It is the object of desire—belief—that reproduces obedience in the somnambulist. The somnambulist succumbs to the power of hypnosis because of involuntary fascinations, attractions, allures and absorptions, and active emotional engagements involved in the process of becoming hypnotized and believing in what is suggested to him. The obedience of the somnambulist is, as such, drawn to the virality of a love that is persistently invested in but never truly satisfied.

For Tarde, the desires and beliefs of the somnambulist appeared to originate in all-out chaos, but today the capturing of this accidental potential is ever more a reality, it seems. Indeed, marketers and political strategists are increasingly interested in the production of Thrift's premediated worlds, in which small flows can be cultivated into becoming significant waves. These new Tardean industrial nurseries prime imitative momentum, steering desire and belief and guiding end user attention toward a specified goal, "without a guiding hand."[43] Like the momentary appearance of phantom clouds, which can appear as mountains and giants, the marketer must carefully prearrange the encounter so that the discharged forces of desire and belief can be nursed into being. Again, like Milgram's Manhattan experiment, the hypnotist must keep her distance and bide her time. But with enough affective priming, added fascination, hormonal splashes, intoxicating glory, love, and celebrity worship, the attention (and distraction) of the lovelorn wasp will eventually be drawn to the imitations of his beloved orchid.

Persuasion and Absorption

The force of imitative encounter is a difficult event to grasp insofar as it is by and large insubstantial. The imitative ray is indeed a constituent of "unknown and unknowable . . . universal repetitions."[44] This is because a social contagion has a subrepresentational affective charge that seems to pass through social atmospheres, entering into the biology of the contaminated body via the skin before it triggers social actions, emotions, and thoughts.[45] The *organizing* principle (if that is the right word to use) of affective contagion is after all its deterritorialized flow and the capacity of that flow to contaminate whatever it comes into contact with. But what matters to the marketer today does not necessarily need to have a substance to persuade. Although imitation-suggestibility is, it would seem, without a body, the intensity of its flow is not entirely untraceable or, indeed, immeasurable.

Technological innovations have allowed business enterprises to detect flows of influence at the surface of the skin and regions of the brain even before a decision is made. As follows, the Tardean trajectory becomes traceable in the efforts marketers make to tap into the affective absorbency a consumer has to imitation-suggestibility. For example, so-called neuromarketers are deploying a combination of eye tracking, galvanic skin response (GSR), and electroencephalography (EEG) to develop new methods of persuasion. These practices map out correlations between what draws a consumer's spontaneous attention and changes in skin conductance and brain activity linked to inferred emotional states to better prime a "propensity to buy."[46] This is a deeper intensification of the technological unconscious currently entering into the realm of neuropersuasion, where the pretesting of involuntary and spontaneous consumption helps to ensure that marketing messages move more rapidly to memory, without the need for costly posttest surveys.

Of course, this technoexpansion into neurological unconsciousness raises big ethical questions concerning social power. Indeed, the technologies used to tap into the visceral relations consumers have with brands and products intervene in a seemingly entrenched ocularcentric Western paradigm. The pure reason of Enlightenment Man, linked as he so often is to a visual bias, representational objectivity, and the exclusion of subjective affect, comes into direct conflict with the idea that irreducible subrepresentational flows might actually have a mind of their own. There is nothing new in such a challenge. The notion of an unaffected ocularcentric reason has already been confronted by questions concerning the problematic distancing function the visual system establishes between subject and object,[47] and here I similarly approach problems relating to the pureness of the objective pathway that is assumed to relate objects to eyes and minds.

In his book *Downcast Eyes,* Martin Jay sets out how sight has been regarded as the noblest of the senses from Plato to Descartes.[48] Along these lines, the eye was supposed to separate out the objects we perceive from the stream of subjective affects absorbed in the general atmosphere. The visual apparatus is therefore, as Kant contended, "the purest intuition since it gives an immediate representation of an object without admixture of noticeable sensation."[49] Kant sought, as such, to determine attentiveness by screening out the meaningless reverie and distractions that disrupt visual attention. Kant's work certainly typified an eighteenth-century "imperative for thinkers of all kinds to discover what faculties, operations, or organs produced or allowed the complex coherence of conscious thought."[50] Arguably, though, as late as the mid-1990s, the mainstream sciences of the mind continued to neglect these disruptions to reasoning. Behavior, cognition, and, later on, computational neuroscience were all preferred to emotions, feelings, and affects. This was until 1994, when the neuroscientist Antonio Damasio's book *Descartes' Error* prompted a gradual shift in focus toward the significant role such disruptions play in cognitive processes. Damasio's approach argues that "reason may not be as pure as most of us think it is or wish it were."[51] Following on the heels of *Descartes' Error,* there has indeed been a prominent turn in the sciences of the mind to the relation between embodied (somatic) emotions and cognitive decision making. Over time, these ideas have inevitably perhaps become translated into design methodologies and technological innovations, most of which have supported business interests keen to tap into the mind and emotions of the consumer.

The Glint in the Eye of the Consumer

An interesting way in which to grasp how this shift in ideas concerning emotion and cognition has had an impact on methods of persuasion is to focus for a while on the technological detail of eye-tracking tests. This is because, although the supporting hypothesis behind eye tracking is fundamentally a Kantian proposition, its use in neuromarketing, alongside EEG and GSR, in particular, informs new methods of persuasion that aim to capture multisensory data from consumer testing.

The visual apparatus is thus regarded as an affective processor rather than an idealist representational mirror of the mind. Like this, then, persuasion strategies move away from seeing ideas and images as shapers of opinion toward the exploitation of the multisensory transmissions between humans and the objects to which they attend.

Eye-tracking tests quite literally measure what is attended to by following a glint in the eye of the consumer. Eye-tracking devices emit an infrared light, which is then reflected onto the eye (a corneal reflection). Two types of eye-tracking technology are currently in common use. In head-mounted systems, the glint in the eye is measured in relation to head movement, and in remote systems, its measurement is relative to the location of a fixed unit, meaning the head must remain still during testing. However, newer remote systems use multiple units, allowing for increased head movement. It is this latter kind of device that is frequently used in testing of on-screen eye motion. Data collected during tracking are broken down into *fixations, saccades,* and *scanpaths.* Fixations are measured according to duration (lasting between 250 and 500 milliseconds) and record attention (quite literally, when the eye becomes fixated). Saccades measure movement from one fixation to another (lasting 25–100 milliseconds). When fixations and saccadic movements are linked together, they form scanpaths. Eye-tracking data are captured and represented in either video format or as x–y coordinates on a screen. Most eye-tracking research presents data in the form of a heat map (see Figure 5.1), which shows the regions of most attention as hot and other less attended areas as cold.

What is ostensibly being measured in eye tracking is *thought* attention. As follows, its theoretical underpinnings are generally linked to Just and Carpenter's eye–mind hypothesis established in 1976, which states that "there is no appreciable lag between what is fixated and what is processed."[52] The usability researchers Poole and Ball describe in the following terms: "what a person is looking at is assumed to indicate the thought 'on top of the stack' of cognitive processes." Accordingly, they claim that the eye–mind hypothesis "means that eye-movement recordings can provide a dynamic trace of where a person's *attention* is being directed in relation to a visual display."[53]

Following this distinctly ocularcentric notion, then, the eye–mind

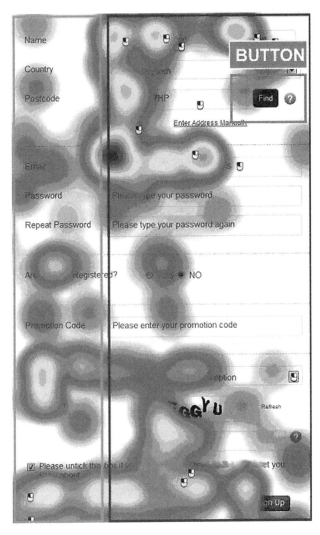

FIGURE 5.1. Eye-tracking heat map.

hypothesis traces a direct pathway of what enters the mind via the eye. However, there are anomalies present in visual research that suggest that the relation between sight and the mind is not as direct or seemingly conscious as it would seem. I'll refer here to just three. To begin with, a condition known as *blindsight* demonstrates how individuals with damaged primary visual cortex can unconsciously discern the shape and location of mental content without actually seeing it or, indeed, knowing about it.[54] Mental representations are apparently received via subcortical pathways and responded to by motorized responses like involuntary pointing.[55] The study of pupillometrics further relates the unconscious reception of a multitude of sensory stimuli, triggered by smell, taste, touch, and hearing, to pupil dilations, suggesting again that the journey between what is seen and what is thought is not a one-way street.[56] To be sure, the eye is not only tracked for movement and the fixing of attention, but by combining pupil dilation with blinking and gazing, some researchers claim that pupillometrics can reveal the eyes' interpretation of affective valence.[57] Although measurements of pupil dilation are often contaminated by cognitive overload or rogue sources of light, in conjunction with other ocular measurements, some eye-tracking manufacturers claim to be able to go "behind the cognitive curtain" to measure emotional engagement by recording the functioning of the visual system.[58] Last, the fairly recent identification of involuntary "microsaccades," which persist in attentive states like reading, watching TV, searching the web, and other activities requiring prolonged visual alertness, suggests that sight, like all other senses, is hardwired to unconscious neurological responses and is not simply a thought observation that separates an individual from his sensory environment.[59] So although eye movement reflects some kind of ongoing processes of information encoding, it does not necessarily reflect mental processes, nor does it indicate what is happening on the path to the mind after encoding has taken place.[60]

Eye tracking has become part of the methodological tool bag of product designers and neuromarketers, the latter of whom are increasingly using it in combination with EEG and GSR to make correlations between attentive states and what a consumer "feels about a product."[61] The aim is to substitute the biased inaccuracies of older marketing techniques reliant on self-reporting with objective measurements of eye movement, electrical activity in the brain, heart rate, and skin conductance and temperature to more effectively prime consumer arousal and manipulate memory.

One software innovation from the company iMotions flags a general turn to affect in eye-tracking technology. Rather than presupposing that what is being looked at equates to what is being thought, the Emotion Tool system has been developed to work with eye tracking to analyze the relation between cognitive and emotional consumption. Distinct from older systems that tend to measure user responses according to either voluntary attention or involuntary inattention, the Emotion Tool is intended to tap into the relation between the two. This signals a shift away from an older distinction. On one hand, the measurement of bodily gestures and orientation, voice intonation, eye contact, and evasion, and even nervous responses, was regarded as voluntary reactions associated with attentive cognitive reflection on what is attracting the eye. On the other hand, increases in heart, pulse, and breathing rates and body temperature and sweating were regarded as involuntary. The thinking behind the *Emotion Tool* conversely considers the relation between the *implicit,* unconscious part of the brain (the limbic system), which is widely recognized as being hardwired to the nervous system, and physical reactions of the *explicit,* conscious system (the frontal cortex). It is the somatic memory, physical responses, and emotions of the implicit system that are assumed to guide the explicit system.[62] As the developer of the Emotion Tool claims,

> It is now generally accepted that emotions dominate cognition, the mental process of the ability to think, reason and remember. Therefore, there is a rapidly increasing interest in methods that can tap into these mostly subconscious emotional processes, in order to gain knowledge and understanding of consumer behavior.[63]

To measure the emotional engagement of an attentive subject, the Emotion Tool tracks facial expressions, particularly those that occur around the eyes, the amount of blinking, the duration of the gaze, and pupil dilation. It also incorporates an algorithmic assessment of two dimensions of the emotional response: *emotional strength* and *valence*. The first is gauged by the level of excitement an external stimulus provokes in the consumer, whereas the second measures the feelings that follow the stimulus—the degree of attraction or aversion that an individual feels toward a specific object or event. Scores are calculated from a range of pleasant, unpleasant, or neither pleasant nor unpleasant. High scores are defined as "affective," low scores as "unaffective."

These new developments in marketing technology sidestep the explicit cognitive realm of visual representation and exploit instead the implicit, unconscious affective systems of consumption. The neuromarketer thus measures the streams of affect the consumer somatically absorbs in the atmosphere. As the enthusiastic CEO of one U.S.-based neuromarketing company puts it, these techniques help the marketer go beyond conscious consumer engagement with a product and actively seek out what unconsciously attracts him. "Absorption is the ideal," A. K. Pradeep claims. This is because it "signifies that the consumer's brain has not only registered your marketing message or your creative content, but that the other centers of the brain that are involved with emotions and memory have been activated as well."[64] Along these lines, persuasion and absorption seemingly involve priming the sensory experiences of consumption to achieve at least three design goals. First, designs must draw the attention of the consumer by "cultivating the ability to change what is focused on by intervening directly in perception."[65] Second, once attention is magnetized, the consumer must remain emotionally engaged in the product or brand. Finally, product designers need no longer survey the memory retention of the consumer. They can now anticipate purchase intention and steer it toward other predetermined points of fascination.

Product and brand design has for a long time now been saturated in sensory experiences, including the entrancing narratives of celebrity intended to cultivate purchasing decisions. But the turn to affect has also manifested itself more explicitly in so-called emotional design techniques in which the seizing of consumer attention begins at the "visceral level" of consumer experience.[66] As emotional design gurus assert, "brands are all about emotions [which] draw the consumer towards the product."[67] Fledgling designers are consequently encouraged to begin with the "affective processing" and "automatic, prewired layer of human interaction" that unconsciously influence behavior and reflective cognitions.[68] Again, this is not an entirely new approach. The goal of the marketer has always been to induce the consumer by illusory means. However, these many appeals to cognitive neuroscience provide an intriguing explanation of how subliminal advertising may in fact function[69] and how, in effect, the hypnosis can be perfected.

Noncognitive Capitalism

Similar innovations in political campaigning suggest that it may be possible to steer the affective contagions of the voter too. Echoing to some extent Lakoff's concern about the manipulation of the political unconscious, Thrift remarks,

> Modern political consultants now understand enough of the dynamics of imitative processes and brain–body chemistry to be able to make reasonably predictable interventions in the political unconscious of the democratic political process. . . . The result is that it is possible to tug on the behavior of voters by transferring these narratives into the political domain as forms of habitual response which the individual voter is plainly susceptible to.[70]

In the United States already, researchers have attempted to intervene in the moods of the voter using functional MRI to measure neural activity in the brains of Democrats and Republicans while they viewed pictures of the faces of George Bush, John Kerry, and Ralph Nader during the 2004 presidential campaign.[71] By studying emotion regions of the brain, such as the insula and anterior temporal poles, researchers were able to compare neural activity to a voter's self-reporting of feelings toward particular candidates. They claim that when a voter views a politician's face, cognitive control networks are activated that regulate emotional reactions according to political allegiance. Similar work has been carried out on swing voters' emotional responses to the candidates in the 2008 election and on Democrats viewing G. W. Bush's campaign commercial featuring the events of 9/11 and Lyndon Johnson's "daisy chain" advertisement from 1964.

If the destinies of emotion, feeling, affect, and political persuasion are indeed coupled to decisions in this way, then we might be observing the twenty-first-century realization of the imitative ray. Here we see how the mirror neuron hypothesis in neuroscience may come into the picture. Lakoff argues, as such, that people are connected by a brain circuitry that "fire[s] when we either perform a given action or see someone else perform the same action."[72] As follows, the activation of mirror neurons adds theoretical support to explanations of how empathic contagions spread through social networks, particularly in terms of the sharing of feelings, obsessions, compassions, admiration, and even mind reading. As Thrift asserts, the unearthing of the mirror neuron confirms

> a plausible neurophysiological explanation for the means by which the existence of the other is etched into the brain so that we are able to intuit what the other is thinking—we are able to "mind read"—not only because we see others' emotions but because we share them.[73]

With a similar focus on the mirror neuron hypothesis and contagious empathic transfers, Barbara Maria Stafford makes a radical intervention into the old dichotomy between rational freewill and ideological false consciousness, noting how the imitative echoic relation with the other begins entirely with the involuntary encounter.[74] It is arguably the volatility of this encounter that makes the somnambulist open to imitation-suggestibility. Indeed, the potential for marketers and politicians to mind read consumers and voters at this point in time and in the future is perhaps part of a shift in capitalism itself—a postcognitive or noncognitive capitalism, if you like. There is certainly a move away from a cognitive model of subjectivation, in which the information inputs and outputs of the black-box mind are managed and put to work, toward a neurological management of the unconscious, increasingly monitored and absorbed into a technological dream of action—no longer a model of the mind-as-digital-computer but an overstimulated twenty-first-century neurosomnambulist: someone who confuses what she believes, desires, and decides on with her own eyes and mind with what she dreams about.

Discerning the Indiscernible

This resuscitation of Tarde observes how his trajectory closely follows the line of flight of contemporary biopower. This is a distinctive exercise of control that occurs at the intersection point between conscious volition and involuntary, mechanical habit. It is at these vulnerable intersections that the mostly unconscious desire to imitate the suggestions of others is appropriated by social invention, becoming the infinitesimal imitation of imitation. This is the social according to Tarde and arguably a kind of social model becoming ever more the strategic focus of business enterprises and political machines. This is the Tardean dream of action—*a dream state that must surely be resisted*, or at least repotentialized. By way of a conclusion to this chapter, and the book as a whole, I therefore want to refer back to a number of ideas already introduced and ask the question, how is it possible to discern the mesmeric flows of twenty-first-century somnambulism? To provoke further discussion, I will look briefly at the revolutionary potential of empathy, love, attention, deception, capture–escape, and contamination. The problem here, though, is that Tarde's imitative ray functions as an action-at-a-distance. It is a force of contagious encounter that is separated in space with no known mediator of interaction. It is evidently tricky to discern the indiscernible.

Empathy

Lakoff's project makes a useful distinction between the neo-Con control of a "political unconscious" and Obama's strategic use of empathy.[75] On one hand, there is the cold, egolike self-interest of the G. W. Bush administration: a self-centeredness that, as the events of Hurricane Katrina demonstrated, is incapable of sharing in the feelings of others. Nonetheless, the neo-Con is expert in spreading his political influence via the emotions of fear and anxiety triggered by increasing contact with the [Islamic] Other. He maintains, as such, a dubious defense of an equally dubious version of democratic freedom to justify, among other things, domestic spying, torture and rendition, denial of habeas corpus, invading a country that posed no threat to the United States, and the subsequent killing and maiming of innocent civilians.[76] On the other hand, Obama-love talked directly to the electorate as a Progressive rendering of empathy. It characterized a shift away from the enlightened minds of the Democrats to an emphasis on *appearing* to put oneself in other people's shoes, or seeing the world through the eyes of others, and consequently giving the impression of caring about people. Lakoff certainly points optimistically to how Obama's concern with a love of difference had the potential to lead to new democratic equalities and changes in foreign policy.

Following what Lakoff flamboyantly refers to as the New Enlightenment project, it would seem that resistance to the control of the political unconscious requires the insertion of shared feelings into reasoned judgments.[77] The aim is to blend the small slice of conscious thought with the vast "invisible realm of neural circuitry not accessible to consciousnesses."[78] In sharp contrast to Kant's appeal to apathy, then, as a way to screen out meaningless reverie and distraction, empathy is supposed to intervene in the political unconscious, fending off the emotionally impaired judgments of Cheney and Rumsfeld. Resistance to the many attempts made by the paranoiac neo-Con to exploit the unconscious political mind is therefore assisted by "neuroscience, neural computation, cognitive linguistics, cognitive and developmental psychology, and so on."[79] This is perhaps an emergent democracy in which consumers and voters are able to discern the mind reading technologies deployed by the corporation and the politician.

The events leading to the election of the first black U.S. president were certainly marked by a global outpouring of viral love. But in hindsight, this moment in history has proved to be a capricious and ephemeral force of encounter. With no end to the War on Terror in sight, Obama-love is fast becoming a contemptible love gone bad. From those early Flickr election images to the computer game (first-person shooter) assassination of Bin Laden, Obama-love has certainly changed. However, while empathy makes the people feel good for a time, it has not delivered the political transformations it promised to. Indeed, empathy may have won an election, but it has not closed down Guantánamo!

Living Attention!

Brennan's concept of affective transmission similarly returns us to the virality of love. However, the focus is not so much on love in itself but rather on love's capacity to become a vehicle that transmits living attention.[80] As follows, love as an affect is different, Brennan contends, from envy, greed, anxiety, fear, and rage, which are negative affects requiring an independent medium of transmission. Love, in contrast, is both affect and the medium through which positive affect travels.[81] This makes it perhaps the ultimate and all-consuming mesmeric contagion in the sense that it is both virus and viral environment enfolded into one time–space. Yet, while the interventions of neuroscience have perhaps made it easier to quantify the emotional state of love in terms of affective valence and arousal, the problem of discerning whether living attention is part of a dream state or a legitimate action is not so easily addressed.

Like Lakoff to some extent, Brennan moves away from the psychoanalyst's tendency to balance conscious and unconscious states. She notes as such how Freud, overgenerously perhaps, implies a 50–50 split between conscious thought and subliminal unconscious. He readies himself, Brennan recounts, for psychoanalysis, sitting poised between actions and passions. On one hand, he is aware and reflective, while on the other, he is receptive and therefore open to affect.[82] In contrast, though, the discernment of the flows of living attention does not belong to well-balanced and self-contained individuals but facilitates instead a social relation without boundaries: a porous relation between self and other.

Whatever gathers attention or makes the transmission of affect discernable relates more readily to mechanical rather than reflective experiences. Like driving a car while daydreaming at the same time, living attention is a more imbalanced, in-between state, one in which the maintenance of what constitutes an awareness of self and environment is always open to, even overwhelmed by, affect. Therefore the unity of self subsists not in spite of but because of the spontaneity of affects.[83] For this reason, being able to discern affect is not about hard-line resistance but rather concerns being able to transform transmissions into something positive—in other words, adjust the valance of affective contagion from unpleasant to pleasant or from fear to love. As Brennan puts it, *resistance to affects is their transformation*.[84] Contrary, then, to the Trojan nature of Tardean love, Brennan emphasizes that love in itself carries with it positive affects. "Love is different in that it directs positive feelings towards the other by attending to the specificity of the other," she contends.[85] Living attention is, it would seem, a joyful encounter that passes through a medium of love. Love is indeed a vehicle: a transmitter of positive affect.[86]

Although affective transmissions are mostly unconscious, being able to transform incoming and outgoing affects requires some level of conscious intervention. This involves an effort to *educate* all the senses to discern what is socially absorbed (e.g., the feelings of others), via affective atmospheres, into the skin and the biology of infected subjectivities. Brennan's lesson is thus:

> Discernment begins with considering sensing (by smell, or listening, as well as observation)—the process of feeling that also operates, or seems to operate, as the gateway to emotional response. When we do not feel, we open the gates to all kinds of affective flotsam. We cease to discern the transmission of affect.... Uneducated, unconscious senses are not aware of any psychical, intelligent connection with the internal invisible body, and this unconsciousness extends to the rest of the environment.... Understanding the influences to which we are subjected in terms of passions and emotions, as well as living attention, means lifting of the burden of the ego's belief that it is self-contained in terms of the affects it experiences. Lifting off this burden liberates it ... allowing it to explore communication by smell and sound in ways that can heal it.[87]

The turn to affect may indeed prove to be an invaluable resource in challenging how Western cultures have made passion retreat into the blind love of the unconscious.[88] Nonetheless, following the trajectory of the Tardean diagram, viral love increasingly passes through a far more indistinct and inseparable conscious–unconscious state, which is becoming all the more vulnerable to Trojanlike flows of spontaneous joyful encounter intended to guide subjective attention and decisions to certain goals. Here the difference between the neo-Con manipulation of a political unconscious by way of fear and terror and the empathic flows of Obama-love is negotiable. Evidently, the problem for educators of the senses is how to discern the many efforts to persuade through direct and indirect appeals to the gut rather than the mind. The hypnotic dictatorship of the somnambulist is, as such, reproduced over and over again as a dream of action that manipulates beliefs and desires in mostly pleasurable and impulsive ways.

The Attentive Subject

Crary's historical account of attentive subjectivation turns the notion of living attention on its head. He introduces a Foucault–Tarde–inspired docile subjectivity falling under the hypnotic influence of an ever more media-saturated urban landscape. There is nothing enlightened about the attentive subject! Rather than contrasting inattention, distraction, reverie, and trance with the narrowing of an unaffected, attentive reason,[89] these two states become part of a continuum. Indeed, the failure of Kant's trajectory, particularly in his nineteenth-century reincarnation in scientific psychology, to isolate attention and make it distinct from flows of affect ends up as little more than a "modern dream of autonomy."[90] In contrast to the Enlightenment proposition that self-mastery can lead to liberation,[91] the attentive subject's trancelike state perfectly encapsulates "the ambivalent status of attention."[92]

Key to understanding this ambivalence is hypnosis, which, in the late nineteenth century, provided remarkable insight into what lies beyond conscious thought and "made clear that attentive states could be delineated in terms of absorption, dissociation, and suggestibility."[93] The hypnotist paradoxically reaches into the unconscious to expand awareness and effectively make the hypnotized subject "see and remember more."[94] The hypnotization of the attentive subject is endemic to the folding of a Foucauldian disciplinary diagram into a Deleuzian control society. It is a continuous diagram of control that renders behavior ever more automatic and predicable. At the turn of the century, the invention of new attentive media technologies began to replace hypnosis as a form of leisure time. Cinema, for example, incidentally corresponds with the demise of hypnosis from mainstream entertainment.[95] Nonetheless, the mesmeric principles remain embedded in the abstract diagram. Television subsequently "emerge[s] as the most pervasive and efficient system for the management of attention,"[96] followed by the Internet, which is now the latest extension of Edison's project to distribute attentive technologies to every corner of social and cultural life. As follows, this diagram needs to be seen in the distribution of the technological unconscious, where the all-pervasive track and trace computing and new persuasion methodologies are clandestinely deployed by a new media business enterprise. The neuromarketer's triangulation of emotional engagement, memory retention, and purchase intent is endemic to a disciplinary regime that conditions sensory experiences by way of revolutionizing the means of perception to paradoxically deploy distraction and guide attention.[97] Neuromarketing is part of a trend toward the emotional design of products and brands, thus providing the cultural logic of capitalism (incorporating the business school inventions of experience and attention economies) with a powerful mode of persuasion that engages the attentive subject like never before. Although, as Crary points out, statements concerning persuasion, along with addiction, habit, and control, have all but disappeared from recent mass media discourses,[98] they have, in the guise of neuromarketing, in particular, returned to haunt the end users of the new media. The reinvention of persuasion requires a "new" media theory or "evil" media study: one part of which scrutinizes the deceptive means by which attention is captured, while the other plans for the eventual subversion of the gaze.

"I Am Deceived, Therefore I Am"

What sets apart the concept of viral love from living attention is a complete lack of respect for the categorization of good and evil.[99] The evilness of Tardean love is apparent only insofar as the trickery, deception, and manipulation evident in its practices expose an indiscernible and paradoxical relation it has with goodness. The imitative radiations of viral love are embedded in relational networks as a sophistry. They feel like (*are* like) consciously appropriated natural flows. As Tarde argued, "*there is nothing more natural than that those who love each other should copy each other.*"[100] Yet it is in premeditated worlds that the imitative spontaneity of love can become absorbed into the skin and attention steered via mostly unconscious points of attraction–distraction to predefined destinations. Remember, the end user of evil media becomes fatigued, overworked, and stressed. It is in these lapses of concentration that she becomes attracted by distraction. As Fuller and Goffey point out, it is the sophistry apparent in the "paradoxical strategies" of evil media that breaks down the discernability of categories in which the distinction between good and evil (and attention and inattention) disintegrates.[101]

Here we observe the virality of present-day marketing, not simply in the hype of memetics or medical metaphors but also in the lessons learned from computer virus writing and, more recently, botnets. The viral declarations of the Love Bug, for instance, were not explicitly evil. It appealed to the passions, vanities, and obsessions of those users it contaminated. Computer viruses are indeed a pervasive evil media of persuasion that deploy Trojan traps and the wearing of masks of someone (or something) lovable to capture end users. Once caught up in the everyday repetitions, routines, and mechanical habits of computer usage, a user can easily drift toward potential windows of opportunity, which, when opened, spread contagion without a guiding hand. The botnet is the latest upgrade of this twenty-first-century Tardean dream of command and dream of action. A botnet paradoxically engages the end user's attention to distract her from the goal of infection. The user is steered toward an innocuous-looking .exe file, which, when opened, surreptitiously contaminates the user's machine, making it an unwitting zombie–actor in the spreading of further iterations of the infected code. The user and her machine thus become an involuntary intervallic node of exchange in a topology of command and control.[102]

How to Make "Getting Lost" a Valued User Experience

Concluding his book *Knowing Capitalism,* Thrift thinks through various methods of subversion and resistance to the ubiquity of the technological unconscious.[103] To be sure, the ushering in of the corporate-led *Internet of Things,* an RFID embedded world in which everyone and everything (a tuft of a carpet or grain of sand) can be wirelessly addressed, tracked, and traced, makes this struggle imperative. The site of resistance should move to the so-called Smart City model, where the power of the open-ended repetitions of biocapitalism will be most felt. Once upon a time, the study of web user navigation emphasized the need to let the user know exactly where he was in a system, but things are seemingly about to change. The user will no longer navigate the computer, but the body of the user will become the trigger for embedded interactions, in all manner of locations. It is now the system that needs to know where the user is. Here the making of a multiple social subject takes a sinister turn. Users will become subjects again, but in ways that are even more unknown to them and hidden in layers of often unwanted device-to-device interaction.

In this premediated world of sensors and triggers, "getting lost," Thrift contends, "will increasingly become a challenging and difficult task." Yet, if the ubicomp paradigm is anything like the breakable and bug-infested systems alongside which we have been working for the past couple of decades, then there is at least the potential for struggle. Thrift refers, as such, to "new kinds of 'excursions'" that can be "coaxed into existence." This new path to resistance may be discovered in exploitable flaws in security systems or source code hacks. Digital contagions and glitches will seep in from time to time and remind the end user of what a messy, patch-up job the network can be. To be sure, the rise of the network security breach suggests that if the network is indeed a distributed panopticon, then it resembles what Goffey and Fuller have more aptly described as a "more or less clumsily designed open prison."[104] So, although in the technological unconscious, the direction of attention is increasingly guided by an unseen hand, *at-a-distance,* perhaps we can, Thrift contends, "make a change in the direction of our attention, sensing possible emergences and new embodiments."

Tardean Antipatheia: Resisting the Biopolitical Contamination of Mood

The age of contagion is no longer synonymous with the age of networks. In the past five years or so, there has been a marked shift away from the discourses of the network age toward the age of austerity. In contrast to the threats and affordances of abundant connectivity, socioeconomic reality is shaped by the overspills of the subprime contagion. It is perhaps not surprising, then, to discover that the neo-Con economist is keen to gauge the mood of the nation. As one news report recently put it, against the backdrop of deep cuts and growing unemployment, the United Kingdom's neo-Con government intends "to make happiness the new GDP."[105] "There is more to progress," they say, "than narrow economics."[106] Well, one aim of this stratagem of well-being is arguably to appeal to the political unconscious in times of hardship for the poor and fat bonuses for the rich and to convince voters that "there's more to life than money." The proposed "big society" project is nothing more than an unconvincing endeavor to contaminate the mood of the nation with the feeling that *we are all in this together*. With similar embryonic political incursions into the feelings of the voter already under way in the U.S. research community, questions concerning resistance to contamination need to move beyond the problem of discerning the affective valence between fearsome or joyful encounters. The challenge now is to drill down into the molecularity of what spreads so as to determine the political deceptions of present-day biopower.

What lessons can be learned from Tarde? The question of how to resist the many efforts to contaminate mood is, of course, complicated by his insistence that what spreads from self to other can infect the entire affective valence. So while both Brennan and Hardt have similarly forwarded love as a way of learning to feel the sensations of others and discern the negative affect of a love gone bad, the virality of a Tardean love seems to be able to evade the power of living attention by appealing indirectly to the gut. Viral love is noncognitive but has a mind of its own. This leaderless hypnotist can steer unconscious beliefs and desires, guide attention via passions and fascinations, and influence decision-making processes by way of a visceral contamination that elides cognition. For this reason, a potential resistance movement may need, as Thrift contends, to become actualized from within the biopolitics of imitation itself: a social invention organized around the very "speed and imitative capacities" of the networks that function to otherwise denigrate democracy.[107] What this infers is a counterpolitics of imitation that spreads not by way of love but similarly through sympathy. We might consider here attempts to trigger countercontagions in the shape of vigils, gatherings, protests, online petitions, campaigns, and fund-raising events. Yet, once again, Tarde's skepticism concerning counterimitation needs to be noted:

> In counter-imitating one another, that is to say, in doing or saying the exact opposite of what they observe being done or said, they are becoming more and more assimilated, just as much assimilated as if they did or said precisely what was being done or said around them. . . .

There is nothing more imitative than fighting against one's natural inclination to follow the current of these things, or than pretending to go against it.[108]

In short, then, by becoming an adversary, one simply becomes more associated in the assemblage of imitation. This is how, in the process of nonverbal communication, for example, opposing facial expressions do not simply oppose people but unconsciously associate them in an assemblage of imitation and counterimitation. In other words, there is, in a crowd, an open repetition of facial expressions (anger, surprise, shock, disgust, contempt, and sadness) all relating one face to the next, and so on.

One way in which we might become disconnected from the affective grip of these associative chains is through the suppression of empathy: a refusal to engage in the transmission of affects, emotions, and feelings of others. But of course, Tarde would not accept the Kantian proposition of apathy either. Such a break in communication with affective capacities would be regarded as impossible. On the contrary, to break from these associative chains, he makes a crucial distinction between counterimitation and nonimitation.[109] In sharp contrast to sympathy, empathy, and indeed apathy, Tarde's nonimitation is achieved through pure antipathy. This is not therefore a disconnection or nonsocial relation but a nonimitation of, and thus antisocial relation with, a "neighbor who is in touch."[110]

What Tarde proposes as an alternative seems to counterintuitively reject Hardt's love of difference as a way to achieve spontaneous democracy insofar as he offers a distinctly cognizant "refusal . . . to copy the dress, customs, language, industry, and arts which make up the civilization of [this or that] neighborhood."[111] Nonimitation requires a constant assertion of antagonism, "obstinacy," "pride," and "indelible feelings of superiority" that empowers and produces a "rupture of the umbilical cord between the old and the new society."[112] It involves a declaration that all other societies are "absolutely and forever alien" and an undertaking never to reproduce the rights, usages, and ideas of any other society. It is indeed nonimitation that Tarde contends purges the social of the contagions of the other. It is only after this purge that old customs can be replaced by truly new fashions. For Tarde, then, it is the long-term maintenance of nonimitation that ensures that those who wish to resist the contagions of the present political climate will in a moment of spontaneous revolution "no longer find any hindrance in the way of [their own] conquering activity."[113]

Tarde's recourse to antipathy returns this book to the central theme of the network and the various claims made that regard contemporary contagions as the result of "too much connectivity" or "increased contact" (see the introduction). These claims seem to lead logically to resistance through either outright disconnection or a global call to action through empathy with the other. However, it is important to note at least two prerequisites Tarde forwards to support how antipathy and nonimitation might resist the magnetisms of imitative flows without becoming necessarily disconnected or connected. The first concerns the paradox of the dream of action. That is to say, the somnambulist condition subsists in paradoxical in-between spaces in which subjectivities are seemingly voluntarily connected, yet, at the same time, involuntarily associated. It is in this absurd neighborhood of dreams that hypnotized subjects willingly engage in the deceptions of others. Second, and in contrast to empathy, resistance to somnambulism—antipathetic nonimitation—is quite literally a refusal to share the feelings of others to "purge the social mass of mixed ideas and volitions."[114] Indeed, to eliminate discrimination and discord, Tarde forwards the idea that the nonimitation of "extraneous and heterogeneous" social invention helps "harmonious" groups spread out and extend themselves and to "entrench themselves in the custom-imitation of which they are the object."[115]

Have we come all this way to discover that resistance to contagion necessitates a dictatorship of love rather than an anarchic and spontaneous mode of democratic self-rule? Well, not quite, since Tarde's in-between space of nonimitation, sooner or later, supports novel social inventions that move away from the harmonious mainstream of organized molar states toward a potential molecular revolution. The old customs are generally replaced by the nonperiodic forward motion of new fashions, which insert themselves, like Trojans, into the periodic and mechanical habits of rituals, beliefs, behaviors, and so on. These "anterior models" are ready to spread, "when the moment has come for civilizing revolution," to "cut a path for fashion-imitation."[116] The education of the senses should not, according to Tarde, result in impassive or apathetic responses or the sharing of feelings via empathy or sympathy but rather through *antipatheia*: antifeelings that may fend off the contaminations of unwanted and mostly unconscious epidemics of viral love. Antipatheia and nonimitation might, as such, help to sustain the propagation of molecular anterior social inventions, which will, in time, spontaneously, and promiscuously, grow into revolutionary contagions too big to be constrained to any molar organization.

Acknowledgments

This book is the product of a capricious series of imitative encounters beginning in the late 1990s with my good friend Jairo Lugo, with subsequent inspiration from Luciana Parisi and Tiziana Terranova (who first suggested Tarde). From this point on, the concept of virality started to spread, and following a network encounter with Jussi Parikka around 2004, these ideas developed into a wider project on spam and viral culture. Thanks all.

Special thanks to Sian, Harry, Daisy, Sam, and my parents for their support during the painful process of writing. Thanks also to the editorial team at the University of Minnesota Press.

No thanks whatsoever go to the ConDem coalition government for their butchering of the already limited opportunity for social and cultural mobility in the United Kingdom. Shame on all the privately educated MPs who voted to turn widening access to a public university sector into a marketplace that favors the rich. *No ifs, no buts, no education cuts!*

Notes

Introduction

1. Jan Van Dijk, *The Network Society* (London: Sage, 2006), 187.

2. Michael Hardt and Antonio Negri, *Empire* (Cambridge, Mass.: Harvard University Press, 2000), 136.

3. Former U.K. prime minister Tony Blair's speech on the Iraq crisis in the House of Commons on Tuesday, March 18, 2003, http://www.guardian.co.uk/politics/2003/mar/18/foreignpolicy.iraq1. See also Barry Johnston and Oana M. Nedelescu, "The Impact of Terrorism on Financial Markets," working paper WP/05/60, International Monetary Fund, http://www.imf.org/external/pubs/ft/wp/2005/wp0560.pdf.

4. E.g., Duncan Watts, *Six Degrees: The Science of a Connected Age* (London: Vintage, 2003); Albert-László Barabási, *Linked* (London: Plume, 2003). On emotions as disease, see Alison L. Hill, David G. Rand, Martin A. Nowak, and Nicholas A. Christakis, "Emotions as Infectious Diseases in a Large Social Network: The SISa Model," *Proceedings of the Royal Society, Series B,* e-pub before print, http://rspb.royalsocietypublishing.org/content/early/2010/07/03/rspb.2010.1217.full.

5. Gilles Deleuze, *Foucault* (London: Athlone Press, 1988), 36, 34–44.

6. Ibid., 36.

7. Gilles Deleuze, *Difference and Repetition,* trans. Paul Patton (New York: Columbia University Press, 1994), 288.

8. Eugene Thacker, "Living Dead Networks," *Fibreculture Journal*, no. 4 (2005), http://journal.fibreculture.org/issue4/issue4_thacker.html. For more on viral discourse, see Stefan Helmreich, "Flexible Infections: Computer Viruses, Human Bodies, Nation-States, Evolutionary Capitalism," *Science, Technology, and Human Values* 25, no. 4 (2000): 472–491, http://web.mit.edu/anthropology/

faculty_staff/helmreich/PDFs/flexible_infections.pdf; Jussi Parikka, "Digital Monsters, Binary Aliens—Computer Viruses, Capitalism, and the Flow of Information," *Fibreculture Journal,* no. 4 (2005), http://journal.fibreculture.org/issue4/issue4_parikka.html; Tony D. Sampson, "Dr Aycock's Bad Idea: Is the Good Use of Computer Viruses Still a Bad Idea?" *Media and Culture Journal* 8, no. 1 (2005), http://journal.media-culture.org.au/0502/02-sampson.php.

9. Nigel Thrift, *Non-representational Theory: Space/Politics/Affect* (London: Routledge, 2008), 239.

10. Ibid.

11. Nigel Thrift, "Space," *Theory, Culture, and Society* 23, nos. 2–3 (2006): 139.

12. Gilles Deleuze, *The Fold: Leibniz and the Baroque,* trans. Tom Conley (Minneapolis: University of Minnesota Press, 1993). Bruno Latour has similarly linked Tarde's "many interlocking monads" to actor network theory. Bruno Latour, "Gabriel Tarde and the End of the Social," in *The Social in Question: New Bearings in History and the Social Sciences,* ed. Patrick Joyce, 117–32 (London: Routledge, 2002).

13. Nigel Thrift, "Pass It On: Towards a Political Economy of Propensity," 14, http://wrap.warwick.ac.uk/1085/1/WRAP_Thrift_0170426-150709-pass_it_on_towards_a_political_economy_of_propensity_nigel_thrify_asof15_7_09.pdf, later published in Matei Candea, ed., *The Social after Tarde: Debates and Assessments* (London: Routledge, 2010), 248–70.

14. Ibid., 5.

15. See, e.g., Candea, *Social after Tarde,* 248–70.

16. "Toute chose est une société, que tout phénomène est un fait social." Gabriel Tarde, *Monadologie et sociologie* (Paris: Les empêcheurs de penser en rond, 1895), 58.

17. Bruno Latour, "Tarde's Idea of Quantification," in Candea, *Social after Tarde,* 155.

18. Gilles Deleuze and Félix Guattari, *A Thousand Plateaus* (London: Continuum, 1987), 218–19.

19. Brian Massumi, *A User's Guide to Capitalism and Schizophrenia: Deviations from Deleuze and Guattari* (Cambridge, Mass.: MIT Press, 1992), 192–93.

20. Ibid., 54.

21. Manuel DeLanda, *A New Philosophy of Society: Assemblage Theory and Social Complexity* (London: Continuum, 2006), 5, 12–13.

22. Deleuze, *Difference and Repetition,* 223.

23. Massumi, *A User's Guide to Capitalism and Schizophrenia,* 55.

24. Ibid., 192; emphasis added.

25. See David Hume on this unbreakable contract between nature and

society in which all society can do is "pretend to . . . give new direction" to the passions of human nature. David Hume, *A Treatise of Human Nature* (1888; repr., Oxford: Oxford University Press, 1980), 521. See also Deleuze's "indissoluble complex" in Gilles Deleuze, *Empiricism and Subjectivity: An Essay on Hume's Theory of Human Nature,* trans. Constantin V. Boundas (New York: Columbia University Press, 1991), 46.

26. Teresa Brennan, *The Transmission of Affect* (Ithaca, N.Y.: Cornell University Press, 2004), 62–63.

27. Thrift, "Pass It On," 6.

28. Gabriel Tarde, *The Laws of Imitation,* trans. E. C. Parsons (New York: Henry Holt, 1903), preface to the 2nd ed., xv; Thrift, "Pass It On," 6.

29. A reenactment of which occurred at the Tarde/Durkheim: Trajectories of the Social Conference, St. Catharine's College, Cambridge, March 14–15, 2008, http://www.crassh.cam.ac.uk/events/2007–8/tardedurkheim.html.

30. Ibid.

31. Paul Marsden, "Forefathers of Memetics: Gabriel Tarde and the Laws of Imitation," *Journal of Memetics: Evolutionary Models of Information Transmission* 4 (2000), http://cfpm.org/jom-emit/2000/vol4/marsden_p.html.

32. Deleuze and Guattari, *A Thousand Plateaus,* 29–30.

33. Gabriel Tarde, "Economic Psychology," trans. Alberto Toscano, *Economy and Society* 36, no. 4 (2007): 633.

34. Ibid.

35. Ibid.

36. Thrift, *Non-representational Theory,* 236–37.

37. George Lakoff, *The Political Mind: A Cognitive Scientist's Guide to Your Brain and Its Politics* (London: Penguin, 2008).

38. Gabriel Tarde, *Laws of Imitation,* 202.

39. Ibid., 218–19.

40. Maurizio Lazzarato, *Puissances de l'Invention: La Psychologie Économique de Gabriel Tarde contre l'Économie Politique* (Paris: Les Empêcheurs de Penser en Rond, 2002).

41. Latour, "Gabriel Tarde and the End of the Social"; Bruno Latour and Vincent Antonin Lépinay, *The Science of Passionate Interests: An Introduction to Gabriel Tarde's Economic Anthropology* (Chicago: Prickly Paradigm Press, 2009); Thrift, "Pass It On"; Lisa Blackman, "Reinventing Psychological Matters: The Importance of the Suggestive Realm of Tarde's Ontology," *Economy and Society* 36, no. 4 (2007): 576; Christian Borch, "Urban Imitations: Tarde's Sociology Revisited," *Theory Culture Society* 22, no. 81 (2005): 83.

1. Resuscitating Tarde's Diagram in the Age of Networks

1. Manuel DeLanda, *A New Philosophy of Society*.

2. Gilles Deleuze, *Foucault*, 36.

3. Ibid.

4. "What fundamentally distinguishes humans from animals is not language but the capacity to imitate and this ability to imitate is innate: babies as young as 41 minutes have been shown to imitate. In other words, imitation provides a novel evolutionary pathway for learning. Babies do not learn to imitate, they learn by imitating, and imitation is the prelude to and facilitator of verbal communication." Thrift, "Pass It On," 9.

5. Anne Sauvagnargues, as cited in Francois Dosse, *Gilles Deleuze and Felix Guattari: Intersecting Lives* (New York: Columbia University Press, 2010), 159.

6. Gabriel Tarde, *Social Laws: An Outline of Sociology* (Ontario, Quebec: Batoche Books, 2000), 136.

7. Tarde, *Laws of Imitation*, 77.

8. Bruno Latour, "Tarde's Idea of Quantification," in Candea, *Social after Gabriel Tarde*, 116.

9. Tarde, *Social Laws*, 187.

10. Ibid., 135–36; emphasis added.

11. Ibid., 4.

12. Thrift, *Non-representational Theory*, 235–39.

13. Gilles Deleuze, *Bergonism* (New York: Zone Books, 2002), 44.

14. Deleuze and Guattari, *A Thousand Plateaus*, 218–19. *Invention*, as it is used here, perhaps corresponds with Tarde's own somewhat "overstretched" meaning of the word. Tarde, *Laws of Imitation*, xiv. See also Latour and Lépinay, *Science of Passionate Interests*, 34–35.

15. Latour and Lépinay, *Science of Passionate Interests*, 46.

16. Ibid., 42–43.

17. Tarde, *Social Laws*, 136–37.

18. Ibid., 136–39.

19. Ibid., 143.

20. Andrea Mu Brighenti, "Tarde, Canetti, and Deleuze on Crowds and Packs," paper presented at the Tarde/Durkheim: Trajectories of the Social Conference, St. Catharine's College, Cambridge, March 14–15, 2008.

21. Tarde, *Social Laws*, 171.

22. Deleuze and Guattari, *A Thousand Plateaus*, 219.

23. Tarde, *Laws of Imitation*, 43–44.

24. Ibid., 44.

25. Ibid., 17.

26. Tarde, *Social Laws*, 171.

27. Tarde, *Laws of Imitation*, 109.

28. Latour, "Tarde's Idea of Quantification," 116.

29. Thrift, "Pass It On," 2.

30. Latour and Lépinay, *Science of Passionate Interests*, 68.

31. Christian Borch, "Crowds and Economic Life: Bringing an Old Figure Back In," paper presented at the Centre for the Study of Invention and Social Processes, Goldsmiths College, London, November 21, 2005, http://www.gold.ac.uk/media/borch_crowds_economic.pdf. See also Borch, "Crowds and Economic Life: Bringing an Old Figure Back In," *Economy and Society* 36, no. 4 (2007): 549–73.

32. Lisa Blackman, "Reinventing Psychological Matters: The Importance of the Suggestive Realm of Tarde's Ontology," *Economy and Society* 36, no. 4 (2007): 576.

33. David Toews, "The New Tarde: Sociology after the End of the Social," *Theory, Culture, and Society* 20, no. 81 (2003): 86.

34. Ibid.

35. Eric Alliez, as cited in ibid., 81–98.

36. Borch, "Urban Imitations," 83.

37. Tarde, *Social Laws*, 84.

38. Ibid., 83–84.

39. Tarde, as cited in Borch, "Urban Imitations," 83.

40. Tarde, *Laws of Imitation*, 53–54.

41. Borch, "Urban Imitations," 92.

42. Ibid., 92–93.

43. Ibid.

44. Elias Canetti, *Crowds and Power* (New York: Farrar, Straus, and Giroux, 1984), 31–32.

45. Ibid.

46. Ibid.

47. Tarde, *Laws of Imitation*, 70, 288.

48. Tarde, *Social Laws*, 178.

49. Bruno Latour, "Gabriel Tarde and the End of the Social," in *The Social in Question: New Bearings in History and the Social Sciences*, ed. Patrick Joyce, 117–32 (London: Routledge, 2002), http://www.bruno-latour.fr/sites/default/files/82-TARDE-JOYCE-SOCIAL-GB.pdf.

50. Gabriel Tarde, preface to the second edition of *Laws of Imitation*, xiv.

51. See "Facebook Helps You Connect and Share with the People in Your Life," http://www.facebook.com/pages/Freindship/111892948828649 (*sic*).

52. S. Harrison, D. Tatar, and P. Sengers, "The Three Paradigms of HCI," in

Proceedings of CHI, http://people.cs.vt.edu/~srh/Downloads/TheThreePara-digmsofHCI.pdf.

53. Deleuze, *Difference and Repetition,* 314.

54. Émile Durkheim, *The Rules of the Sociological Method,* trans. W. D. Halls (1895; repr., New York: Free Press, 1982). See chapter V.

55. Latour, "Gabriel Tarde and the End of the Social."

56. Tony D. Sampson, "Error-Contagion: Network Hypnosis and Collective Culpability," in *Error: Glitch, Noise, and Jam in New Media Cultures,* ed. Mark Nunes (New York: Continuum, 2010), 239–40.

57. Émile Durkheim, preface to the second edition of *The Division of Labor in Society,* trans. W. D. Halls (New York: Free Press, 1984), xxxv–ivii.

58. Robert Keith Sawyer, *Social Emergence: Societies as Complex Systems* (Cambridge: Cambridge University Press, 2005), 1–9, 63–124; Elias L. Khalil and Kenneth Ewart Boulding, eds., *Evolution, Order and Complexity* (London: Routledge, Taylor, and Francis, 1996); Jennifer M. Lehmann, *Deconstructing Durkheim: A Post-post-structuralist Critique* (London: Routledge, 1993), 129; and N. J. Enfield and Stephen C. Levinson, eds., *Roots of Human Sociality: Culture, Cognition, and Interaction* (Oxford: Berg, 2006), 377.

59. Émile Durkheim, *The Elementary Forms of the Religious Life,* trans. Joseph Ward Swain (London: George Allen and Unwin, 1915), 444.

60. Émile Durkheim, *The Rules of the Sociological Method,* trans. W. D. Halls (1884; repr., New York: Free Press, 1982), chapter V.

61. Ibid., 129.

62. It is claimed, for example, that as much as 98 percent of attention, deci-sions, and intent derives from the unconscious functioning of the brain. Lakoff, *The Political Mind.*

63. Maurizio Lazzarato, as cited in Thrift, *Non-representational Theory,* 230.

64. Gabriel Tarde, preface to the second edition of *The Laws of Imi-tation,* xi.

65. Thrift, *Non-representational Theory,* 237.

66. Marsden, "Forefathers of Memetics."

67. Ibid.

68. Ibid.

69. Tarde, *Laws of Imitation,* 361.

70. Richard Dawkins, *The Selfish Gene* (Oxford: Oxford University Press, 1977), 202–33.

71. Tarde, *Laws of Imitation,* xvii.

72. Latour, "Gabriel Tarde and the End of the Social."

73. Ibid.

74. Ibid.

75. Ibid.

76. Ibid.

77. Ibid.

78. Tarde, "Economic Psychology," 618.

79. Ibid., 622.

80. Tarde, *Laws of Imitation*, 61.

81. Jonathan Crary, *Suspensions of Perception: Attention, Spectacle, and Modern Culture* (London: MIT Press, 2001), 45–46.

82. Thrift, *Non-representational Theory*, 243.

83. Alex R. Galloway and Eugene Thacker, "On Narcolepsy," in *The Spam Book: On Viruses, Porn, and Other Anomalies from the Dark Side of Digital Culture*, ed. Jussi Parikka and Tony D. Sampson (Cresskill, N.J.: Hampton Press, 2009), 251–53.

84. Deleuze and Guattari, *A Thousand Plateaus*, 29–30.

85. Bruno Latour, *Pandora's Hope: Essays on the Reality of Science Studies* (Cambridge, Mass.: Harvard University Press, 1999), 9.

86. Thrift, *Non-representational Theory*, 110.

87. Ibid., 110–111.

88. Deleuze and Guattari, *A Thousand Plateaus*, 226.

89. François Dosse, *Gilles Deleuze and Felix Guattari: Intersecting Lives*, trans. Deborah Glassman (New York: Columbia University Press, 2010), 15.

90. Deleuze and Guattari, *A Thousand Plateaus*, 10.

91. Ibid., 407.

92. Ibid.

93. Derek W. Dunn et al., "A Role for Parasites in Stabilising the Fig–Pollinator Mutualism," *PLoS Biology* 6, no. 3 (2008), http://www.plosbiology.org/article/info%3Adoi%2F10.1371%2Fjournal.pbio.0060059.

94. Samuel Butler, *Erewhon; or, Over the Range* (New York: E. P. Dutton, 1872), http://etext.lib.virginia.edu/toc/modeng/public/ButErew.html.

95. Gilles Deleuze and Félix Guattari, *Anti-Oedipus* (London: Athlone Press, 1984), 285.

96. Deleuze and Guattari, *A Thousand Plateaus*, 241.

97. Massumi, *A User's Guide to Capitalism and Schizophrenia*, 96, 192.

98. Tarde, *Laws of Imitation*, 38.

99. Félix Guattari, *Chaosmosis* (Sydney, Australia: Power, 1995), 27.

100. Ibid., 41.

101. Thrift, "Pass It On," 8.

102. Thrift, *Non-representational Theory*, 221–25, 232.

103. Anne Gaskett, Claire Winnick, and Marie Herberstein, "Orchid Voyeurs," *The American Naturalist*, June 2008.

104. Luciana Parisi, *Abstract Sex* (London: Continuum, 2004), 45.

105. Ibid., 12.

106. Ibid., 145, 201.

107. Tarde, *Laws of Imitation*, xi.

108. Thrift, *Non-representational Theory*, 231–32.

109. Tarde, *Laws of Imitation*, 83–84.

110. Crary, *Suspensions of Perception*, 49.

111. Thrift, *Non-representational Theory*, 232–33.

112. Ibid., 243.

113. Ibid., 247–50.

114. Teresa Brennan, *The Transmission of Affect* (Ithaca, N.Y.: Cornell University Press, 2004), 54.

115. Thrift, *Non-representational Theory*, 220–21, 236.

116. Stanley Milgram, Leonard Bickman, and Lawrence Berkowitz, "Note on the Drawing Power of Crowds of Different Size," *Journal of Personality and Social Psychology* 13, no. 2 (1969): 79–82.

117. April Mara Barton, "Application of Cascade Theory to Online Systems: A Study of Email and Google Cascades," *Minnesota Journal of Law, Science, and Technology* 10, no. 2 (2009): 474.

118. Stanley Milgram, *Obedience to Authority* (New York: Harper and Row, 1974), 144–15. As Milgram defines imitation, "conformity is imitation but obedience is not. Conformity leads to homogenization of behavior, as the influenced person comes to adopt the behavior of peers. In obedience, there is compliance without imitation of the influencing source. A soldier does not simply repeat an order given to him but carries it out."

119. Charles Mackay, *Memoirs of Extraordinary Popular Delusions and the Madness of Crowds* (London: Office of the National Illustrated Library, 1852, 1848), http://www.econlib.org/library/Mackay/macExCover.html.

120. Sadie Plant, foreword to Parikka and Sampson, *The Spam Book,* ix.

121. Barbara Maria Stafford, *Echo Objects: The Cognitive Work of Images* (Chicago: University of Chicago Press, 2007), 75–81; Lakoff, *Political Mind*, 39–40. See also Thrift, "Pass It On."

122. Stafford, *Echo Objects*, 75–81.

123. Lakoff, *Political Mind*, 125.

124. Christopher Lydon, "Obama in a Bind," interview with George Lakoff, Radio Open Source, Watson Institute for International Studies, Brown University, July 10, 2008, http://www.radioopensource.org/george-lakoff-obama-in-a-bind/.

125. "The same part of the brain we use in seeing is also used in imagining that we are seeing, in remembering seeing, in dreaming that we are seeing, and in understanding language about seeing." Lakoff, *Political Mind*, 39.

126. Ibid., 9.

127. Thrift, "Pass It On," 4.

128. Thrift, *Non-representational Theory*, 235–36.

129. Thrift, "Pass It On," 14.

130. Thrift, *Non-representational Theory*, 236.

131. Ibid., 229–30, 237.

132. Ibid.

133. Tarde, "Economic Psychology," 627.

134. Thrift, *Non-representational Theory*, 230.

135. Ibid.

136. Thrift, "Pass It On," 6.

137. Thrift, *Non-representational Theory*, 231.

138. Ibid., 238.

139. Thrift, "Pass It On," 2.

140. Ibid., 5.

141. Thrift, *Non-representational Theory*, 238.

142. Ibid., 236–37.

143. Ibid., 241.

144. Thrift, "Pass It On," 23.

145. Ibid.

146. Thrift, *Non-representational Theory*, 229–30.

147. Thrift, "Pass It On," 14.

148. Ibid., 5.

149. Ibid., 20–22.

150. Tarde, *Laws of Imitation*, 77.

2. What Spreads?

1. Susan Blackmore, *The Meme Machine* (Oxford: Oxford University Press, 1999), 204–18.

2. Gustave Le Bon, *The Crowd: A Study of the Popular Mind* (New York: Dover, 2002), 15.

3. Ralph F. Wilson, "The Six Simple Principles of Viral Marketing," *Web Marketing Today,* February 1, 2005, http://www.wilsonweb.com/wmt5/viral-principles-clean.htm. See also Seth Godin, *Unleashing the Idea Virus* (London: Free Press, 2000).

4. Esther Dyson, "Second Sight," *The Guardian,* April 8, 1999, http://www.guardian.co.uk/Archive/Article/0,4273,3850829,00.html. See also David Harley, Robert Slade, and Urs E. Gattiker, *Viruses Revealed* (New York: Osborne/McGraw-Hill, 2001), 409.

5. Aaron Lynch, *Thought Contagion: How Belief Spreads through Society* (New York: Basic Books, 1996).

6. Charlie Cook, "Got Meme? How to Attract Your Clients and Customer's

Attention," *Add Me Newsletter,* October 8, 2003, http://www.addme.com/issue304.htm.

7. Ibid.

8. Godin, *Unleashing the Idea Virus,* 25–26.

9. Thrift, *Non-representational Theory,* 243–45.

10. Thrift, "Pass It On," 16.

11. Blackmore, *Meme Machine,* 24.

12. Richard Dawkins, *The Selfish Gene* (Oxford: Oxford University Press, 1977), 192.

13. Dawkins, as cited in Blackmore, *Meme Machine,* vxi.

14. Richard Dawkins, "Viruses of the Mind," in *Dennett and His Critics: Demystifying Mind,* ed. Bo Dalhbom, 13–27 (Cambridge, Mass.: Blackwell, 1993).

15. Ibid., 19.

16. Daniel Dennett, *Consciousness Explained* (London: Penguin, 1991); Douglas Hofstadter, *Metamagical Themas: Questing for the Essence of Mind and Pattern* (New York: Basic Books, 1985); Lynch, *Thought Contagion*; and Blackmore, *Meme Machine.*

17. Mario Vaneechoutte, "The Memetic Basis of Religion," *Nature* 365 (1993): 290.

18. Alejandro Lynch and Allan Baker, "A Population Memetics Approach to Cultural Evolution in Chaffinch Song: Meme Diversity within Populations," *American Naturalist* 141 (1993): 597–620.

19. David Rowe and Joseph Rogers, "A Social Contagion Model of Adolescent Sexual Behavior: Explaining Race Differences," *Social Biology* 41 (1994): 1–18.

20. Adam Westoby, "The Ecology of Intentions: How to Make Memes and Influence People: Culturology," Working Paper Series, Center for Cognitive Studies, 1994, http://ase.tufts.edu/cogstud/papers/ecointen.htm.

21. Liane Gabora, "Meme and Variations: A Computational Model of Cultural Evolution," in *Lectures in Complex Systems,* ed. Lynn Nadel and Daniel Stein, 471–85 (Reading, Mass.: Addison-Wessley, 1993).

22. Hans-Cees Speel, "Memetics: On a Conceptual Framework for Cultural Evolution," http://imagomundi.com.br/cultura/memes_speel.pdf.

23. *Journal of Memetics: Evolutionary Models of Information Transmission,* http://www.jom-emit.org/.

24. Blackmore, *Meme Machine,* 4.

25. Ibid., 55.

26. Dawkins, "Viruses of the Mind," 14.

27. Dennett, *Consciousness Explained,* 207.

28. Blackmore, *Meme Machine,* 204–18.

29. Ibid., 204.

30. Lynch, *Thought Contagion,* 5–6.

31. Ibid., 107.

32. Blackmore, *Meme Machine,* 2, 233–34.

33. Ibid., 234.

34. Keith Ansell Pearson, *Philosophy and the Adventure of the Virtual: Bergson and the Time of Life* (London: Routledge, 2002), 82.

35. Bruce Edmonds, "The Revealed Poverty of the Gene–Meme Analogy—Why Memetics Per Se Has Failed to Produce Substantive Results," *Journal of Memetics: Evolutionary Models of Information Transmission* 9 (2005), http://cfpm.org/jom-emit/2005/vol9/edmonds_b.html.

36. Richard Dawkins, as cited in Blackmore, *Meme Machine,* xii.

37. Ibid., x.

38. Ibid., 215.

39. Claude Shannon and Warren Weaver, *The Mathematical Theory of Communication* (Urbana: University of Illinois Press, 1949).

40. Jeremy Campbell, *Grammatical Man: Information, Entropy, Language, and Life* (New York: Simon and Schuster, 1982), 97–98.

41. Pearson, *Philosophy and the Adventure of the Virtual,* 79–86.

42. Examples of the imitation video clips that followed Lonelygirl15 are archived at http://www.youtube.com/results?search_query=lonelygirl15&search_type.

43. Godin, *Unleashing the Idea Virus,* 19.

44. Blackmore, *Meme Machine,* 193, 246.

45. Ibid., 193.

46. Ibid., 246.

47. Matthew Fuller and Andrew Goffey, "Towards an Evil Media Studies," in Parikka and Sampson, *The Spam Book,* 155.

48. Ibid.

49. Ibid.

50. Godin, *Unleashing the Idea Virus,* 47.

51. Fuller and Goffey, "Towards an Evil Media Studies," 155.

52. YouTube Comments and responses to LonelyGirl15 REVEALED video, http://www.youtube.com/watch?v=5XSld5qwqjQ (accessed April 20, 2007).

53. Matthew Fuller, *Media Ecologies: Materialist Energies in Art and Technoculture* (Cambridge, Mass.: MIT Press, 2005), 111–16.

54. Ibid., 115.

55. Ibid., 116.

56. Ibid., 132–33.

57. Ibid., 144.

58. Parisi, *Abstract Sex,* 50.

59. Geneticist Gabriel Dover speaking at the Creative Evolution Conference at Goldsmiths College, University of London, February 12–13, 2005.

60. Brennan, *Transmission of Affect,* 74.

61. Ibid., 74–75.

62. Gustave Le Bon, as cited in Sigmund Freud, *Group Psychology and the Analysis of the Ego* (New York: Liveright, 1951), 6.

63. Le Bon, *The Crowd,* 7.

64. Ibid.

65. Ibid., 29.

66. Brennan, *Transmission of Affect,* 52–54.

67. Edward Bernays, *Propaganda* (New York: Liveright, 1928).

68. Le Bon, *The Crowd,* 26–27.

69. Freud, *Group Psychology and the Analysis of the Ego,* 13.

70. Le Bon, *The Crowd,* 7.

71. Ibid., 6–7.

72. Brennan, *Transmission of Affect,* 53–54.

73. Ibid., 54.

74. Freud, *Group Psychology and the Analysis of the Ego,* 15.

75. Ibid., 20.

76. Ibid.

77. Ibid., 16–22.

78. Le Bon, *The Crowd,* 15.

79. Ibid., 16.

80. Ibid., 4, 46.

81. Ibid., 79.

82. Ibid., 4.

83. James Surowiecki, *The Wisdom of Crowds: Why the Many Are Smarter Than the Few and How Collective Wisdom Shapes Business, Economies, Societies, and Nations* (New York: Random House, 2004), xv–xvi.

84. Le Bon, *The Crowd,* 30.

85. Ibid.

86. Ibid., vi.

87. Ibid., 45.

88. Ibid.

89. Brennan, *Transmission of Affect,* 49.

90. Ibid.

91. Ibid., 56–57.

92. Ibid., 49.

93. Ibid.

94. Ibid., 68.

95. DeLanda, *A New Philosophy of Society,* 8–25.

96. Ibid., 4.

97. Ibid., 10–11.

98. Massumi, *A User's Guide to Capitalism and Schizophrenia,* 192.

99. DeLanda, *A New Philosophy of Society,* 40.

100. Ibid., 50.

101. Michael Hardt and Antonio Negri, *Multitude* (London: Penguin Books, 2005), 99–100.

102. Tarde, as cited in Marsden, "Forefathers of Memetics."

103. Louise Salmon, "Gabriel Tarde and the Dreyfus Affair: Reflections on the Engagement of an Intellectual," Champ Pénal/Penal Field, June 19, 2009, http://champpenal.revues.org/document7185.html.

104. Tarde, *Laws of Imitation,* 84.

105. Ibid.

106. Ibid.

107. Ibid., 84–85.

108. Ibid., 78.

109. Ibid.

110. Ibid., xviii.

111. Ibid., xiii.

112. Deleuze and Guattari, *A Thousand Plateaus,* 29–30.

113. Le Bon, *The Crowd,* 26–27.

114. Tracy H. Koon, *Believe, Obey, Fight: Political Socialization of Youth in Fascist Italy, 1922–1943* (Chapel Hill, N.C.: University of North Carolina Press, 1985), 4–5.

115. Deleuze and Guattari, *A Thousand Plateaus,* 33. See also Canetti, *Crowds and Power,* 91–124.

116. Philip Goodchild, *Deleuze and Guattari: An Introduction to the Politics of Desire* (London: Sage, 1996), 78.

117. Brian Massumi, *Parables of the Virtual: Movement, Affect, Sensation* (Durham, N.C.: Duke University Press, 2002), 16.

118. Ibid., 130.

119. Ibid., 129.

120. Gilles Deleuze, *The Logic of Sense* (London: Continuum, 1990), 241–57.

121. Ibid., 242.

122. Ibid., 312.

123. Thrift, "Pass It On," 5–6.

3. What Diagram?

1. Deleuze, *Foucault,* 36, 34–44.

2. See, e.g., Hardt and Negri, *Empire,* 134–36, and Alexander R. Galloway and Eugene Thacker, *The Exploit: A Theory of Networks* (Minneapolis: University of Minnesota Press, 2007).

3. Galloway and Thacker, *The Exploit,* 27.

4. Duncan Watts, *Six Degrees: The Science of a Connected Age* (London: Vintage, 2003), 50.

5. Thrift, *Non-representational Theory,* 110.

6. Thrift, "Pass It On," 18.

7. Massumi, *Parables of the Virtual,* 86.

8. Ibid.

9. Parikka, "Digital Monsters, Binary Aliens."

10. World Bank, Policy Research Working Papers series, http://ideas.repec.org/cgi-bin/htsearch?q=contagion&ul=%2Fwbk%2Fwbrwps.

11. Former U.K. prime minister Tony Blair's speech on the Iraq crisis in the House of Commons on Tuesday, March 18, 2003, http://www.guardian.co.uk/politics/2003/mar/18/foreignpolicy.iraq1.

12. R. Barry Johnston and Oana M. Nedelescu, "The Impact of Terrorism on Financial Markets," working paper WP/05/60, International Monetary Fund, http://www.imf.org/external/pubs/ft/wp/2005/wp0560.pdf.

13. Jamie Doward, "Antidepressant Use Soars as the Recession Bites: Experts Warn on 'Quick Fix' after a Rise of 2.1m Prescriptions in 2008," *The Observer,* June 21, 2009, http://www.guardian.co.uk/society/2009/jun/21/mental-health-antidepressants-recession-prescriptions.

14. Sanjeev Bhojraj, Robert J. Bloomfield, and William B. Tayler, "Margin Trading, Overpricing, and Synchronization Risk," *Review of Financial Studies,* forthcoming, http://ssrn.com/abstract=786008.

15. As one former New Labour adviser in the United Kingdom recently argued to this effect, "the *Credit Crunch* will generate a wave of anomie" in which rates of suicide and depression will inevitably go up. Mathew Taylor, "The credit crunch will generate a wave of anomie," blog post to the *Daily Telegraph* website, October 14, 2008, http://blogs.telegraph.co.uk/news/matthewtaylor/5449617/The_credit_crunch_will_generate_a_wave_of_anomie/.

16. Jeffrey C. Alexander and Philip Daniel Smith, *The Cambridge Companion to Durkheim* (Cambridge: Cambridge University Press, 2005), 142.

17. Craig Calhoun and Joseph Gerteis, *Classical Sociological Theory* (New York: John Wiley, 2007), 197.

18. Brian L. Mishara, "Suicide and Economic Depression: Reflections on

Suicide during the Great Depression," *International Association for Suicide Prevention (IASP) New Bulletin*, December 2008, http://www.iasp.info/pdf/papers/mishara_suicide_and_the_economic_depression.pdf.

19. Ibid.
20. Borch, "Crowds and Economic Life."
21. Thrift, "Pass It On," 4.
22. Tarde, as cited in ibid., 3.
23. Ibid., 5.
24. Ibid., 4.
25. Ibid., 14.
26. Ibid., 21.
27. Ibid.
28. Ibid., 24.
29. See further discussion in Tony D. Sampson and Jussi Parikka, "The Accidents of Influence: Learning from Dysfunctionality and Anomaly in Network Environments," in *The Blackwell Companion to New Media Dynamics*, ed. J. Hartley, J. Burgess, and A. Bruns (New York: Wiley-Blackwell, 2012).
30. Stanley Milgram, "The Small World Problem," *Psychology Today* 1, no. 1 (1967): 60–67.
31. Malcolm Gladwell, *The Tipping Point* (London: Abacus, 2000), 34–36, 7–9.
32. Ibid., 3–4.
33. Ibid., 141.
34. Clive Thompson, "Is the Tipping Point Toast?" *Fast Company Magazine*, February 1, 2008, http://www.fastcompany.com/magazine/122/is-the-tipping-point-toast.html.
35. Albert-László Barabási, *Linked* (London: Plume, 2003), 123.
36. Ibid., 131.
37. Romualdo Pastor-Satorras and Alessandro Vespignani, "Epidemic Spreading in Scale-Free Networks," *Physical Review Letters* 86, no. 14 (2000): 3200–3.
38. Jeffery Kephart et al., "Computers and Epidemiology," *IEEE Spectrum*, May 1993, 20–26, http://www.research.ibm.com/antivirus/SciPapers/Kephart/Spectrum/Spectrum.html.
39. Mark Buchanan, *Nexus* (New York: W. W. Norton, 2002).
40. Barabási, *Linked*, 71.
41. Ibid., 67–69.
42. Ibid., 152–53.
43. Ibid., 174.
44. Watts, *Six Degrees*, 200–1.
45. Ibid., 50.
46. Ibid., 52–53.

210 NOTES TO CHAPTER 3

47. Duncan Watts, as cited in Thompson, "Is the Tipping Point Toast?"
48. Thrift, "Pass It On," 20.
49. Ibid.
50. Ibid., 21–22.
51. Tarde, *Laws of Imitation*, 109.
52. John Stuart Mill, "On the Definition of Political Economy, and on the Method of Investigation Proper to It," in *Essays on Some Unsettled Questions of Political Economy*, 2nd ed., 86–114 (London: Longmans, Green, Reader, and Dyer, 1874).
53. Thrift, "Pass It On," 3.
54. Ibid., 3–4
55. Borch, "Crowds and Economic Life," 19–22.
56. Ibid., 17–18.
57. Ibid. See also Canetti, *Crowds and Power*, 179–82.
58. Canetti, *Crowds and Power*, 186–87.
59. Thrift, "Pass It On," 19.
60. Tarde, "Economic Psychology," 620.
61. Thrift, "Pass It On," 18.
62. Ibid.
63. Ibid., 18–19.
64. Ibid., 18.
65. Borch, "Crowds and Economic Life," 19.
66. Thrift, "Pass It On," 20.
67. Tarde, *Laws of Imitation*, xxiv.
68. Paul Virilio, "Interview with Virilio," in *From Modernism to Hypermodernism and Beyond*, ed. John Armitage, 40–41 (London: Sage, 2000).
69. Ibid.
70. See references to Virilio's accidents in Jussi Parikka, *Digital Contagions: A Media Archaeology of Computer Viruses* (New York: Peter Lang, 2007).
71. Paul Virilio, as cited in Patrick Crogan, "The Tendency, the Accident, and the Untimely," in Armitage, *From Modernism to Hypermodernism and Beyond*, 171.
72. Paul Virilio, as cited in ibid., 171.
73. Steve Redhead, ed., *The Paul Virilio Reader* (New York: Columbia University Press, 2004), 262.
74. Alfred North Whitehead, *Process and Reality: Corrected Edition*, ed. David Ray Griffin and Donald W. Sherburne (New York: Free Press, 1978), 21.
75. Ibid., 18.
76. Events engaged in "[a] double battle . . . to thwart all dogmatic confusion between event and essence, and also every empiricist' confusion between event and accident." Deleuze, *Logic of Sense*, 64.

77. Pierre Levy, *Becoming Virtual: Reality in the Digital Age*, trans. Robert Bononno (New York: Plenum Trade, 1998), 178, 171.

78. Ibid., 178; emphasis added.

79. Bertrand Russell, as cited in Peter Farleigh, "Whitehead's Even More Dangerous Idea," in *Toward a Science of Consciousness II: The Second Tucson Discussions and Debates*, ed. Stuart R. Hameroff, Alfred W. Kaszniak, and Alwyn C. Scott (Cambridge, Mass.: MIT Press, 1998), 129.

80. Michel Foucault, as cited in Massumi, *Parables of the Virtual*, 298.

81. Manuel DeLanda speaking at the Creative Evolution Conference at Goldsmiths College, University of London, February 12–13, 2005, author's notes.

82. Manuel DeLanda, *Intensive Science and Virtual Philosophy* (London: Continuum, 2002).

83. Massumi, *Parables of the Virtual*, 5.

84. As Deleuze proposes, "The Great Pyramid is an event, and its duration for a period of one hour, thirty minutes, five minutes . . . [is] a passage of Nature." Gilles Deleuze, "What Is an Event?" in *The Fold: Leibniz and the Baroque* (Minneapolis: University of Minnesota Press, 1992), 86.

85. Massumi, *Parables of the Virtual*, 225–26.

86. Massumi, *A User's Guide to Capitalism and Schizophrenia*, 18.

87. Ibid., 19.

88. Massumi, *Parables of the Virtual*, 86.

89. Ibid.

90. Ibid., 87.

91. Ibid., 219.

92. Ibid., 88.

93. Jussi Parikka, "Contagion and Repetition: On the Viral Logic of Network Culture," *Ephemera: Theory and Politics in Organization* 7, no. 2 (2007): 287–308.

94. Tarde, "Economic Psychology," 627.

95. Ibid.

96. Tarde, *Laws of Imitation*, 250.

97. Guattari, *Chaosmosis*, 16.

98. Ibid., 2.

4. From Terror Contagion to the Virality of Love

1. The stratagem approach is very loosely borrowed from Fuller and Goffey, "Towards an Evil Media Studies."

2. Thrift, "Pass It On," 18.

3. Tarde, *Laws of Imitation*, 196.

4. Sean Cubitt, "It's Life Jim, but Not as We Know It," in *Fractal Dreams,* ed. Jon Dovey (London: Lawrence and Aishart, 1996), 36–37. See also Parikka, *Digital Contagions,* 153.

5. Deleuze and Guattari, *A Thousand Plateaus,* 86.

6. See, e.g., David S. Bennahum, "Heart of Darkness," *Wired,* November 1997, http://www.wired.com/wired/archive/5.11/heartof.html.

7. Parikka, *Digital Contagions,* 183–84.

8. Stefan Helmreich, "Flexible Infections: Computer Viruses, Human Bodies, Nation-States, Evolutionary Capitalism," *Science, Technology, and Human Values* 25, no. 4 (2000): 472–91, citing from the online version: http://web.mit.edu/anthropology/faculty_staff/helmreich/PDFs/flexible_infections.pdf.

9. Ibid.

10. Following a statement made in 1999 (and cited in ibid.). The U.S. Defense Department Advanced Research Projects Agency (DARPA) set up CERT as a tactical response to the computer virus problem in 1988.

11. Tiziana Terranova, *Network Culture: Politics for the Information Age* (London: Pluto, 2004), 99–101.

12. For a good summary, see Jeremy Campbell, *The Improbable Mind* (New York: Touchstone, 1982), 104, 108–17.

13. A. K. Dewdney, "In the Game Called Core War Hostile Programs Engage in a Battle of Bits," *Scientific American,* May 1984, 14–22.

14. A. K. Dewdney, "A Core War Bestiary of Viruses, Worms, and Other Threats to Computer Memories," *Scientific American,* March 1985, 14–19.

15. Fred Cohen, "Computer Viruses—Theory and Experiments," paper presented at DOD/NBS 7th Conference on Computer Security, http://www.all.net/books/virus/index.html. See also Tony D. Sampson, "Dr Aycock's Bad Idea: Is the Good Use of Computer Viruses Still a Bad Idea?" *Media and Culture Journal* 8, no. 1 (2005), http://journal.media-culture.org.au/0502/02-sampson.php.

16. See, e.g., Eric Louw and Neil Duffy, *Managing Computer Viruses* (Oxford: Oxford University Press, 1992).

17. Ibid., 43.

18. See, e.g., Jeffrey Kephart et al., "An Immune System for Cyberspace," paper presented at the IEEE International Conference on Systems, Man, and Cybernetics—Artificial Immune Systems and Their Applications, Orlando, Fla., October 12–15, 1997. See also Jungwon Kim et al., "Immune System Approaches to Intrusion Detection—A Review," paper presented at the Artificial Immune Systems: Third International Conference, ICARIS, Sicily, Italy, September 2004, http://arxiv.org/ftp/arxiv/papers/0804/0804.1266.pdf.

19. Kephart et al., "An Immune System for Cyberspace."

20. Kim et al., "Immune System Approaches to Intrusion Detection."

21. Tony D. Sampson, "Senders, Receivers, and Deceivers: How Liar Codes Put Noise Back on the Diagram of Transmission," *Media and Culture Journal Transmit* 9, no. 1 (2004), http://journal.media-culture.org.au/0603/03-sampson.php.

22. Kephart et al., "An Immune System for Cyberspace."

23. Ibid.

24. Symantec press release, http://www.symantec.com/press/1999/n990511.html.

25. Michel Foucault, *Power/Knowledge: Selected Interviews and Other Writings 1972–1977*, ed. C. Gordon (Brighton, U.K.: Harvester Press, 1980), 92–108.

26. Norbert Wiener, *Cybernetics: or Control and Communication in the Animal and the Machine* (1948; repr., Cambridge, Mass.: MIT Press, 1961), 130, 161.

27. Interview with John Perry Barlow, "Go Placidly amidst the Noise and Haste," *New Perspectives Quarterly,* n.d., http://w2.eff.org/Misc/Publications/John_Perry_Barlow/.

28. Deleuze and Guattari, *A Thousand Plateaus,* 422.

29. Robert Baer, "This Deadly Virus: In a Searing Analysis of the Wave of Suicide Bombings, Former CIA Agent Robert Baer Warns Britain of the Grave Dangers Ahead," *The Observer,* August 7, 2005.

30. Parikka, *Digital Contagions,* 93–96.

31. Sampson, "Senders, Receivers, and Deceivers."

32. Eugene Thacker, "Cryptobiologies," *ArtNodes: E-Journal on Art, Science, and Technology,* November 6, 2006, http://www.uoc.edu/artnodes/6/dt/eng/thacker.html.

33. Eugene Thacker, "On the Horror of Living Networks," paper presented at the Exploring New Configurations of Network Politics Conference, Cambridge, March 2010, http://www.networkpolitics.org/request-for-comments/dr-thackers-position-paper.

34. Ibid.

35. Ibid.

36. Michel Foucault, *Madness and Civilization: A History of Sanity in the Age of Reason* (London: Routledge, 1989), 3.

37. As Thacker argues, "in this regard nothing is more exceptional than the inability to distinguish between epidemic and war, between emerging infectious disease and bioterrorism." Eugene Thacker, "Living Dead Networks," *Fibreculture: Internet Theory, Criticism, Research* 4 (2005), http://journal.fibreculture.org/issue4/issue4_thacker.html.

38. Paul Virilio, *The Original Accident* (Cambridge: Polity, 2007), 15–22.

39. Thacker, "Living Dead Networks."

40. John Arquilla and David Ronfeldt, *The Advent of Netwar* (Santa Monica, Calif.: RAND, 1996), 96.

41. Richard Forno, "Disclosure of Risk Is an Ethical Dilemma," *Financial Times*, September 20, 2005, http://www.ft.com/cms/s/2/48307322-28d9-11da-8a5e-00000e2511c8.html#axzz1JV5nQLTU.

42. Lakoff, *Political Mind*.

43. Ibid., 39–40, 28.

44. Ibid., 41.

45. Ibid., 125.

46. Antonio Damasio, *Descartes' Error: Emotion, Reason, and the Human Brain* (London, Vintage, 2006), xxii.

47. Stafford, *Echo Objects*, 75–81.

48. David Patrick Houghton, *Political Psychology: Situations, Individuals, and Cases* (London: Routledge, 2009), 143–54. A. K. Pradeep, "Persuasion: The Science and Methods of Neuromarketing," white paper, http://www.neurofocus.com/pdfs/DrPradeepPersuasion.pdf.

49. Thacker, "On the Horror of Living Networks."

50. Lakoff, *Political Mind*, 56.

51. Brennan, *Transmission of Affect*, 62–63.

52. Ibid., 49.

53. Ibid.

54. As Deleuze infers, it is best not to confuse affect with such fantasy. Gilles Deleuze, *Two Regimes of Madness: Texts and Interviews, 1975–1995* (New York: Semiotext(e), 2007), 102.

55. Canetti, *Crowds and Power*, 26, 53.

56. Brennan, *Transmission of Affect*, 32.

57. Tarde, *Laws of Imitation*, 80.

58. Ibid., 196–202.

59. Ibid.

60. Gabriel Tarde, *Underground Man*, trans. Cloudesley Brereton (London: Duckworth, 1905), 105.

61. Tarde, *Laws of Imitation*, 215.

62. Caleb Smith and Enrico Minardi, "The Collaborator and the Multitude: An Interview with Michael Hardt," *Minnesota Review* 61–62 (2004), http://www.theminnesotareview.org/journal/ns61/.

63. Michael Hardt, "About Love," a lecture given in 2007 at the European Graduate School, http://www.youtube.com/watch?v=ioopkoppabI.

64. For more in-depth insight into Negri's use of Lenin's concepts of spontaneity and organization, see Michael Hardt, "Into the Factory: Negri's Lenin and the Subjective Caesura," in *The Philosophy of Antonio Negri: Resistance in*

Practice, ed. Timothy S. Murphy and Abdul-Karim Mustapha (London: Pluto Press, 2005), 7–39.

65. As Pope John Paul II made clear to the poor of Latin America, the love of God is wholly inconsistent with political revolution. "Be careful," he warned them. Do not "accept nor allow a Vision of human life as conflict nor ideologies which propose class hatred and violence to be instilled in you." See Pope John Paul II, "Option for the Poor," sermon in Mexico, 1990, http://www.bbc.co.uk/religion/religions/christianity/beliefs/liberationtheology.shtml.

66. Freud, as cited in Michael S. Kimmel, *Revolution: A Sociological Interpretation* (New York: Polity Press, 1990), 42.

67. See, e.g., Lisa Pine, *Nazi Family Policy, 1933–1945* (New York: Berg, 1997), 179.

68. CNN/Opinion Research Corporation Poll, "Terrorism," November 2–4, 2007, http://www.pollingreport.com/terror.htm, and World Public Opinion, "Muslim Public Opinion on US Policy, Attacks on Civilians and al Qaeda," April 24, 2007, http://www.worldpublicopinion.org/pipa/pdf/apr07/START_Apr07_rpt.pdf.

69. Tarde, *Laws of Imitation,* 281–82.

70. Ewen MacAskill, "George Bush: 'God Told Me to End the Tyranny in Iraq': President Told Palestinians God Also Talked to Him about Middle East Peace," *The Guardian,* October 7, 2005, and Andy McSmith, "Blair: 'God Will Be My Judge on Iraq,'" *The Independent,* March 4, 2006.

71. Cyberpunk author Bruce Sterling, writing for *Antivirus Online* 2, no. 1, http://vx.netlux.org/lib/mbs00.html; emphasis added.

72. Tarde, *Laws of Imitation,* 78–79.

73. Ibid., 202.

74. Ibid.

75. Vesselin Bontchev, "Bulgarian and Soviet Virus Factories," paper presented at the First International Virus Bulletin Conference, Jersey, U.K., September 12–13, 1991, 11–25, http://www.people.frisk-software.com/~bontchev/papers/factory.html.

76. Ibid.

77. Bennahum, "Heart of Darkness." See also *Copy Me—I Want to Travel,* a film by Pauline Boudry, Brigitta Kuster, and Renate Lorenz (zdf/arte, 2004).

78. Ibid.

79. Sarah Gordon, "Inside the Mind of Dark Avenger, an Interview with the Bulgarian Virus Writer Dark Avenger," *Virus News International,* January 1993, http://researchweb.watson.ibm.com/antivirus/SciPapers/Gordon/Avenger.html.

80. Harley et al., *Viruses Revealed,* 32.

81. Bennahum, "Heart of Darkness."

82. A network culture that Tiziana Terranova points toward in *Network Culture: Politics for the Information Age*, 67.

83. The LoveBug author Onel De Guzman was interviewed in a CNN chat room on September 25, 2000, http://archives.cnn.com/2000/TECH/computing/09/26/guzman.chat/.

84. Andrew Sullivan, "Barack Obama Is Master of the New Facebook Politics," *Sunday Times*, May 25, 2008, http://www.timesonline.co.uk/tol/comment/columnists/andrew_sullivan/article3997523.ece.

85. Obama images archived at http://flickr.com/photos/barackobamadotcom/sets/72157608716313371/.

86. Specific Obama image and Flickr user comment archived at http://www.flickr.com/photos/barackobamadotcom/3008254887/.

87. Global Project, "Behind This Victory, the Great Multitudinarian Struggle," interview with Antonio Negri, Global Project, http://archive.globalproject.info/art-17685.html; transl., http://anomalia.blogsome.com/2008/11/06/negri-obamas-victory-the-multitude/.

88. Thrift, *Non-representational Theory*, 139.

89. Brennan, *Transmission of Affect*, 74.

5. Tardean Hypnosis

1. "Society is imitation and imitation is a kind of somnambulism." Tarde, *The Laws of Imitation*, 77, 87.

2. See, e.g., April Mara Barton, "Application of Cascade Theory to Online Systems: A Study of Email and Google Cascades," *Minnesota Journal of Law, Science, and Technology* 10, no. 2 (2009): 474.

3. Watts, *Six Degrees*.

4. Malcolm Gladwell, *Blink: The Power of Thinking without Thinking* (New York: Little, Brown, 2005).

5. David Patrick Houghton, *Political Psychology: Situations, Individuals, and Cases* (New York: Routledge, 2009), 51–52.

6. Thrift, "Pass It On."

7. Ibid., 5.

8. Tarde, *Laws of Imitation*, 199.

9. Ibid., xi; emphasis added.

10. Yemeni president Ali Abdullah Saleh, in a news report in the *Kurdish Globe*. "Yemen's President Compares Protests to 'Influenza,'" *Kurdish Globe*, February 22, 2011, http://www.kurdishglobe.net/display-article.html?id=4FBB6B1254488A1CC2B8ED5604B294D7.

11. Thrift, "Pass It On," 8.

12. Nigel Thrift, *Knowing Capitalism* (London: Sage), 223.

13. Galloway and Thacker, "On Narcolepsy."

14. Nigel Thrift, "Remembering the Technological Unconscious by Fore-grounding Knowledges of Position," *Environment and Planning: Society and Space* 22 (2004): 175–90.

15. Galloway and Thacker, "On Narcolepsy."

16. Ibid.

17. Fuller and Goffey, "Toward an Evil Media Studies."

18. Ibid., 152.

19. Crary, *Suspensions of Perception,* 49. The problem of attention is insepa-rable from inattention. They are not polar opposites—they are a continuum.

20. Ibid., 242–43. See also Fuller and Goffey, "Toward an Evil Media Studies," 147.

21. Fuller and Goffey, "Toward an Evil Media Studies," 143.

22. Crary, *Suspensions of Perception,* 77.

23. Fuller and Goffey, "Toward an Evil Media Studies," 147.

24. Tarde, *Laws of Imitation,* 199.

25. Nigel Thrift, "Halos: Making More Room in the World for New Po-litical Orders," http://nigelthrift.files.wordpress.com/2008/09/halos7.pdf. Also published in *Political Matter: Technoscience, Democracy, and Public Life,* ed. Bruce Braun and Sarah J. Whatmore (Minneapolis: University of Minnesota Press, 2010).

26. Ibid.

27. Ibid.

28. Thrift, *Non-representational Theory,* 243.

29. Ibid., 240–43.

30. Ibid., 241.

31. Ibid.

32. Rosalind D. Williams, *Dream Worlds: Mass Consumption in Late Nine-teenth-Century France* (Berkeley: University of California Press, 1982), 18.

33. Ibid., 373.

34. Borch, "Crowds and Economic Life," 19.

35. Thrift, "Pass It On," 20.

36. Deleuze and Guattari, *A Thousand Plateaus,* 29–30.

37. Deleuze and Guattari, *Anti-Oedipus,* 3.

38. Rae Beth Gordon, "Unconscious Imitation," in *The Mind of Modernism: Medicine, Psychology, and the Cultural Arts,* ed. Mark S. Micale (Stanford, Calif.: Stanford University Press, 2004), 118–20. Ibid., 118.

39. Ibid.

40. Sjoerd Van Tuinen, "Is There a Contemporary Use for Tarde's Con-cepts of Magnetism, Somnambulism and Hypnosis?" paper presented at

the Tarde/Durkheim Conference, Cambridge, March 14–15, 2008.

41. Richard Gross, *Psychology: The Science of Mind and Behaviour,* 3rd ed. (London: Hodder and Stoughton, 1996), 87–89.

42. Tarde, *Laws of Imitation,* 77.

43. Thrift "Pass It On," 5–6.

44. Tarde, *Laws of Imitation,* 365.

45. Brennan, *Transmission of Affect,* 3.

46. Thrift, "Pass It On," 22.

47. Martin Jay, *Downcast Eyes: The Denigration of Vision in Twentieth-Century French Thought* (Berkeley: University of California Press, 1993).

48. Ibid., 21–81.

49. Immanuel Kant, *Anthropology from a Pragmatic Point of View,* ed. Robert B. Louden (Cambridge: Cambridge University Press, 2006), 48.

50. Crary, *Suspensions of Perception,* 15.

51. Antonio Damasio, *Descartes' Error: Emotion, Reason, and the Human Brain* (New York: G. P. Putnam, 1994), ii. See also Robert Zajonc, "Feeling and Thinking: Preferences Need No Inferences," *American Psychologist* 35, no. 2 (1980): 151–75.

52. M. A. Just and P. A. Carpenter, "A Theory of Reading: From Eye Fixations to Comprehension," *Psychological Review* 87 (July 1980): 329–54.

53. A. Poole and L. J. Ball, "Eye Tracking in Human–Computer Interaction and Usability Research: Current Status and Future Prospects," in *Encyclopedia of Human Computer Interaction,* ed. Claude Ghaoui (Hershey, Pa.: Idea Group, 2005), 211–19.

54. Sandra E. Leh, Heidi Johansen-Berg, and Alain Ptito, "Unconscious Vision: New Insights into the Neuronal Correlate of Blindsight Using Diffusion Tractography," *Brain: A Journal of Neurology* 129, no. 7 (2006): 1822–32, http://brain.oxfordjournals.org/cgi/content/full/129/7/1822.

55. P. Winkielman and J. Schooler, "Unconscious, Conscious, and Metaconscious in Social Cognition," in *Social Cognition: The Basis of Human Interaction,* ed. F. Strack and J. Foerster (Philadelphia: Psychology Press, 2008), 49–69.

56. Richard D. Zakia, *Perception and Imaging* (Boston: Focal Press, 2002), 240–41.

57. Eric Granholm, "Pupillometric Measures of Cognitive and Emotional Processes," *International Journal of Psychophysiology* 52 (2004): 1–6.

58. Although a good number of commercially inclined reports actively promote measuring pupil dilation as an effective way in which to gauge consumer arousal to a given product, it is generally accepted in scientific journals that it is not a reliable form of measuring emotional responses in isolation. As de Lemos et al. from the Danish company iMotions concede, pupil dilation "has

been coupled with activation of the sympathetic nervous system. However, the relationship is complex because pupil size is also related to cognitive processing load, and the amount of light or hue in visual stimuli." Jakob de Lemos et al., "Measuring Emotions Using Eye Tracking," Research and Technology Department, iMotions, Copenhagen, Denmark, http://www.noldus.com/mb2008/individual_papers/FPS_eye_tracking/FPS_eye_tracking_deLemos.pdf.

59. *Health Journal,* "Microsaccades—Unconscious Eye Movements Help Our Vision!," March 5, 2009, http://www.dirjournal.com/health-journal/microsaccades-unconscious-eye-movements-help-our-vision/.

60. J. R. Anderson, D. Bothell, and S. Douglass, "Eye Movements Do Not Reflect Retrieval Processes: Limits of the Eye–Mind Hypothesis," *Psychological Science* 15 (2004): 225–31.

61. A. K. Pradeep, "Persuasion: The Science and Methods of Neuromarketing," industry white paper published on *NeuroFocus,* September 2007, http://www.neurofocus.com/pdfs/DrPradeepPersuasion.pdf.

62. Jakob de Lemos, "Measuring Emotionally 'Fuelled' Marketing," *Admap Magazine,* April 2007, 40–42.

63. Ibid.

64. Pradeep, "Persuasion."

65. Ibid., 27.

66. Donald A. Norman, *Emotional Design: Why We Love (or Hate) Everyday Things* (New York: Basic Books, 2004).

67. Ibid., 59–60.

68. *Ibid.,* 22–23.

69. Thrift, "Pass It On," 22.

70. Ibid., 18.

71. Houghton, *Political Psychology,* 144.

72. Lakoff, *Political Mind,* 39.

73. Thrift, "Pass It On," 8.

74. Stafford, *Echo Objects,* 76–77.

75. George Lakoff, "The Obama Code," *Huffington Post,* blog comment posted February 24, 2009, http://www.huffingtonpost.com/george-lakoff/the-obama-code_b_169580.html.

76. Ibid.

77. Ibid., 13–15.

78. Ibid., 14.

79. Ibid.

80. Brennan, *Transmission of Affect,* 41.

81. Ibid., 32.

82. Ibid., 128.

83. Ibid., 129.

84. Ibid.

85. Ibid., 32.

86. Ibid. There is in fact some support for this claim insofar as the discernment of loving attention in human and animal relations affects both the biological and intellectual growth of offspring in what would be aptly described as positive ways.

87. Ibid., 94–95.

88. Ibid., 116–17.

89. Crary, *Suspensions of Perception,* 1.

90. Ibid., 45–46.

91. Ibid.

92. Ibid., 65.

93. Ibid., 67.

94. Ibid., 68.

95. Ibid., 69.

96. Ibid., 71.

97. Ibid., 29–30, 13.

98. Ibid., 71.

99. Quote in heading is from Damasio, *Descartes' Error,* 249.

100. Tarde, *Laws of Imitation,* 215.

101. Fuller and Goffey, "Toward an Evil Media Studies," 158–59.

102. See more discussion on the *Storm Worm* botnet in Sampson, "Error-Contagion," 239–40.

103. Nigel Thrift, *Knowing Capitalism* (London: Sage, 2005), 226.

104. Goffey and Fuller, "Towards an Evil Media Studies," 147.

105. Allegra Stratton, "David Cameron Aims to Make Happiness the New GDP; Prime Minister Acts on Pledge to Find Out What Makes the Nation Content," *The Guardian,* November 14, 2010, http://www.guardian.co.uk/politics/2010/nov/14/david-cameron-wellbeing-inquiry.

106. Toby Helm, "Small Is Beautiful: The Father of David Cameron's Big Society: The Prime Minister's Political Philosophy Shows Repeated Similarities to EF Schumacher's Famous Work," *The Observer,* March 27, 2011, http://www.guardian.co.uk/politics/2011/mar/27/small-beautiful-david-cameron-big-society.

107. Thrift, *Non-representational Theory,* 253.

108. Tarde, *Laws of Imitation,* xvii.

109. Ibid., xix.

110. Ibid.

111. Ibid.

112. Ibid.
113. Ibid.
114. Ibid.
115. Ibid.
116. Ibid.

Index

absorption, 13, 82, 90, 95, 114, 117, 139, 141, 159, 161–62, 167, 169, 171–73, 178, 180, 184, 185, 186

abstract diagram, 3, 97–98, 134, 161, 185

accidents, 6, 10, 16, 18, 19, 26, 34, 42–43, 44, 46, 57, 65, 74–75, 78, 84–85, 95, 99, 106–7, 111–22, 127, 162, 165, 167, 171, 209n29, 210n70, 211n76

accumulation, 6, 22, 25, 29, 31, 43, 83, 98, 104, 121

action-at-a-distance, 27, 30, 39, 41–42, 57, 59, 94, 116–17, 126, 149, 168–69, 170, 181

actor network theory (ANT), 15, 17, 20, 37, 39–41, 43, 196n12

adaptation, 18, 20–23, 25–26, 30, 35, 38, 56, 119, 126, 140–41, 154, 157

affect: and absorption, 172–73; and assemblage, 87, 153–54; and atmospheric transmissions, 13, 85–86, 90, 139, 142–43, 182–84, 220n86; and contagion, 3, 19, 28, 29, 46–47, 52, 55, 57–60, 92, 94–95, 125, 139, 149, 157, 160–64, 166–68, 172, 179; and encounter, 12–13, 15, 127, 138–39, 140–41,

185, 189–90; and eye tracking, 173–78; and human computer interaction, 32–33; and markets, 30, 98, 99, 104–5, 114–15; and memes, 70, 75–76, 77, 78–79 (*see also* memetics); and priming, 5, 42, 54–55, 58–59, 95, 105, 112–13, 115, 126, 140, 162, 171; and virality, 3–5, 17

Agambenian zone of indistinction, 137

agency, human, 9, 17, 28–29, 34, 38–41, 43, 53, 56, 69, 86, 98, 141

agentic state, 28, 29, 52, 160, 161

age of austerity, 100–103, 188, 208n15

age of contagion, 2–3, 188

algorithms: evolutionary algorithms, 10, 11, 39, 66, 68–69, 72, 74, 77–78; dreaming of the algorithm, 165; financial algorithm, 102

Alliez, Eric, 29

Amazon, 58

analogy: analogical thinking, 2–5; biological analogy, 2, 15, 24, 129, 131–32, 135; immunological analogy, 4, 132–33; meme/gene analogy, 11, 14, 61–62, 64–67, 70,

77–78, 86 (*see also* memetics)
anomaly: anomalous economic
bubbles and shocks, 53, 100,
102, 104, 111, 114, 118, 124–25;
anomaly detection, 5, 132–33, 134
anomie (Durkheim), 27, 34–35, 79,
103, 104, 208n15
anterior models (Tarde), 191–92
antipatheia (antipathy or antifeelings), 188, 190–92
antivirus (AV), 128, 132–34, 151,
153
apathy (Kant), 182, 190
appropriation (desire appropriated
by invention), 6, 18, 19, 24, 25,
29–30, 31, 104, 113–14, 142, 150,
154, 161–62, 163–64, 168, 181
assemblage: assemblages of
imitation, 190; assemblage
theory, 7–9, 17–18, 20, 23–24,
37, 44–48, 62–63, 87, 148–49;
machinic assemblages (desiring
machines), 12, 24, 168–69; social
assemblages, 3, 6–7, 12–13, 25,
29–31, 40, 57, 87–90, 91–92;
social and technical assemblages,
152–54; wasp–orchid assemblage,
11, 44–48, 58, 117, 144–45, 148
assimilation, process of, 38, 54–55,
59, 84, 91–92, 189–90
association: inscribed association,
41; monadological association,
40–42; network association, 42.
See also unconscious association
attention: crowds and attention,
90, 160–61; eye tracking and
attention, 174–77; living
attention, 182–85, 186, 220n86;
management of attentive subjects,
33, 42, 48–50, 80, 81, 95, 135,
160–61, 162, 165–66, 171, 173,

178, 185–89, 200n62, 217n19;
user/consumer, 164, 171, 172, 178
attraction, 30–31, 32, 54–55, 57–58,
91, 95, 113–14, 171, 177–78, 186.
See also magnetism

Baer, Robert, 135
Baldwin, James, 66
Barabási, Albert-László, 106, 108–
10, 112
becoming other and becoming the
same, 8, 45–46, 62, 79, 121, 145
belief (the object of desire), 5–6, 12,
18–19, 23, 25–26, 49, 69, 91, 104,
122, 127, 138, 143, 146, 161–62,
170–77, 184–85, 189, 191
Belle Poule, 82–83, 94
Bell Labs, 131
Bennahum, David S., 154
Bergson, Henri (Bergsonism), 22–23
bin Laden, Osama, 157, 182
biopower, 5, 22–23, 48, 60, 106, 113,
126, 127, 137, 159, 167, 181, 189
Blackman, Lisa, 15, 28
Blackmore, Susan, 39, 67–69, 71–72,
74
Blair, Tony, 2, 101, 150
Bontchev, Vesselin, 151–52
Borch, Christian, 15, 28, 29, 30, 104,
115, 117, 168
botnets, 187
Brennan, Teresa, 9, 78–79, 85–86,
141–43, 157, 182–84, 189
bubble phenomenon, 1, 35, 51, 53,
58, 98, 99, 101–4, 110–11, 113–14,
118, 124–25, 160
Bulgarian Virus Factory, 129, 130,
135, 150, 151–54
Bush, George W., 54, 150, 155, 179, 181
business enterprise, 1, 2, 6, 16,
31–32, 58–59, 60, 98–99, 105–6,

167, 171, 183, 184, 186; emotion and cognition, 13, 42, 53–55, 95, 102, 141, 160, 218–19n58 (*see also* cognitive processes). *See also* contagion; design

empathy, 32, 53–55, 139, 155, 181–82, 190–92

encounters: accidental and capricious encounters, 23, 24, 26, 46, 78, 84–85, 99, 115–17, 182; crowd encounters, 50–52, 62, 142; epidemiological encounters, 1, 56; fake encounters, 160–62; force of relational and contagious encounters with events, 3–5, 12–15, 18–19, 20, 22–23, 24, 26, 30, 46, 56, 57, 90, 93–94, 98, 110–12, 115–17, 118, 119, 121, 122–23, 125, 171–72, 181; hypnotic (unconscious and involuntary) encounters, 63–64, 78, 79, 91, 117, 160, 180; imitative encounters (contagious), 3, 25–26, 29–30, 35, 40, 44–46, 48, 49–50, 56, 61, 90–91, 94, 95, 118, 151–54, 160–62; joyful and fearsome encounters, 5–6, 14, 48, 127–28, 136, 138–45, 148–50, 155–57, 184, 189; priming of encounters, 95, 16, 162, 165, 171; viral encounters, 85. *See also* affect: contagion

epidemiology (as applied to social, digital, corporate, and political spaces), 1–3, 5, 17–18, 20–21, 23, 24, 27, 29, 31, 33, 35–39, 56, 58–60, 62–63, 83, 85, 95, 105–13, 117–18, 119, 123, 124, 127, 135, 137, 139, 149, 169, 171

escape: 65–66, 159, 164, 181, 187–92. *See also* capture

event philosophy, 118–26, 210n76, 211n84; actor networks and events, 43–44; actual occasions, 120; aperiodic or nonperiodic events (chance, happenstance, spontaneous, unforeseen, and accidental), 6, 34, 46, 53, 74–75, 85, 98–99, 100–101, 109–12, 113–14, 116–20, 122–26, 130; body and events, 49–50, 121–23, 164–65; events in passage, 111–12; hypnotic events, unconscious mesmerism of, 43, 104, 168, 170; image-event, 82–83, 91–92; imitative encounters with events, 41, 90–91, 140–41; incorporeal events, 120–21; language events, 128–29; memetic event, 77–78 (*see also* memetics); money event, 2, 32–33, 74, 104–5, 113, 115, 123; periodic events, 99, 113–14, 116–18, 122–26; phantom events, 63, 92–94, 137, 169; repetition of imitative ray as a desire-event, 6, 12, 13, 14, 19, 23, 21–22, 24–27, 29–32, 56–58, 104 (*see also* imitation); subrepresentational flow of events, 6, 7, 91–92; suppression of real events (hallucinogenic), 62–63, 75–76, 79, 82–83, viral events, 75, 77, 95, 151. *See also* networkability of the event

evil media studies, 165–66, 186–87, 211n1

evolutionary theory (Darwinism and neo-Darwinian), 2, 10–11, 15, 22–23, 37–39, 52, 62, 65–74, 76–79, 83, 85–86, 94, 130–31, 141–42, 198n4 eye tracking, 172–77, 218–19n58

Facebook, 155–56, 163–64, 168
factory models: Fordist and post-
  Fordist, 124; Freudian, 93;
  schizoid, 63–64, 93–94, 169–70
family unit, 11, 69, 92, 145–48;
  Obama's family, 155–56
fascination, 13–14, 25, 48–49, 52, 58,
  81, 90–91, 95, 125, 127, 149–53,
  155, 160–61, 162, 166–69, 171,
  178, 189
fascism, 81, 83, 92–93, 144, 147
fashion-imitation: and fads, 1, 2,
  20, 24–25, 29–30, 37–38, 52, 83,
  98–99, 100, 107–8, 113, 125, 160,
  191–92. *See also* imitation
fear contagion, 3, 5, 9, 14, 16, 49–50,
  54, 57, 77, 105, 127–29, 134–43,
  148, 150, 155–57, 163, 170–71,
  181, 183–84, 189; Le Bon's fear of
  revolutionary contagion, 83–84
financial contagion. *See* contagion
Flickr, 155–56, 182
Foucault, Michel, 97, 121, 134, 137,
  185
Freud, Sigmund, 10, 11, 36, 43, 62,
  79–81, 83, 89, 92–93, 146–47, 165,
  169, 183
friendship, 24, 32, 58, 155–56
Fuller, Matthew, 75–77, 95, 165–66,
  186–87, 189, 211n1

Galloway, Alex, 43, 97, 165
Gladwell, Malcolm, 83, 85, 106–8,
  112
Godin, Seth, 65–66, 75
Goffey, Andrew, 75, 95, 165–66,
  186–87, 188, 211n1
good and evil, 34, 81, 129, 145, 186–87

Gordon, Rae Beth, 170
graph theory, 97, 109–10
Great Depression, 103
group psychology, 10, 11, 43, 62,
  80–81, 90, 147, 169–70
Guattari, Félix, 7–8, 11, 15, 22,
  23–24, 43–48, 92–93, 125–26,
  135, 169

hallucination, 62, 76, 81–82, 95. *See
  also* collective; contagion; event
  philosophy
Hardt, Michael, 2, 144–50, 189, 190,
  214n64
Hegel, G. W. F., 22
Helmreich, Stefan, 129–39, 134
herding theory, 51, 53, 58, 81, 100–
  101, 110, 114–15, 160
heterogeneity, 43, 45, 79, 82–83, 84,
  87, 191
hierarchy, 52, 97–98, 143–44
Hofstadter, Douglas, 67
homeostasis, 35, 134–35
homogeneity, 8, 82–83, 87, 98, 109,
  202n118
hope, 5–6, 14, 54, 104–5, 127–28,
  143, 155
hormones, 5, 49–50, 59–60, 95,
  104–5, 116–17, 167, 171
host (playing), 47, 64, 66–67
Hume, David, 196–97n25
Hurricane Katrina, 155, 181
hypnosis, 11, 13, 27, 29, 30, 34, 36,
  39, 42–43, 48, 49–50, 52, 55, 57,
  59–60, 62, 76, 77, 78, 79–80, 85,
  89, 90–95, 117, 125, 149, 157,
  159–71, 179, 184–85, 189, 191

ideas, 25, 29, 31, 34–35, 54, 60,
  65, 66–69, 71, 72–75, 77, 78, 82,

30, 53–54, 59–60, 65–66, 76, 95,
98, 100–105, 112–13, 116–17,
125–26, 127, 140, 142–43,
155–56, 157, 179, 188–89. *See also*
collective
Morris Worm (computer worm), 130
multiplicity (molar/molecular
relation), 9, 24, 26, 88, 93, 116,
120, 145–46
multitude, 145, 147, 149, 157
mutualism, 11, 20, 45, 47, 48, 55, 59,
78, 91, 105, 169–71

nature/culture/society artifice, 9, 46,
57, 141, 157, 162
Negri, Antonio, 1–2, 145, 157,
214–15n64
neo-Darwinism, 3, 10–11, 14, 22–
23, 37–38, 44, 47–48, 61–62, 65,
66, 70–71, 74, 76–79, 131–32
networkability of the event, 29, 99,
118, 123
networks, 1–5, 7, 10, 13, 14–16,
17, 19, 24, 28–30, 31–32, 42–43,
45, 49, 50, 51, 53, 55–56, 58–59,
60, 61, 63, 64, 65, 67, 75–76, 85,
88, 95, 97–102, 104–13, 114–15,
117–18, 118–19, 121, 123, 124–25,
128–30, 132, 134–38, 144, 150,
151–56, 159, 160, 161, 163–68,
180, 186–88, 189, 191, 216n82.
See also event philosophy: actor
networks and events; Internet
neuromarketing, 12, 32–33, 36, 42,
60, 161–62, 172, 173–79, 186
neuroscience, 13, 17, 33, 50, 55, 60,
139–40, 173, 178–80, 182, 183
noncognitive, 19, 36, 114, 165–67,
179–80, 189
nonhuman, 136–37, 140
nonrepresentation, 3–4, 49–50, 91–

92, 161. *See also* representation;
subrepresentation
nonself, 127, 128, 133–35, 161. *See
also* self
nurseries of industry, 12, 31–32, 95,
171

Obama, Barack. *See* Obama-love
Obama-love, 54, 150, 155–57, 168,
181–82, 184. *See also* love
Oedipal: crowds, 93–94; families,
147, 148; unconscious, 93, 169.
See also love
ontological approach, 2–5, 10–11,
14, 17, 22, 29, 33–34, 41, 55, 79,
87–89, 97–98, 119–23, 148
opposition (relation), 4, 7–8, 18,
20–23, 26–27, 29, 30, 38, 46, 88,
117, 148
organizational forces, 4–6, 8–10, 11,
13–14, 19–22, 26, 30, 35, 43–44,
49–50, 62, 69–70, 77–78, 79, 81,
83–85, 109, 113–14, 117, 126, 128,
129–30, 134–36, 146–47, 164, 169,
172, 189, 190–91, 214–15n64

pack mentality, 93
panic, spreading of, 5, 54, 57, 100,
102, 110, 115, 127–28, 133–34,
138, 142–43, 150
Parikka, Jussi, 99, 124, 129, 209n29
Parisi, Luciana, 47–48, 77–78
passion, 12, 14, 25, 27–28, 35, 48,
52–53, 56–57, 59, 79, 90, 94,
113–14, 125, 145, 148–50, 151–53,
167, 170–71, 183, 184, 187, 189,
196–97n25
pass-on power, 106–7, 112, 159
Pearson, Keith Ansell, 70, 72
persuasion, 42, 49–50, 54–55, 74,
79–81, 127, 140, 159, 165–66,

Trojans, 37–38, 64–65, 75, 94, 101, 154, 183–84, 187, 191–92
tulipomania (MacKay), 52–53, 102, 104, 111
Twitter, 163–64, 168

ubiquitous computing (ubicomp), 164, 187–88
unconscious: associations, 10, 11, 13, 18, 19–20, 23, 27, 28–29, 36, 42, 56–57, 104, 159–60, 190–91; consumption, 32, 168, 172; Freud's notion of group communication, 11, 43, 80–81, 92–93, 165, 183. *See also* consciousness
Underground Man (Tarde), 143–44

Van Dijk, Jan, 1, 100
video viral, 63–65, 67, 72, 74–76
vigilambulism, 170
viral: atmospheres, 58–60, 113; viral capitalism (*see* capitalism); viral love (*see* love); viral marketing, 3, 32, 64–66, 74–76, 95, 105
virality: defined as a theory of contagion and assemblage, 1–15, 17, 24, 29, 31–32, 161; differs from ANT, 41–44; molar and molecular virality, 5–6; network virality, 60, 106, 110, 113, 124, 135; neurological approach, 43; nonconscious, 93; rejection of memetics, 62–66, 78–79; universality of virality, 87; virality of love, 144, 155, 157, 171, 182–83, 189; virality of money, 115, 123
Virilio, Paul, 118–20, 122–23, 137. *See also* accidents; riddle of technology, the

Von Neumann, John, 130–31, 150
vulnerability: to suggestibility, 13, 29, 77, 81, 138–39, 141, 181; to virality, 1, 5, 46, 60, 61, 100, 110, 160, 162, 184

Wall Street crash, 103
War on Terror, 2, 14, 54, 128–29, 135–36, 137–39, 141, 145, 147, 157, 182
War on Viruses, 128–29, 135–36
Watts, Duncan, 106, 108, 110–12
Weismannian inheritance mechanism, 71–72
whatever enemy, 135
Whitehead, Alfred North, 120
Wiener, Norbert, 134–35
Williams, Rosalind D., 68
World Bank, 2, 100
World Wide Web and Web 2.0, 31, 109–10, 153–54, 155–56, 164, 176, 187–88

Xerox's Palo Alto Research Center, 131

Yahoo, 112
Yemen, 163
YouTube, 63–65, 73–75, 78, 94, 95
Y2K bug, 133–34

zero cost marketing, 65
zombies, 165, 187
zoocentric doctrine of neo-Darwinism, 77–78

Tony D. Sampson is a London-based academic and writer currently lecturing at the University of East London. A former musician, he studied computer technology and cultural theory before receiving a PhD in sociology from the University of Essex. He is coeditor of *The Spam Book: On Viruses, Porn, and Other Anomalies from the Dark Side of Digital Culture* (2009).